Problem Solving

A Top-Down Approach

Problem Solving

A Top-Down Approach

James Adair

Scott, Foresman and Company
Glenview, Illinois
Boston

Library of Congress Cataloging in Publication Data

Adair, James,
    Problem solving.

    Includes index.
    1. Electronic digital computers--Programming.   2. Problem solving.   I. Title.
QA76.6.A32   1989   005.1   89-5932
ISBN 0-673-18607-5

1   2   3   4   5   6   KPF   94   93   92   91   90   89

ISBN 0-673-18607-5

Contents

Preface

Programming is the translation of physical processes into computerized form. Its purpose is to transform data into useful information. It is more than just computerizing a mechanical process. It is in fact a problem-solving process, which involves describing and determining the details of how things will be done. If this is done appropriately, the process of making this determination can lead to improved solutions. The problem-solving process includes data gathering, inputting, processing, outputting/storing, and using information. All of these processes are also a part of the practice of programming.

Program Life Cycle Organization

Programming is concerned with the bringing together of various components—people (users), hardware, software, procedures, and data/information—to help solve problems. This book is written around the problem-solving steps in the program life cycle:

1. defining the problem
2. feasibility
3. designing
4. coding
5. testing/debugging
6. documenting
7. implementing
8. maintenance

Modularity Used in the Solution Process

This book uses modular design as a problem-solving technique in the solution process. As they work through each of these steps, students are introduced to the detailed substeps that break up the problem into parts or modules. This demonstrates that problems are solved—and programs are written—in small segments, so that when a program is modified, only those modules that are affected must be changed rather than the whole program.

Courses and Approach

This book is intended for an introductory course in programming for business student and/or computer information systems students. It is applications oriented and takes a structured and top-down approach, first exposing students to overall programming concerns, then examining specific problem-solving situations found in business and industry.

Each chapter defines a problem, then describes the problem in terms of a real-world business computing situation. These problem-solving situations include payroll, newsletters, mailing lists, database maintenance, and inventory control. A solution that illustrates problem-solving using a top-down approach follows each problem.

BASIC and Pascal examples show the specific programming code. The illustrations, graphs, and charts are provided to enhance student interest and understanding.

Specific Text Features

The text has a number of features designed to assist students in learning to solve business problems:

- An emphasis on logic and program design concepts, as opposed to a language-dependent approach, so that the problem-solving techniques the student learns can be used in any language.

- BASIC and Pascal are used to illustrate how programming techniques might be executed in these languages, but the text does not depend on them to explain programming techniques.

- A top-down approach that reduces programming to simple logic modules. The early emphasis on subprograms as a technique for modularization makes initial construction and debugging easier for new programmers.

- Real-world applications illustrate programming techniques, creating situations similar to those that students will encounter in the workplace.

- Pseudocode is used to outline the program and/or segment, so that students can work exclusively with logic and program design; this eliminates the confusion that often occurs when specific language syntax is used to describe program design.

- Demonstration programs and illustrations appear throughout the text, reinforcing screen and printed output techniques and assisting in student comprehension.

- End-of-chapter pedagogical features include a chapter summary, list of key terms, review questions, and problem-solving assignments.

Supplements

The Instructor's Manual contains numerous teaching suggestions and possible course outlines, as well as answers to all end-of-chapter questions and problems.

Acknowledgments

I would like to acknowledge the contributions of Janet Spears of Black Hawk College, Sydney Newell of Docutech, Carla Hall of St. Louis Community College, and Ken Knecht, John Angermeyer, and Saul Aguiar.

I'd also like to thank my wife Patty, my son Evan, and my daughter Susan for inspiring me in my endeavors.

Application Programming: A Problem-Solving Approach

The scenario that follows is imaginary, but it represents the type of information processing problems that users face daily.

One month ago the principal of Anglewood Junior High School, J.T. Salinger, purchased a personal computer system for use by school administrators. At that time the administrators at Anglewood had a general knowledge of the capabilities of personal computers, yet they weren't certain how to go about putting their new system to work.

The computer salesperson had assured them that the *software,* or programs, included with the computer hardware would satisfy all their administrative needs. The salesperson had even given J.T. and several administrators a convincing demonstration of the power of the system they were about to purchase.

The administrative secretary, Persephone Childersleeve, set up the new system and immediately began to use the new application. (An application program is a program written to perform a specific task, such as report card preparation.) After a few days she realized that many features of the software were of no use to the Anglewood administrators. In turn, the software could not perform many of the tasks the administrators needed to do.

For instance, J.T. and her employees had hoped to computerize the production of grade reports (the dreaded report cards) that could be mailed directly to students' homes. The filing software that came with the hardware system provided an acceptable method for recording student grades from the grade sheets turned in by teachers at the end of each semester. This program could also produce a simple grade report.

However, the filing package could not perform the math that was necessary to determine the grade point average for each student. Also, the package required different types of information to be recorded in separate files, so the software could not merge student addresses with grade reports. The adminstrators could not produce the grade reports they needed.

In an attempt to solve these and other problems, J.T. hired a free-lance computer programmer, Dorian Cohen. Cohen spent about half a day reviewing Anglewood Junior High's hardware and software. The result of his analysis was not comforting: "Your computer hardware is fine," Dorian said. "You can meet most of your processing requirements with this system. But standard application packages often don't provide the versatility that users need to handle specialized needs. I'm afraid that, if you really want to use your hardware to full capacity, you're going to have to spend some money.

"You need a custom system," Cohen continued. "In other words, your processing problems are unique, and they require some specialized solutions. You should realize I'll have to take some time analyzing the problems involved in handling your administrative processing requirements. After we've evaluated these requirements, I can begin to design some custom programs that will work for you. But my approach involves following a step-by-step process. And, to be successful, I'll need your cooperation."

PROBLEM-SOLVING METHODS

In the Anglewood scenario users relied on packaged software to handle all their processing needs. As users at Anglewood and many other organizations have discovered, however, processing requirements can be unique, and packaged software may be too limited to meet them. Unique requirements call for unique solutions. To provide these solutions, users and computer programmers have to work together to analyze needs and problems and then to develop solutions. The point is that *computer programming is a problem-solving process.* Programming requires careful thought and creativity.

In general, a computer program is a set of instructions that a computer can follow in solving a problem or meeting a processing need. A *computer programmer* is a person who designs solutions and describes the instructions that can be followed in carrying out these solutions.

In essence, the job of a computer programmer is to design a computer-based solution that replaces manual steps. For instance, at Anglewood Junior High, instructors enter final grades for students on class roster sheets. Administrators then use these sheets to type grade reports that are mailed to students' homes. All information for each student has to be typed on a separate grade report.

In this scenario computers could streamline the reporting process. Administrators could use a specialized program that processes and prints grade reports automatically. With this system, it would be necessary to enter only the student's name. In response, the computer screen would display a form listing the classes in which the student is enrolled. The administrator would enter the letter grade next to each class name. Following data entry, the program would format and print a grade report for each student. The report would include the student's name and address, class names, teacher names, and letter grade. For each student, the program could also calculate and print the semester grade point average.

The Role of Programs and Programmers

At Anglewood, Cohen is responsible for translating manual procedures into a process that a computer can follow effectively. However, in using his skills, Cohen is doing much more than computerizing a set of mechanical processes. The way people handle a problem usually differs from the way in which a computer handles the same problem. Computers do not think. They must be provided with detailed step-by-step instructions for completing even the simplest problem.

Consider a fundamental activity you perform daily, such as tying your shoelaces. This activity seems so easy that you perform it seemingly without thinking. Yet your brain is actually working through the steps required to guide your muscles, hands, and other parts of your body. In doing so, your brain is performing *problem decomposition, or partitioning.* It decomposes, or partitions, an overall problem into smaller subproblems that can be solved separately. This concept of problem decomposition is central to program design. In any program design effort, you first decompose an identified problem into smaller, manageable subproblems. You then determine the steps that your program must take to solve each subproblem. All the programming steps that make up a subproblem are referred to as a *module.* A structured program is composed of modules that a computer processes separately, until the overall programming problem has been solved.

As a point of interest: Even the basic shoelace-tying task would be extremely difficult for most computers. The programming required to decompose the problem into the separate movements and calculations for manipulating each shoelace would require months of effort and tremendous computing power. Engineers have attempted to get computer-driven robots to perform similar precision activities, but with only moderate success.

The human brain cannot always outperform a computer, however. Computers can be extremely efficient at performing the repetitive calculations and processing operations that take place routinely in a business. Computers can record and transform basic facts and figures about people, places, and events—usually in a fraction of the time required by people using manual methods. For instance, to produce the several thousand grade reports due at the end of each semester, several Anglewood administrators must work full time for more than a week. An efficiently programmed computer could complete this activity in a matter of hours. And the value of computers increases as the volume of work increases.

Note the phrase "efficiently programmed" in the preceding paragraph. It is up to people to evaluate a programming problem and then to describe the basic steps that a computer must carry out to solve the problem. So, computer programming is a creative, problem-solving process. The term *process* implies that a series of steps can be followed in developing a solution. Five steps describe this problem-solving process:

1. Gathering data
2. Inputting data
3. Processing data (including primary storage)
4. Outputting information (including secondary storage)
5. Using information

Gathering Data. Data are facts that describe some person, event, product, or other measurable or quantifiable entity. For instance, to process registration information about you, your school needs to gather several items of data: your full name; your street address, city, and ZIP code; your identification or Social Security number; your class ticket numbers; and so on. Each of these data items represents a fact that will help describe you to the computer system that handles registration processing.

The first step in any programming effort is always the same: Describe techniques that can be followed to gather the items of data required to carry out processing. Typically, programmers ask a series of questions:

- What items of data are required by the program?
- What is the most efficient method for gathering these data items?
- On what medium should the data be recorded, and in what format?
- Do any data items currently exist in a computer-readable form?

The importance of the first two questions should be obvious. However, to understand the third and fourth questions, you need some explanation. A medium is simply a means for storing or transmitting data and information. With a *computer information system* (CIS), the most popular media for data recording are magnetic tape and magnetic disks. These media provide a way to record data in a format that can be understood by computers.

Obviously, it would be inefficient to gather data that already exist in a computer-readable form. Therefore, a capable programmer always determines if data items are available for immediate use. For instance, in the registration example, your school might already have a record of your name, address, I.D. number, phone number, and similar items. In fact, many registration systems mail current students a preregistration form, which contains known data items. The student then has the opportunity to update items that have changed. During registration, then, processing can be simplified by gathering only those data items that are new—class ticket numbers, class standing, and so on.

No matter the programming task, programmers have two responsibilities when it comes to data gathering: Programmers must identify all data required for processing and then they must collect it.

Inputting Data. *Data input* refers to techniques required to enter data into a computer system in preparation for processing. Note the difference between gathering and inputting data. With data gathering, the major concern is identifying and collecting data. With data inputting, however, the focus is on making data available to a program for processing.

A *programming language* is a system of vocabulary and rules used to control a computer. Most programming languages require that the programmer define characteristics about data to be processed. The programmer must establish categories of related data. These categories are called *fields*.

For instance, your street address represents a field that describes you for registration processing. Your city is a second field, your state a third, your ZIP code a fourth, and your phone number a fifth. The terms *data item* and *field* are, for the most part, synonymous. From this point the text will use the term *field* to describe items of data.

Typically, programming languages also require programmers to define the *data type* for each field. The data type describes how the data is represented in the programming language. For instance, your name might be represented as an *alphanumeric field*. In other words, this field is composed of alphabetic and numeric characters. The amount you pay for tuition might be labeled a *numeric field*. This field is composed entirely of numbers (along with an optional decimal point) that can be used in numeric calculations.

Why is it important to define data types? Data typing helps a programming language identify the way a certain processing operation will be handled. Consider an "addition" operation: When you define two fields as type numeric and then specify that you want your program to add the two field values 1032 and 1212, the program develops a total—the value 2244. However, if you define two alphanumeric fields such as "by" and "gone" and then specify an addition operation, the program strings the two fields into a combined field—"bygone."

To illustrate data typing a bit further, consider a third data type. A program used by your school might have a separate *logic field* for residency status. A logic field is one that has two possibilities—yes/no, true/false, or on/off. For instance, if you are a resident of the state in which you are attending school, your residency status is Y (for yes). If you are not a resident, your residency status is N (for no, of course). In other words, a logic field works like a simple on/off switch. This data type helps to simplify processing by limiting the input possibilities for a particular item of data.

Like data gathering, data inputting involves specifying the basic formats in which data will be read into a program. These formats tell a program how to classify and group input data. Here is a simple analogy: In a toolbox you could organize items according to type and size. For instance, you could separate screws from nails. Then you might separate sheet-metal screws from wood screws, masonry nails from finishing nails, and so on. If you are really a stickler for organization, you might organize each separate item according to size—number 4 screws would be grouped together, number 8 screws would be grouped together, and so on. Organizing your fasteners in this manner turns out to be a blessing when it comes time to work on a major construction project. Who wants to waste 20 minutes looking for a half dozen number 16 screws?

The same concept of organization holds true in programming. It is easier to develop a solution to a programming problem if you have identified and organized data and information in a way that leads to efficient processing. You already know one basic data format—the field. In addition, all the fields that describe a particular entity— such as yourself, a product, an event, and so on—can be grouped to form a *record*. A record is a collection of related fields. A collection of related records is a *file*. In the registration example, all fields that describe you make up one student record. All student records for all freshmen make up the freshmen student file, all student records for registered sophomores make up the sophomore student file, and so on. Figure 1.1 shows how fields, records, and files relate in the registration example.

Keep in mind that input formats must be organized according to type. For instance, in a student file, a separate field is AMOUNT PAID, which describes tuition paid to the registrar's office. This field is type numeric so that calculations can be performed. Therefore, all values in this field, for all student records, must be composed entirely of what the programming language defines as numbers.

Size, too, is an important factor in defining data formats. For instance, almost all programming languages require you to define the maximum size allowed for each field within each record of a file. Programs require these size specifications so that addressable areas of computer memory can be set up to store input data.

Processing Data. So far, you have seen the term *processing* in several contexts. In general, *processing* refers to any operation that causes data to undergo a change—either in content or format—that will lead to desired, meaningful information.

Note the qualifying phrase, "desired, meaningful information." If you turn off your computer's power while a program is running, the data currently in memory certainly undergo a change—the data may be lost. But the change doesn't lead to desired, meaningful information. Consider another example: Imagine that you have designed a program that automatically identifies and reports on low stock levels in a warehouse. Through a programming error all stock levels are printed in hexadecimal code. Hexadecimal code is understandable to some programmers, but it is probably meaningless to the inventory manager. So, in this case, processing operations produce the desired result—an inventory exception report. However, the report isn't meaningful. Or suppose that, through a different programming error, your program adds one hundred to each quantity under the heading "ON HAND." In this situation the report has meaning to the inventory manager, but it doesn't provide the desired information.

Seven types of processing operations can be performed on data to produce desired, meaningful information:

- Sorting
- Classifying
- Calculating
- Summarizing
- Comparing
- Merging
- Reporting

Figure 1.1

Relationship of fields, records, and file

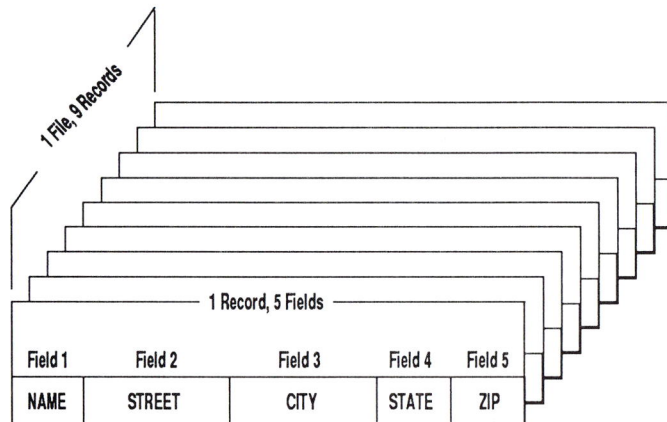

As a programmer, you will use these basic operations to design programming solutions. In fact, many programming languages contain English verbs—such as SORT, MERGE, and PRINT—that indicate the type of processing operations they perform. This book describes ways to use these basic types of processing operations to design effective programs.

Outputting Information. Note that the first four steps of the problem-solving process emphasize data rather than information. There is a basic distinction between these two. Data usually refers to separate facts that have little, if any, meaning of their own.

For instance, what does your street address mean? On its own, a data item such as 4325 Mockingbird Lane really does not provide any meaning to people. However, when that data item is processed along with name, city, state, and ZIP code fields, the result provides a meaningful address for postal employees and other people who want to locate the residents at this address. So, *information* refers to data items that have been processed to provide meaning. Thus, your street address is an item of data, but your full address can be considered information to certain users.

The term *data* describes items gathered and input to a program for processing. As you might expect, the term *information* tends to be used to refer to the results of processing, or *output*. Keep in mind, however, that information outputs can also be used as input. For instance, information in the files that result from your school's registration processing can be input later to a program that creates grade reports.

Processed information can be output in human-readable form or it can be stored in machine-readable form for future use. Human-readable outputs are usually made by two devices: a display screen or a printer. A screen, of course, provides only a temporary version of an output. A printer, on the other hand, produces a permanent, hard-copy version.

When information is stored for future use, it is often written to a magnetic medium, such as tape or disk. Other machine-readable storage media are available (punched cards, for instance), but tape and disk are by far the most common storage media used with computer systems. If you work only with microcomputers, you might work solely with disk storage devices.

The distinction between outputting and storing information is important to you as a programmer. Many languages require you to specify within your program the type of output or storage device(s) to use. Different device types may suggest or require different output or storage formats. For instance, if you want your program to print or display a report, you have to devise a readable, attractive output format. This involves creating and formatting heading lines, columns and column headings, and other report features.

Printed and displayed reports can present some special programming problems. For instance, if your program outputs a 70-line report, you cannot fit the entire report on one printed page or on a single screen. To handle this problem, you have to build your program to accommodate multiple-screen displays and page breaks.

Using Information. In English composition classes instructors usually encourage students to heed a basic decree: "Know your audience!"

This same decree holds true in programming, because all computer systems exist to support people. From a programmer's perspective, the people who rely on computer-produced outputs are known as *users*. In tackling any programming problem, you should first consider this basic question: Who are my users and what solution will best meet their needs?

If you know your users, you will be in a good position to evaluate their needs. Discussion of techniques for determining user needs appears in a later chapter. For now, consider that users expect four things from any program: reliability, timeliness, readability, and relevance.

- **Reliability.** Users should be able to rely on the information they receive. A reliable program is one that produces accurate and consistent outputs. Users can count on the results of a program each time they use it.

- **Timeliness.** Information should be delivered within an acceptable time frame. Countless application programs have been discarded by users simply because they run too slowly or cannot operate within normal business reporting cycles. So, when you design a program, it is a good idea to recognize when users need information as well as the type of information they need.

- **Readability.** You probably would not consider showing up for a job interview in jeans and a T-shirt. Businesspeople are professionals and expect a professional appearance. Yet it is surprising to note the number of professional programmers who display a lack of care in designing screen and printed report formats. A good product is only as good as its presentation. As a programmer, it is up to you to control the presentation of program outputs. It makes sense to design output formats that users will find readable and attractive.

- **Relevance.** Perhaps most important, a program should provide relevant information—that is, information that meets the needs of users. The history of computer systems is filled with stories of programs that produced beautiful, timely outputs, but they had one important flaw. The outputs did not provide the information that users expected. A program design that fails to meet the expectations of users does not solve the problem for which it was intended. Such a program is worse than having no program at all, because time and money have been wasted in developing a useless product.

THE PROBLEM-SOLVING ENVIRONMENT

When a programmer is asked to solve a programming problem, he or she has to consider the environment in which the program will be created and used. Any computer program must operate within the context of an integrated system of components. You certainly don't want to design a program only to find that it will not run on the user's computer system. Still worse, imagine a program that makes no provision for gathering data prior to input. (A program without data to process is just as useless as data that lack a working program.) Such situations have actually occurred. Therefore, this is a good place to review the basic components that make up an operational computer system:

- People
- Hardware
- Software
- Procedures
- Data
- Information

Figure 1.2 shows how these elements relate.

People

People involved in a computer system include the individuals who gather data, input the data, monitor the operations of the system, and—of course—those who use system outputs. As part of the programming process, a programmer must often describe the roles of all these people. For instance, to gather data a programmer might find it necessary to design special data input forms that can be scanned by optical reading devices. In another project, the programmer might have to provide prompts, or screen-displayed instructions, that guide people through the steps of inputting data. In any case the programmer will certainly have to interview users to determine input, output, and processing requirements.

Hardware

The term *hardware* refers to the physical devices that make up a computer system. The actual computer itself, a collection of circuits that perform transformations on data, is called the *processor unit*. This unit has two basic parts: *memory* and the *central processing unit* (CPU). Memory refers to the circuits that store data and programs temporarily, while a computer is in operation. The CPU contains the circuits that carry out the basic processing operations described earlier. This textbook stresses

Figure 1.2

Relationships among people, hardware, software, data, and information

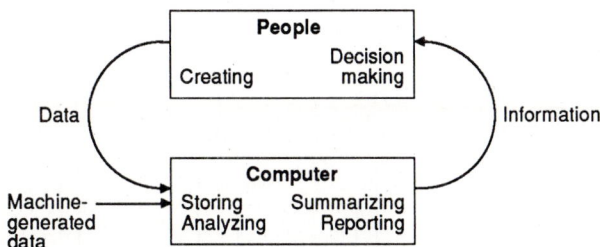

the dominant role that personal computers play in computer information systems today. For this reason it makes sense to describe computer hardware within a personal computer context.

In a microcomputer the CPU is stored on a single microprocessor chip. The CPU has two functional parts: the *control unit* and the *arithmetic/logic unit* (ALU). The control unit operates much like a traffic cop, coordinating the flow of data and program instructions to and from the ALU and memory. The ALU performs the arithmetic and comparative functions that are the building blocks of all processing operations. (As you may know, the computer is limited to these two basic functions—processing two numbers arithmetically and comparing the relationship between two values.) The ALU can also store small quantities of data and program instructions in *registers,* which hold those data items and instructions currently being processed. Special registers, called *accumulators,* or general registers, are also available to accumulate totals during processing.

The memory portion of a processor unit is frequently called *main memory* to distinguish it from other devices that can store data and programs. These devices, such as disks and tapes, are often said to provide *secondary storage.* In a personal computer main memory is a series of microchips that are usually plugged into a single circuit board. A memory chip is typically capable of storing about 16,000, 32,000, or 64,000 characters of data and/or program instructions.

Figure 1.3

The components of a CPU

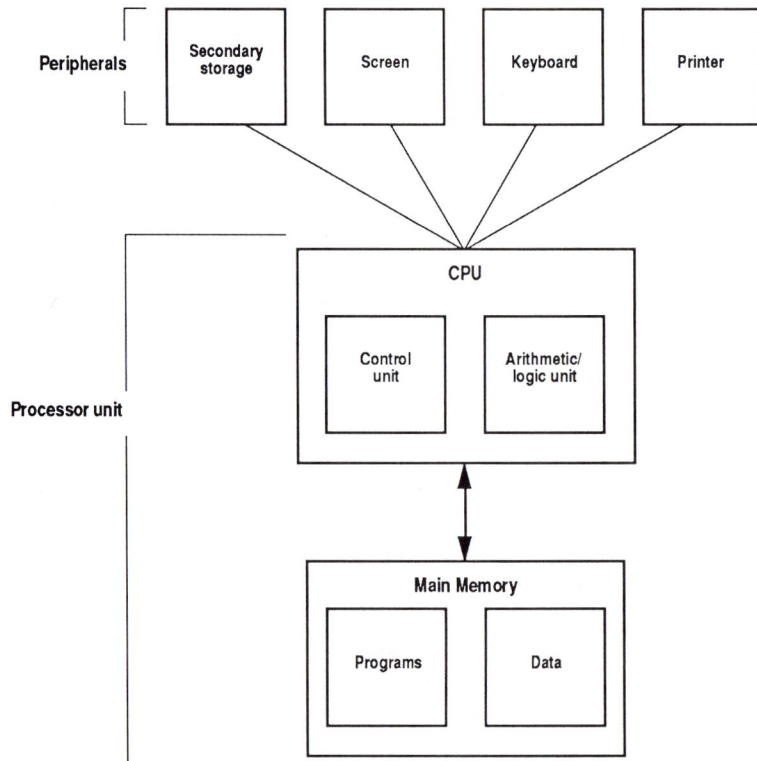

All other devices attached to the processor unit—such as the keyboard, screen, and disk drives—are called *peripherals*. These devices perform most of the input, output, and storage tasks required to move externally stored data and programs into and out of the processor unit. Many people make a distinction among peripherals by referring to them as input devices, output devices, or storage devices. However, these distinctions often tend to be confusing.

For instance, is a screen display an input or an output device? It is both, of course, and in fact is often referred to as an I/O (for input/output) device. As another example, consider a disk drive and its disks. Is this unit an input device, an output device, or a storage device? As you probably realize, a disk drive performs all three of these basic peripheral tasks. The point: It is more important to understand how you, as a programmer, can use a given peripheral than it is to know the labels given to it. Figure 1.3 shows how peripherals, memory, and the CPU relate.

Software

Software, of course, refers to the programs that process data and information. The word *software* is sometimes used to refer to finished and tested programs only. But other than this usage, no important distinction exists between the terms *software* and *programs*. Most programmers use them interchangeably.

Software falls into two general categories: application programs and system programs.

Application Programs. An application program is designed and written to solve a particular problem for users. For instance, a word processing program is an application program that allows users to enter, edit, and print text documents. A filing system is an application program that allows users to organize records into separate files, and it performs processing operations on these files. This book discusses application programs within a realistic business context. Why? Most application programmers today are employed to solve the computer system problems of businesspeople—problems similar to the one provided at the outset of this chapter.

An application program is composed of a set of instructions that the computer can follow in processing data and information. Recall that these instructions exist within different modules, with each module responsible for solving a different part of the overall programming problem. Program instructions are written in programming languages that can be translated into machine instructions, or signals, that a computer can understand. A good programmer understands the information needs and business problems of users as well as the basic hardware operations that a program manipulates to solve a problem.

System Programs. System programs include the operating system of a computer and the many system utilities that work in close coordination with the operating system. An operating system is the set of programs that control and coordinate the flow of application program instructions and data through the processor unit and its peripherals. The language translator for BASIC programming is a part of the system software. System programming is a more technical occupation than application programming, and it is beyond the scope of this book.

Procedures

Procedures are the written instructions that tell users how to operate the hardware and software components of a computer system. Procedures often take the form of user's manuals that guide people, step by step, through the operations of an application program. In years past, programmers tended to de-emphasize the importance of user's manuals and other written procedures. The belief was that, as long as a program operated correctly and efficiently, the programmer had done his or her job. This viewpoint, fortunately, is changing rapidly. The reason: Many powerful application software packages have failed to satisfy users simply because the user's manual was poorly written, overly technical, or incomplete.

Today most programmers recognize the importance of communicating the features of a program to users. In fact, the ability to educate and explain program features to users is considered as important as programming skill. Today program documentation is considered a critical part of program design.

Data and Information

Data and information are the raw materials that computers process to provide useful results to people. However, data and information are also considered valuable resources to businesspeople. Businesspeople at all levels of a company rely on computer-produced information to carry out daily operations and to make important decisions that guide the course of the business. For this reason application programmers today often follow what is called a *data-centered approach*. This means that programmers focus on the information outputs that users require and the raw data that must be identified, gathered, and input into the system to produce the outputs. This approach contrasts markedly with the techniques of the past, which emphasized processing steps. As a programmer, you can benefit by keeping the data-centered approach in mind. That is, consider the information needs of users, determine the data that will be required to produce the desired results, and then develop the processing steps that will transform the raw data into useful information for system users.

THE PROGRAM DEVELOPMENT LIFE CYCLE

You have probably heard anecdotes about scientists who made remarkable discoveries by accident. Penicillin and X-rays are said to be accidental discoveries. Although some scientific advances have been accomplished by stumbling onto important facts, programming never works this way.

This chapter has stressed that programming is a problem-solving discipline. In designing programs, programmers employ creativity within a step-by-step problem-solving process. This process is often said to fit within a life cycle because changes in business operations or technologies can make a program obsolete. When this happens, a new, more effective program is required, and the development cycle begins again.

The program development life cycle contains eight steps. In each step the programmer follows a different imperative:

1. **Define the problem.**
2. **Determine the feasibility of designing a solution.**
3. **Design a solution.**
4. **Code the program in a programming language.**
5. **Test and debug the program.**
6. **Document the program.**
7. **Implement the program.**
8. **Maintain the program.**

Step 1: Define the Problem

In any problem-solving activity you can expect to find a solution only after you have clearly identified and defined the problem. So, the first step in the program development process is to formulate a problem definition. Consider one problem definition: Design a program that allows warehouse personnel to identify understocked items within eight working hours of the time the stock level falls under established minimums. Another example: Design an aging program that the accounting department can use to identify the number of days and the amounts overdue for all customers who are more than 45 days behind in their payments.

Notice that both of these decision statements are user-oriented. They focus on the problem from the standpoint of users, rather than programmers. To achieve a user orientation in the program as well as the definition, programmers next determine the output and input requirements of users. Usually, these requirements can best be determined by interviewing users. The questions that follow typically lead to the identification of appropriate output and input requirements.

Output
- What information is to be output?
- On what media should information be output?
- How should the output appear?
- Who will use the output?
- Why is the information needed?
- When or how often is the information needed?

Input
- What data (fields) are required for input?
- Through what media should data be input for processing?
- How should data be organized, or formatted, for input?
- Who will be performing data gathering and input operations?
- Why are these data required for processing?
- When or how often should data gathering and input take place?

After a programmer has identified and defined a problem by resolving these questions, he or she can assess the time, labor, and thinking skills that will be involved in designing and implementing a solution.

Step 2: Determine Feasibility

The term *feasibility* refers to factors that determine whether a project is worth carrying out. A feasible project is one that managers and other expects believe can be carried out within a reasonable time and budget. Often, managers and programmers evaluate the feasibility of a programming project by commissioning a feasibility study. The people who perform this study determine the scope, or boundaries, of the project. Next they study two or more alternative solutions to the problem. Then they establish a preliminary schedule and budget that reflect the time and amount of money that will have to be invested to follow through on the project. The feasibility study also evaluates the amount of human effort that will be required to design the program.

If management believes that the expense and human resources required to solve the problem are reasonable, the project is set in motion. If the cost of solving a programming problem is too high for the business to support, the project is shelved for the time being. It is better to realize that a project is not feasible during the planning stages rather than midway through program development. The sooner the feasibility or unfeasibility of a program is determined, the less likely the risk of wasting time, money, and human effort on an unrealistic project.

In general, full-blown feasibility studies are conducted for large-scale programming projects that might run into hundreds of thousands of dollars and thousands of programming hours. For small-scale programming projects, a feasibility study might be an hour-long meeting between management, users, and programmers. In any case, keep in mind that your role as a programmer is to give an honest estimate of the time and effort that you believe will be required. It is sad to say, but programmers sometimes become carried away with their own projects and downplay the cost and time that must be expended. In these cases, the results can be disastrous both for the business and for the career of the programmer.

Step 3: Design a Solution

If a program is feasible, the next step is to select a programming alternative and begin program design. This step represents the bulk of the effort for programmers. At this point programmers begin to determine the steps required to transform input (data) into output (information). This procedure is often called algorithm development. An *algorithm* is a description of the steps that can be followed to solve a problem or work through a process. For instance, return for a moment to the shoelace-tying scenario. A partial algorithm to tie shoelaces might look something like this:

Loosen shoelaces of both shoes.
Put shoes on feet.
Tighten lace on one shoe, working from the bottom of the shoe upward.
Pull the ends of the lace straight up, holding the free portions parallel.
Cross the free portions up to form an X.
Loop one portion under and through the intersection of the X.
Pull the ends of the lace outward, until the loop forms a tight half knot, which is snug against the tongue of your shoe.

You can see the level of detail required to describe each basic step. The substeps required for each of these general steps probably might number in the hundreds, if not the thousands. The task the algorithm outlines may seem silly, but the concept it illustrates is not. When you program for computers, it is important to account for each step in the problem-solving processing. Remember: Computers don't think. They are not usually capable of making deductive leaps, as people can. You must provide program instructions for each task to be performed.

During algorithm development it is enough to identify general processing steps. Later, each step can be transformed into a single program module, or subproblem. For instance, to process a registration record for each student, this algorithm might be used:

Read (input) student record into main memory.
Examine each field to make sure it contains valid data.
Add amount in AMT PAID field to accumulator (to calculate total amount of registration income for all students).
Add 1 to counter (to accumulate total number of students registered).
For valid record, write (output) student record to registration file.
For invalid record, print (output) message on audit/error report and add 1 to invalid-record counter.
Repeat for each record to be processed.

Each step in this algorithm can now be treated as a separate module. The programmer can focus on one module at a time, developing the detailed processing steps required for each module, until program design is complete.

So far, you have studied the processing steps that take place once data have been input into memory and until the data are output to a file and/or report. Notice that these steps are repeated for each record. That is, the main processing steps form a loop. However, other steps must be described to prepare the computer system for processing and to prepare the program to terminate after all records have been processed. Think of these set-up and clean-up steps as housekeeping. There are two types of housekeeping tasks: initialization and termination.

Initialization. Recall that most programming languages require you to describe in your program the format of fields and records. With these descriptions the program can allocate space in memory to hold the fields for each input record. In the preceding algorithm, note that three accumulators are required—one to total the amount paid for all registered students, a second to count total number of students registered, and a third to count invalid student records.

As part of initialization your program has to define the accumulators that will store and calculate these amounts. In addition, it is customary to reset these accumulators to 0 or 1 at the outset of processing. This is done in case the accumulators contain values left over from a previous program's processing. If your program were to add new values to the leftover values, output would be invalid. By initializing accumulators to 0 or 1, all registers are cleared. Other initialization procedures will be discussed later in the text.

Termination. To continue examining the preceding algorithm, consider what happens after all records have been processed. Some provision has to be made to output final totals on the audit/error report. In other words, after the last student record has been processed, the program must end its main processing loop and print the totals contained in the accumulators. These totals tell users the total amount of money taken in during registration, the total number of students who attempted to register, and the total number of students who have errors in their record and must take corrective action. In addition to exiting the main loop and printing results, termination often includes closing the input and output files. (These files are set up either at the outset of processing or during the course of processing.) In this example the program would probably close the input registration file and the output registration file and possibly the printer file.

Step 4: Code the Program

After a program design is completed, it is ready to be converted into a high-level programming language. This book codes program design examples in two popular high-level languages: BASIC and Pascal.

All programming languages are composed of a set of language primitives, or terms. Most languages are composed of two types of primitives: *statements* and *functions*. Examples of high-level language statements include READ, WRITE, and PRINT. Functions perform special processing operations, such as converting values from one data type to another. In addition, all languages allow programmers to supply variable names and values that are specific to a particular program. Figure 1.4 contains an example of a BASIC program and an example of a Pascal program.

Statements, functions, and user-supplied elements can be combined in an almost unlimited way to create instructions. Each instruction must adhere to the basic rules of the language, called the language's *syntax*. Syntax rules include allowable spellings and abbreviations for instructions and valid ways to combine statements and functions into complete instructions. In general, a single instruction, or line of code, performs a processing task. A related group of language instructions are then grouped to form a module, which represents a general processing operation such as reading (inputting) a record into memory. An organized set of modules is a completed program.

High-level language programs cannot be understood directly by a computer. Since a computer understands electrical on/off signals only, high-level instructions must be translated (either compiled or interpreted) into corresponding machine-language instructions that contain only strings of the values 0 and 1. A compiled language is one that translates all high-level instructions in a program into machine language prior to processing. An interpreted-language program is translated into machine language one line at a time, when each line is executed by the computer. A translated, executable version of a program is called object code.

The language essentials and syntax of BASIC and Pascal are discussed in some depth in later chapters. For now, you should realize that the coding step is relatively straightforward and requires far less mental effort than program design.

Figure 1.4

BASIC Program

```
10  REM DEMOPROGRAM
20  REM
30  REM INITIALIZATION PROCEDURE ************
40  AP=0
50  N=0
60  IN=0
70  T=10000
80  INPUT PROCEDURE ************************
85  PRINT "ENTER NAME, ID NUMBER, AMOUNT PAID"
90  INPUT N$, ID, A
100 WHILE ID <> 999
110 REM PROCESSING PROCEDURE ***************
120    AP=AP+A
130    N=N+1
140     OUTPUT PROCEDURE ***********************
150    IF A<T THEN PRINT N$,ID, A, "AUDIT ERROR":IN=IN+1
            ELSE PRINT N$,ID, A,"REGISTERED"
160    INPUT PROCEDURE ************************
165    PRINT "ENTER NAME, ID NUMBER, AMOUNT PAID"
170    INPUT N$, ID, A
180 WEND
190 REM TERMINATION PROCEDURE *************
200 PRINT "TOTAL TUITION PAID: ";AP
210 PRINT "NUMBER REGISTERED IS: ";N
220 PRINT "NUMBER TO AUDIT: ";IN
230 END
```

Pascal Program

```
PROGRAM DEMOPROGRAM   REGISTER(INPUT,OUTPUT);
VAR
   NAME: ARRAY[1..20] OF CHAR;
   ID:INTEGER;
   PAID:REAL;
   AMOUNT_PAID:REAL;
   NUMBER:INTEGER;
   AUDIT:INTEGER;
CONST
   TUITION 10000;

PROCEDURE INIT;
 BEGIN
   AMOUNT_PAID:=0.0;
   NUMBER:=0;
   AUDIT:=0;
 END;
PROCEDURE DATAIN;
 VAR
   COUNTER: INTEGER;
```

(continued)

Figure 1.4 (continued)

```
    CHARACTER; CHAR;
    INDEX: INTEGER;
BEGIN
   FOR INDEX:= 1 TO 20 DO
       NAME[INDEX]:=' ';
   COUNTER:=1;
   WRITELN('ENTER NAME');
   REPEAT
       READ(CHARACTER);
       WORD[COUNTER]:=CHARACTER;
       COUNTER:=COUNTER+1;
   UNTIL (CHARACTER=' ') OR (COUNTER>20);
   WRITE('ENTER ID');
   READLN(ID);
   WRITE('ENTER PAID');
   READLN(PAID);
WRITELN(ID,NAME,PAID:6:2,'ERROR-AUDIT');
AUDIT:=AUDIT+1;
 END;

PROCEDURE PROCESS;
 BEGIN
   AMOUNT_PAID:=AMOUNT_PAID+PAID;
   NUMBER:=NUMBER+1;
 END;

PROCEDURE DATAOUT;
 BEGIN
   IF PAID<TUITION THEN
      BEGIN
         WRITELN(ID,NAME,PAID,'AUDIT ERROR');
         IN=IN+1;
      END;
   ELSE
         WRITELN(ID,NAME,PAID:6:2,'REGISTERED');
 END;

PROCEDURE TERMINATE;
 BEGIN
   WRITELN('TOTAL TUITION PAID:',AMOUNT_PAID:10:2);
   WRITELN('NUMBER REGISTERED:',NUMBER:5);
   WRITELN('NUMBER TO AUDIT:',AUDIT:5);
 END;

BEGIN {MAIN PROCEDURE}
 INIT;
 DATAIN;
 WHILE ID<>999 DO
   BEGIN
      PROCESS;
      DATAOUT;
      DATAIN;
   END;
 TERMINATE;
END. {MAIN PROGRAM}
```

Step 5: Test and Debug the Program

A program is considered complete and ready to implement only after it has been thoroughly tested. Testing procedures involve running object code with sample test data to determine if any programming errors have been made. Two types of errors are possible: syntax errors and logic errors.

Syntax Errors. A syntax error violates the syntax rules of the programming language in which it is written. For example, if you code an input instruction as INPT rather than INPUT, the program does not run. Syntax errors are identified by the compiler or interpreter that translates source code into object code. However, the compiler or interpreter recognizes only that an error exists and the general location of the error. It is up to you to isolate and correct each syntax error.

Logic Errors. A logic error is far more serious than a syntax error, because it is more difficult to locate and correct. A logic error is any programming mistake that leads to incorrect processing, even though no syntax rules have been violated. Many novice programmers—and some experienced ones—signal that they have found a logic error by groaning. The reason for such despair is that a logic error may indicate faulty or incomplete design; the programmer may have to rethink the problem. Examples of logic errors include language instructions that are coded out of sequence, unterminated loops, juxtaposed variables, and missing modules.

Procedures that you carry out to correct syntax and logic errors are called *debugging* activities. A debugged program is one in which all identified syntax and/or logic errors have been corrected so that test data produce correct output. Most programs that are designed for professional use contain a few syntax errors and possibly some minor logic errors when they are first tested. Nobody is perfect, and even a pro can make occasional typos and errors in judgment. However, a well-designed program should be relatively easy to test and debug. A program that is riddled with serious errors, especially logic errors, indicates a poor design. If you concentrate on the front-end design steps involved in program development, you will reduce the potential for making serious errors when you code your design in a programming language.

Step 6: Document the Program

Program *documentation* includes any explanations that help other programmers and users understand program operations. The most common form of documentation is a user's manual that people can read to learn about the capabilities and requirements of a program. Another form of documentation is an on-line help screen. These screens guide users through the operation of different program functions.

Another important role of program documentation is to aid *maintenance programmers* in understanding existing source code. A maintenance programmer devotes programming effort to modifying existing programs to accommodate new business techniques, requirements, or equipment. Often, a complex and lengthy source code listing is difficult to understand, even for an experienced programmer. For this reason, considerate programmers include *remark lines,* or internal documentation, within their source code. Remarks are written in English and explain the purpose of a particular module or instruction. In most programming languages it is possible to precede a remark line with a symbol that tells the compiler or interpreter to ignore the comments that follow when the code is translated into object code.

Additional program documentation includes the design itself. As discussed later, copies of flowcharts, structure charts, or pseudocode can assist maintenance programmers in understanding the modular approach used to solve the original programming problem. As a rule, documenting is easiest if you do it continually during program design. That is, as you complete the development of a module, collect and store your design documentation. Then, when you prepare source code, include internal comments in each module to describe your design to other programmers. When it comes time for you or others to prepare a user's manual, the design documentation that you have prepared should be easy to convert into written text.

Step 7: Implement the Program

Finally, you are ready to place your completed and documented program into operation. However, even though you have made it this far, there is no guarantee of user success. Obscure errors are often uncovered after a program is in use. In addition, you may have to modify parts of the program that users find confusing.

Thus, it is important to make yourself available during the implementation stage to answer any questions or to solve problems. With major application programs, however, it isn't always possible to do this. A hundred or more companies may purchase your program, and each may require occasional assistance. In these situations it is common to train a user support group. These are professionals that can make themselves available to users to answer questions and solve minor problems. Even if you train a user support group, however, keep in mind that at any point during implementation you might be called in to make adjustments to your program.

Step 8: Maintain the Program

Businesses are dynamic; the needs of businesspeople are in a state of continual change. As a result, even the best application programs require refinement and minor changes during their operating life. Often, the people who maintain a program are different from the programmers who create the original design. In fact, it has been estimated that more than 70 percent of the jobs assigned to entry-level programmers in businesses involve program maintenance. Therefore, you may find that, as a professional programmer, your first years on the job will be devoted to maintenance programming.

Do not assume, however, that the design principles described in this book are less important to maintenance programmers than to those who design new programs. Maintenance programming can be a major undertaking, and it requires the same modular design approach used in creating new programs. In recognition of the importance of maintenance programming to businesses, the final chapter in this book is devoted to understanding and solving maintenance problems.

MODULAR PROGRAMMING METHODS

At this point in the discussion, it makes sense to consider a basic question: How is a program design represented? In other words, how do you show, on paper, the organization and content of the modules you have identified and the order in which the modules are executed?

Program Design Options

There is no universal technique for representing program design. However, several established methods are available that encourage a structured, modular program approach. Each method is a design tool that stresses a different aspect of programming. Four common tools are:

- IPO charts
- Structure charts
- Pseudocode
- Flowcharts

IPO Charts. An *IPO chart* is an English description of program design. IPO stands for *input, processing, output,* the three categories into which the chart divides operations. The input section lists the data that have to be input to the program, the processing section lists the processing steps that will be performed on each input record, and the output section lists basic output requirements. Figure 1.5 presents an IPO chart for the student registration problem. As you can see, an IPO chart emphasizes a data-centered approach to processing by listing specific input data and output information requirements.

Structure Charts. A *structure chart* organizes programming operations within the three main modular sections: initialization, processing, and termination. Each module is given a name and is enclosed within a box. The chief feature of a structure chart is its ability to show the hierarchical, or top-down, relationships among different modules in a program. These relationships are shown by attaching modules with horizontal and vertical lines. The relationships then appear as a series of levels. A structure chart for the student registration problem is shown in Figure 1.6. This structure chart contains three levels. Read the organization of modules from left to right and from top to bottom.

Figure 1.5

IPO chart for the student registration problem

INPUT	PROCESSING	OUTPUT

Input file of student records	1. Read a record
	2. Verify fields
	3. Add amount paid
	4. Add 1 to record counter
	5. Valid record:
	   Write to output file
	   Invalid record:
	   Print error message
		Student file of valid records
		
		Audit/error report listing records processed and records in error

Pseudocode. *Pseudocode* is an English-like description of initialization, processing, and output procedures. Pseudocode is organized as an outline. Indentations are used to represent the hierarchical relationships among the three main modules, subordinate modules, and individual program instructions. Pseudocode provides a method for describing program design in great detail, using a language that is readable even by non-programmers. In fact, completed pseudocode can often be converted into programming language line by line. Pseudocode for the student registration problem is shown in Figure 1.7.

Flowcharts. A *flowchart* portrays processing steps within a set of symbols that are connected by lines. The symbols are of various shapes, and each shape describes a different processing operation. For example, a diamond represents a decision point in program processing. A parallelogram represents an input or output operation. A rectangle represents a processing operation. Arrows on the connectors show the flow of control that the program follows in carrying out processing operations. Although a flowchart is a useful way to represent processing steps, discerning the structured rela-

Figure 1.6

Structure chart for the
student registration
problem

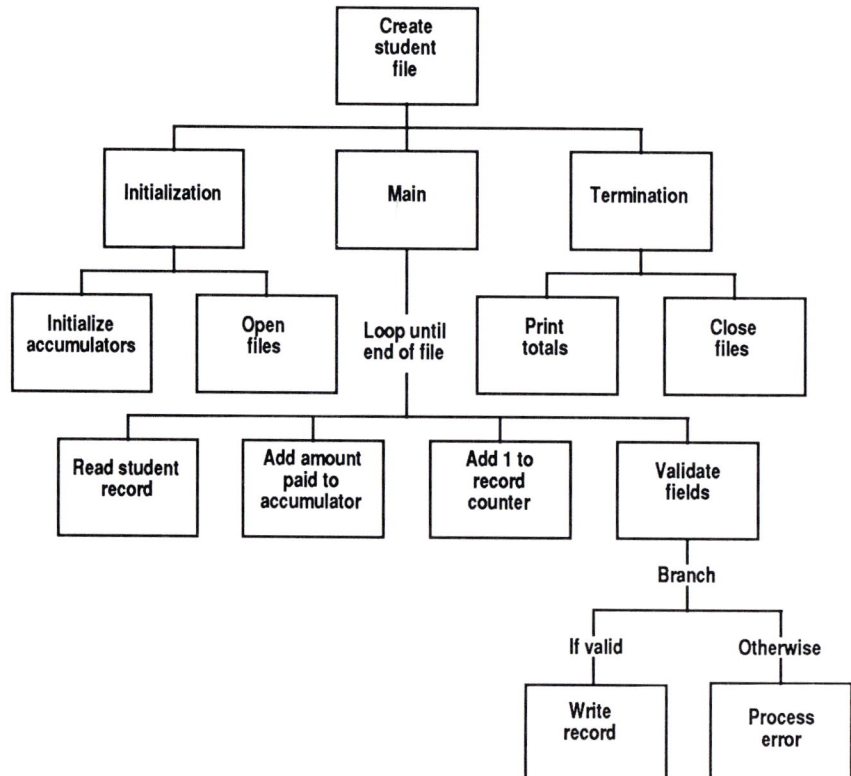

tionships among modules on a flowchart can be difficult. A flowchart for the student registration example is shown in Figure 1.8.

Many programmers developed their design skills at a time when flowcharting was quite popular. For this reason many programmers are adept at creating and reading flowcharts. However, as structured programming methods have evolved, other design methods, such as structure charting and pseudocoding, have all but replaced flowcharts. Thus, this book employs structure charts and pseudocode throughout and uses flowcharts only when necessary.

It is worth pointing out that design tools are often a matter of personal taste. Many excellent programming books use flowcharts exclusively. Other books rely on design techniques that this book does not describe. The problem-solving approach that you follow in designing a program is far more important than the particular tools that you choose to represent your design.

Program Control Structures

All programs execute modules and instructions according to three general *control structures*. A control structure describes the order in which two or more modules are executed. The three possible structures are:

- Sequences
- Branches
- Loops

Figure 1.7

Pseudocode for the student registration problem

```
CREATE STUDENT FILE

DO INITIALIZATION
DO MAIN UNTIL END OF INPUT FILE
DO TERMINATION

        INITIALIZATION
            Initialize accumulators
            Open files

        MAIN LOOP
            Read student record
            Add amount paid to accumulator
            Add 1 to record counter
            Validate fields
                IF Valid
                    DO Write Record
                OTHERWISE
                    DO Process Error
                END IF

        TERMINATION
            Print totals on audit/error report
            Close files
```

Sequences. If a program contains a *sequence control structure,* two or more instructions or modules will be executed in the same order that they appear within a program. For instance, in the pseudocode in Figure 1.7, the two modules in the initialization section form a sequence structure because they are executed in order, from top to bottom.

Branches. *Branch control structure,* sometimes called selection structure, means that normal, sequential execution of modules or instructions is altered. Program control branches, or alters the order of execution, based upon the results of a decision. When the program reaches the decision point, a test is performed to determine which of two or more alternatives will be selected. Based upon the results of the test, program control branches to the appropriate alternative.

Figure 1.8

Flowchart for the student registration problem

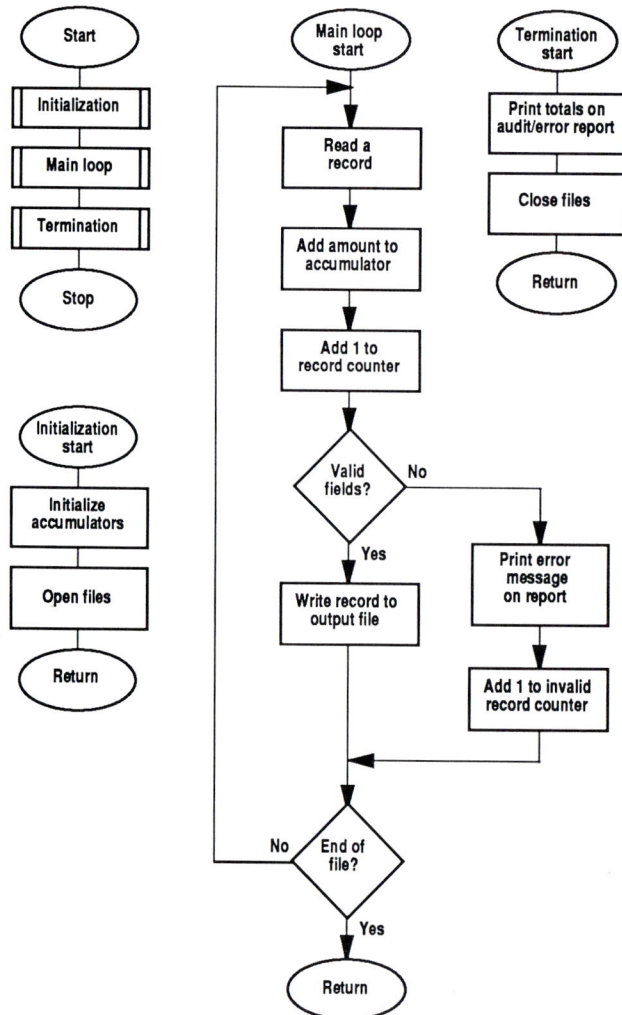

For instance, in Figure 1.8, the program performs a test to determine which of two modules will be executed. If the student record contains all valid fields, the "Write record" module is selected. If the student record contains one or more invalid fields, the "Print error message" module is selected.

Loops. *Loop control structure* means that a set of instructions or modules is repeated until the results of some condition are either true or false (depending upon how the condition test is written). Almost all programs in this text and those that you will design as exercises contain at least one main loop that separates the main processing section of a program from the intialization and termination sections. The reason is simple: After housekeeping procedures prepare a program and its data for processing, the program performs nearly identical processing for each input record. These processing procedures form the main loop.

In general, the main loop inputs a record for processing, processes the record (sorts, calculates, and so on), and outputs the record or writes the record to secondary storage. These three steps repeat for each record to be processed. Notice in Figure 1.6 that the notation "Loop until end of file" is placed after all initialization modules have been completed and before the first record is input. In other words, after the last record in the input file has been processed, control passes to the termination section of the program.

A PROGRAM DESIGN MODEL

The discussion presented so far can be summarized by presenting a general design model that you can follow in organizing modules for just about any program that you write. This model, which follows in pseudocode, portrays the general organization of modules in a structured program and indicates the basic control structures that govern their execution. Within this basic structure, of course, you will design more detailed modules that are executed under other control structures. However, this model can serve as the basic skeleton to which you can add program "meat."

```
Initialization module
    Loop begin
       Inputting module
       Processing module
       Outputting module
    Loop end
Termination module
```

The initialization module defines the variables used in the program and sets their initial value. The inputting module indicates what data have to be entered into the program. It also indicates where the data come from. The processing module changes data input into information output. The outputting module indicates what variables are output as information and to which device the information should go. Finally, the termination module prints summary data and ends the program.

SUMMARY

Chapter 1 introduces the world of programming by showing techniques for solving a problem. In programming, problem solving is often achieved through the top-down approach of problem decomposition. This approach requires you to break down a problem into ever smaller parts until each small part is solvable. Once each part is solved, the whole problem is solved.

Whenever you write a program, you must consider the people involved, the hardware used to run the program, the data and information needs, and the procedures needed. Programming involves problem solving, then coding.

Key Terms

Accumulator	Logic field
Algorithm	Loop control structure
Alphanumeric field	Main memory
Application program	Memory
Arithmetic logic unit (ALU)	Module
Branch control structure	Numeric field
Central processing unit (CPU)	Operating system
Computer information system	Output
Computer program	Peripheral
Computer programmer	Problem decompostion
Control structure	Procedures
Control unit	Processing
Data	Processor unit
Data-centered approach	Programming language
Data input	Pseudocode
Data type	Record
Debugging	Register
Documentation	Remark line
Field	Secondary storage
File	Sequence control structure
Flowchart	Software
Function	Statement
Hardware	Structure chart
Information	Syntax
Initialization	Syntax error
IPO chart	Termination
Logic error	User

1. List the seven processing operations.

2. List the four qualities that users expect in a professionally produced program.

3. What are data types and how do they differ?

4. What are the steps in the problem-solving process?

5. What are the steps in the program development life cycle?

6. What are the differences between an operating system and an application program?

7. List the data hierarchy from smallest to largest.

8. What are the types of program errors? Give an example of each.

9. What are the differences and similarities between debugging and maintenance?

10. What are the control structures? Give an example of each.

11. What is program decomposition and how is it used?

12. What is documentation? Why is it needed? What types are there?

13. What components make up a computer system?

14. What is algorithm development?

15. List the elements in the skeleton program design model.

16. Match the terms that follow with the phrases in this exercise. Terms can be used once, more than once, or not at all. There is at least one term for each phrase.

a. ALU
b. CPU
c. Control unit
d. Disk drive
e. Keyboard
f. Main memory
g. Processor unit
h. Register

_____ Acts like a traffic cop
_____ Performs comparisons and mathematics
_____ Holds data and program instructions
_____ Is a peripheral

17. Following the instructions in question 16, match the terms that follow with the concepts provided.

a. Definition
b. Design
c. Documentation
d. Feasibility

e. Implementation
f. Maintenance
g. Test and debug

_____ Algorithm development
_____ Input/output needs
_____ Syntax error
_____ On-line help screens
_____ Step requiring the most care
_____ Step where most programming time is spent

18. Following the instructions in question 16, match the terms that follow with the concepts provided.

a. Gathering
b. Inputting
c. Outputting

d. Processing
e. Terminating
f. Using

_____ Sorting, classifying, merging
_____ Reporting, providing information
_____ Reliability, timeliness

Problem-Solving Assignments

1. Determine the type of hardware you will be using in this course. Begin to learn its characteristics.

2. Determine the programming language you will be using in this course. This book focuses on BASIC and Pascal. The text will not attempt to show you all the syntax variations of these languages, but it will give you the basics. For more details you will need a reference guide, and you are encouraged to experiment. Problems at the ends of chapters to come will give you code and ask you to work with it.

3. Determine in what form you will develop your programs before translating them into code. Assignments in later chapters will ask you to use one of the program-development tools to plan your programs.

4. Review the list of terms provided in this chapter, even if you think you know the terms. A term in one field may have a different meaning in another.

5. Remind yourself that programming is a combination of problem-solving techniques and coding techniques. Your goal is to first solve problems and then to code the solution. Practice problem-solving techniques by:

a. Directing someone to the library.

- Write down instructions for getting there.
- Test the instructions by using them to go to the library yourself. Did you leave out any steps? If you did, redo your algorithm.
- Give your instructions to another person. Did they end up in the correct location?

b. Writing instructions for making a paper airplane that flies.

- Have someone else follow your instructions. Does the resulting plane fly?

2

Structured Problem Solving

In Chapter 1, you learned that structured problem solving is a process of decomposition. That is, you begin with an overall problem and break it down, or decompose it, into separate parts. You then can manage each step as a separate subproblem.

As a quick example, consider vacation planning. Assume this problem definition: Make all necessary arrangements for a seven-day trip to the Grand Canyon, beginning June 10. After a few seconds of consideration, you come up with several subproblems: notifying employer of vacation date, making airline reservations, making rental car reservations, making hotel reservations, cleaning and organizing hiking gear, packing for trip, arranging for housesitter, and so on.

If you are a realistic person, you realize that each of these steps might involve two or more tasks. Making airline reservations, for instance, might involve calling a travel agent and picking up and paying for the ticket. In programming terms you have decomposed the problem to the level of individual modules.

A module, then, is a task that can be carried out as part of a problem-solving step. Programmers often refer to individual modules as *subprograms*. This book uses the terms *module* and *subprogram* interchangeably. In Latin the prefix *sub* means under. So, a subprogram lies under the control of a main program. In other words, each module, or subprogram, is composed of a set of operations that completes a task for the main program.

Program designs that solve problems by decomposing a problem into problem steps and then decomposing these steps into modules are said to follow a problem decomposition approach. This chapter explores the problem-solving techniques available to you in practicing problem decomposition, which is also referred to as the top-down approach.

A computer program represents a logical solution to a physical problem. For instance, calculating wages and deductions and then writing a paycheck and pay stub for an employee constitute a physical problem. The algorithmic steps that a computer follows in solving this problem represent a logical solution. As a programmer, you design the logic of a program and then instruct the computer to follow this logic in performing a physical solution.

Programming logic is manipulated through the use of control structures. Basically, a control structure describes the order and frequency of module execution. A control structure, then, is a method for organizing problem steps and modules into a working program. As Chapter 1 explained, three types of control structures are available to you:

- Sequence structures
- Branching structures
- Looping structures

This chapter explores the ways you can use these control structures to decompose a problem into steps and subprograms that can be organized into a program. This is called top-down programming.

SEQUENCE STRUCTURES

A sequence structure is a set of program operations that are executed in the same order in which they occur in a program. Figure 2.1 illustrates the generic format for program steps that have been organized into a sequence. Note that steps 2 through 4 are indented. Indentation differentiates between housekeeping tasks and the actual input, processing, and output steps that involve data. In this case all five steps are executed in sequence.

The program begins by executing all the housekeeping, or initialization, instructions required to prepare the computer and data for processing (step 1). Next, program instructions are executed to input data into the computer (step 2). The sequence structure continues by processing data (step 3), then outputting the data (step 4), and—finally—by performing termination activities (step 5).

Sequence structures are valuable in identifying the basic steps that are required to solve a programming problem. However, it is a rare program indeed that follows the strict sequence structure shown in Figure 2.1. Most programming problems are too complex to be handled in this way; decomposing problem steps into separate modules is usually more effective. For this reason, a sequence structure is often just a starting point for decomposing a problem into smaller subproblems that can be designed and executed as separate program units.

Figure 2.1

Format for sequence of program steps

```
Step 1   Begin program
    Step 2   Input data
    Step 3   Process data
    Step 4   Output data
Step 5   End program
```

BRANCHING STRUCTURES

A branching structure allows processing in an order different from the physical sequence of instructions. The two main types of branching techniques are unconditional branching and conditional branching.

Unconditional Branching

You no doubt have heard the phrase "unconditional love," which is often applied to a parent who loves a child no matter what happens or how awful the child might be. Similarly, an *unconditional branch structure* always alters the normal execution of instructions where a branch is specified—no matter what processing results occur.

Figure 2.2 illustrates the general structure of a program that uses an unconditional branch to call subprograms to process input data. Program instructions are executed in sequence until data have been input for processing. After input, control passes to a set of modules that perform separate tasks. This branching activity is unconditional because it always occurs when the computer reaches the specified point in the program.

To demonstrate this branching concept further, Figure 2.3 shows an expanded version of Figure 2.2. Notice that the instructions that constitute the two new modules appear after the overall program structure. However, they are called (executed) before any instructions for steps 4 and 5. Depending on the programming language, branching can be carried out by instructing the computer to search the program for a user-defined line number, module number, or module name.

In step 3 then, the first "Execute" instruction calls the module that contains the instructions that carry out a single task: calculating a student's semester grade point average. After the GPA has been calculated, program control returns to the next instruction in sequence—the second execute instruction of step 3. This instruction, of course, calls the module that calculates a student's overall grade point average. After the instructions within this module have been completed, flow of control returns to step 4. At this point instructions are executed in sequence until the program halts.

Unconditional branching allows you to separate processing into two distinct subproblems. In this case the subproblems correspond with the two chief processing tasks of the program. Having decomposed the processing problem into separate tasks, you can focus on the design of a solution for the first task. After determining the operations that will be performed to calculate a semester GPA, you solve the second task. In this way you design two subprograms that fit neatly within the general algorithm.

Figure 2.2

**Structure for program
using unconditional
branching**

```
Step 1  Begin program
    Step 2   Input data
    Step 3   Process data
        Execute subprograms (modules)
    Step 4   Output data
Step 5  End program
```

Conditional Branching

The programming approaches described so far are a bit unrealistic in that they don't employ a vital computer capacity: the ability to make a comparison and direct program processing flow according to the results of the comparison.

For instance, consider a school that allows students to withdraw from classes temporarily, for as long as one year. Under this plan a student may receive a partial refund for fees paid, but he or she remains enrolled. This plan allows students to take time off to deal with serious family, health, or other personal problems without forfeiting student standing.

Under this program a withdrawal does not cause a student's record to be removed from the student registration file. During grade reporting there is no need to calculate a grade report for a student who has withdrawn from school in mid-semester. So, step 3 begins by testing a status field to make sure the field does not contain a W, which represents *withdrawn*. If the field does contain a W, then the student's record is not processed. This also means that the two modules within step 3 are not executed. This approach is called conditional branching because the program alters sequential flow only if some processing condition is met. As you can see, the top-down approach allows you to first define the general modules. Once they are defined, details can be added.

Figure 2.4 shows a *conditional branch structure* within the general algorithm of program steps. This illustration is an expansion of Figure 2.2. However, notice that Figure 2.4 makes no mention of modules. Step 3 is either executed or not—execution is determined by the results of some condition test. To use modules as the basic

Figure 2.3

How the program directs its flow of control to individual modules

```
Step 1  Begin program
     Step 2   Input data
     Step 3   Process data
          Execute Calculate-Semester-GPA module
          Execute Calculate-Cumulative-GPA module
     Step 4   Output data
Step 5 End program

Calculate-Semester-GPA module
     Instruction 1
     Instruction 2
          .
          .
          .
Return

Calculate-Cumulative-GPA module
     Instruction 1
     Instruction 2
          .
          .
          .
Return
```

building blocks for problem solving and to have as much control over program flow as possible, combine the modular features of Figure 2.2 with the conditional branching of Figure 2.4. Figure 2.5 shows the result.

The problem-solving method is now flexible enough to handle realistic programming problems. For instance, the program structure shown in Figure 2.6 could be used to determine whether a student's status field contains a W.

Notice the use of the term IF in Figure 2.6. IF indicates that a condition test takes place. The END IF notation defines the boundary of the IF statement and the actions that are carried out if the condition test is true. In this case the two "Calculate" modules are carried out only if the status field value is not a W.

Keep in mind that, in an actual program, the semester GPA field would be set to 0 as part of initialization and before each record is input. Similarly, the cumulative GPA field would contain the value that resulted from grade processing for the previous semester. This value would be placed into memory during the input step.

When step 4 outputs a record, these initial values would be printed on a grade report for a student who has withdrawn. For a student currently in attendance, new GPA values would be calculated and printed on the grade report. Figure 2.7 shows how grade reports are generated by following both processing options.

MODULAR TECHNIQUES

Although you have not yet learned about the third control structure (looping), you should begin to develop an understanding of the importance of combining modular coding with branching structures. Modules and branches are the foundation of the top-down approach.

The basic modular coding structure is called a *subroutine*. The terms *subroutine*, *module*, *subprogram*, and *procedure* are used more or less interchangeably. *Module* and *subprogram* are generic terms that relate to a subproblem within an overall pro-

Figure 2.4

Structure for program
using conditional
branching

```
Step 1 Begin program
    Step 2   Input data
    Step 3   Process data if condition is met
    Step 4   Output data
Step 5 End program
```

Figure 2.5

Program structures
using modules with
conditional branching

```
Step 1   Begin program
    Step 2 Input data
    Step 3 Process data
        Execute subprograms if condition(s) is (are) met
    Step 4   Output data
Step 5   End program
```

gram design. *Subroutine* and *procedure* are terms used within specific programming languages.

At this point consider what you know about problem-solving principles: Any problem is divided into solvable steps. Each step is divided into modules. These modular structures carry out the separate tasks for each problem-solving step. Thus, each module is a subprogram that has its own algorithm.

Since a module is a subprogram, you design a module by identifying the algorithmic steps that the module will follow in carrying out its task.

Types of Subprograms

Before you begin designing the algorithm for a particular module, you can simplify your task by determining whether the module already exists. If you have to design and code the module, it is called an *internal module*. If the module already exists, ready for use by your program, it is considered an *external module* in terms of your program design.

With an external module you define the data that will be processed by the module. Then you insert the appropriate command ("Execute" in these examples) that calls the pre-existing module into execution. An external module might be an internal module that you had designed for a previous program, and which also works with your current program. Other external modules might be subprograms that are generic to thousands of programs. Because these subprograms are used so frequently, software companies often sell them to programmers to help simplify programming.

Now take a closer look at internal and external subprograms.

Figure 2.6

Structure for program to determine whether a student's status field contains a W

```
Step 1  Begin program
    Step 2  Input data
    Step 3  IF status field is not W, process data
                Execute Calculate-Semester-GPA module
                Execute Calculate-Cumulative-GPA module
            END IF
    Step 4  Output data
Step 5  End program

Calculate-Semester-GPA module
    Instruction 1
    Instruction 2
        .
        .
        .
Return

Calculate-Cumulative-GPA module
    Instruction 1
    Instruction 2
        .
        .
        .
Return
```

Internal Subprograms. Consider the module to calculate a student's cumulative GPA, which is suggested by the program design in Figure 2.6. At present, instructions for this module do not exist. You need to create an algorithm that lists the steps in solving this sub-problem. Basically, a student's cumulative grade point average is calculated by first adding the semester grade points to the total number of grade points earned during the student's enrollment. (The semester grade points would be calculated and stored in memory as part of the Calculate-Semester-GPA module.) Then the total number of grade points is divided by the total number of semester hours attempted. An algorithm for this subproblem of the grades program looks like this:

Step 1   Add semester grade points to cumulative grade points.
Step 2   Store total number of grade points in new cumulative grade points field.
Step 3   Add semester hours attempted to cumulative semester hours attempted.
Step 4   Store total semester hours attempted in new cumulative semester hours attempted field.
Step 5   Divide new cumulative grade points by new cumulative semester hours attempted.
Step 6   Store result in Cumulative GPA field.

To see how this algorithm might be applied, consider an example: Martha Robbins has earned a total of 53 grade points for this semester. (This amount has already been calculated as part of the Calculate-Semester-GPA module.)

In step 1 of the algorithm, 53 is added to Martha's previous cumulative grade point total, 102.

In step 2, the result, 155, is stored in a computer register.

Step 3 adds the semester hours that Martha has attempted for this semester, 16, to her previous cumulative grade point total, 28. The result, 44, is stored in a computer register as part of step 4.

Figure 2.7

How grades are output by the program

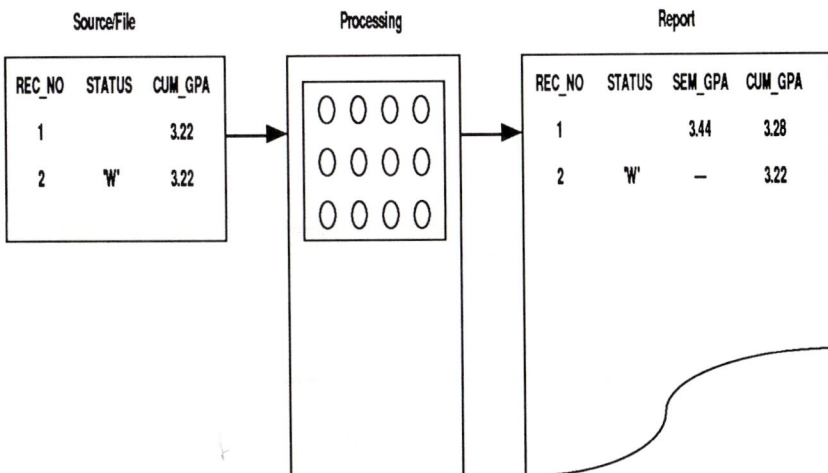

Source/File				Processing		Report			
REC_NO	STATUS	CUM_GPA		0 0 0 0		REC_NO	STATUS	SEM_GPA	CUM_GPA
1		3.22		0 0 0 0		1		3.44	3.28
2	'W'	3.22		0 0 0 0		2	'W'	—	3.22

Step 5 then divides Martha's new cumulative grade points, 155, by her new cumulative grade points attempted, 44. Step 6 stores the result, 3.5, in the cumulative GPA field to await output.

Figure 2.8 illustrates how input, processing, and output for this module work. Notice that the processing steps portray the preceding algorithm in pseudocode form. Return to Figure 2.6 for a moment. As this figure shows, the main program design simply contains a command to execute the Calculate-Cumulative-GPA module. The program design shown by the pseudocode in Figure 2.8 contains the algorithm and, in turn, the logical design that calculates the actual cumulative GPA for a student.

External Subprograms. Now imagine that the president of the university that Martha attends has noticed a disturbing trend in student grades. Specifically, the total GPA for all students has declined slightly over the past three years. In response to this situation, the president wants the data processing staff to design a program to produce mid-semester progress reports for students. These reports are similar to final grade reports, but they are intended to help students evaluate their mid-semester status.

The format of the mid-semester progress report will differ from that of the final semester grade report, but much of the processing will be identical. For instance, the mid-semester report will print a mid-semester GPA and a mid-semester cumulative GPA to show each student his or her standing so far.

Obviously, there is no need to redesign the Calculate-Cumulative-GPA module, since the calculations to be performed are identical to those performed for the final semester grade report. Thus, when the maintenance programmer for this project designs the new program, he or she simply notes that an external module can be called to calculate the mid-semester cumulative GPA. The programmer simply specifies in the main program the data that will be passed to the existing module. It is not necessary to specify any of the processing that will be performed on the data. The code for the existing module can be copied into the new program and then executed as is.

Passing Data to and from Subprograms

The term *passing* refers to transferring items in some manner between main programs and subprograms. Each item to be passed is called an *argument*. Arguments can be used in two ways: locally and globally.

Figure 2.8

Algorithm for the grades program

```
Calculate-Semester-GPA module
        Calculate number of semester grade points
        Add semester grade points to cumulative grade points
            and store in new cumulative grade points field
        Calculate number of semester hours attempted
        Add semester hours attempted to cumulative semester hours
            and store in new cumulative semester hours attempted field
        Divide cumulative grade points by new cumulative semester hours attempted
            and store in cumulative grade point average field
    Return
```

A *local argument* has meaning only to the procedures in which it is *declared,* or defined and placed for use. In other words, you must redeclare a local argument within each procedure that will use the argument. Use of the argument is restricted to procedures in which it is declared.

A *global argument* has meaning to an entire program—that is, to the main program and all procedures. Typically, you establish a global argument by placing it in a specific part of the main program. The placement of a global argument varies for different languages.

The terms *local* and *global* refer to the *scope,* or boundaries for use, of an argument. Thus, the scope of an argument is defined by its placement in a program.

Arguments can also be defined according to the way they are passed. There are two basic techniques that programming languages use to pass an argument: by variable and by value.

Passing Arguments by Variable. In the GPA calculation modules, you can pass the argument by defining its variable name in terms of a procedure. By doing so, you are providing the subprogram with the memory address for a particular variable used in the main program. Thus, when you execute the Calculate-Cumulative-GPA subprogram, you call it in this way:

```
Execute Calculate-Cumulative-GPA (with Semester-Grade-Points, Semester-Hours-
    Attempted)
```

This subprogram call tells the main program to pass the memory location for the variable Semester-Grade-Points to the Calculate-Cumulative-GPA module. The variable Semester-Hours-Attempted is also passed to the Calculate-Cumulative-GPA module. As this example shows, it is possible to pass more than one argument to a procedure at a time. Here the two arguments in parentheses make up the *argument list*. Because argument passing by variable is achieved by referring to a memory location, this approach is often called *passing by reference.*

Passing Arguments by Value. As an alternative, you can pass only the value of a variable to a subprogram, rather than the memory location. With this approach the Calculate-Cumulative-GPA subprogram is called in this way:

```
Execute Calculate-Cumulative-GPA (with Semester-Grade-Points value, Semester-
    Hours-Attempted value)
```

The program passes the values currently stored in the Semester-Grade-Points and Semester-Hours-Attempted variables. Return to Martha Robbins's record for a moment. If you pass arguments to the Calculate-Cumulative-GPA module by value and Martha's record is currently in memory, the subprogram call passes the value 53 (her semester grade points) and the value 16 (her semester hours attempted).

You might have realized that passing by variable has, in this case, the same effect as passing by value. That is, if you pass Martha's arguments by variable, the subprogram uses the addresses for the variables and then references the values 53 and 16. However, passing by value provides a safeguard. Because the subprogram does not have any memory addresses, there is no way for it to pass values back to the main program. This safeguard can be valuable if a subprogram alters a value during processing.

LOOPING CONTROL STRUCTURES

In most processing situations, instructions within one or more modules need to be executed two or more times. Consider the GPA program. As you might have realized, steps 1 through 4 have to be executed for each student record that is input to the program. In other words, for each record, fields have to be input, calculated, and—possibly—output. If you know that 350 student records will be processed, you can instruct the program to repeat these steps 349 times. After the final record in the file has been processed and/or output, the program passes control to step 5 to prepare to terminate processing.

This type of loop—in which input, processing, and output modules are repeated once for each input record—is often called a *main processing loop*. The generic logic for this type of loop appears in the pseudocode in Figure 2.9.

Notice that separate pseudocode entries are provided at the beginning and ending points of the loop. These two entries are mandatory. If you omit either the starting or ending statements of a looping structure, your program may abort or fail to compile. At worst, absence of an end-of-loop instruction can cause the program to enter an *endless loop*. That is, you will not have provided a way for the program to exit the looping structure. In such a case the program continues to process instructions indefinitely. To avoid these kinds of disasters, the program must know when to begin and end the repetition of instructions or modules.

Figure 2.10 expands the generic pseudocode of the previous illustration. It shows the main portion of the program, after a main processing loop has been specified.

The looping approach shown in Figure 2.10 represents one of two basic types of loops. These two types are fixed loops and variable loops.

Fixed Loops

The looping example presented in Figure 2.10 is a *fixed loop*. In other words, the number of passes through the loop is known. In this case, you need to establish a *counter* area in memory to keep track of the number of passes through the loop. This is done by specifying an *initial value* that can be used to maintain a count of passes.

For instance, it is commonplace to set an initial value as 0 or 1. The value 0 is used if the loop will begin counting with the first input record.

The value 1 is preferable if the loop will begin counting after the first record has been input. This approach is called a *trailing read*. In a trailing read, the first record in a file is input as part of the "Begin program" step. Subsequent records are input at the end of the main processing loop. In later chapters you will see why this approach can be efficient—even necessary.

For fixed loops it is also important to include a *termination value*. Suppose you know that 350 records exist in the student file, and that you will use an initial read in the "Begin program" step and a trailing read after each record has been processed. In this case the initial looping value is 1, and the termination value is 350. After each record is processed, you instruct the program to add 1 to the counter value currently in memory. When this counter value reaches 350, the program exits the loop. The pseudocode for this program logic is shown in Figure 2.11.

Notice that Figure 2.11 contains the same number of processing steps as Figure 2.10. However, in Figure 2.11 step 2 has been moved to the end of the loop. The inputting step is now step 4, and it includes instructions to *increment* the counter value—that is, to increase the counter by the value specified. In this case the counter value is 1. Step 4 also inputs the next record in the file. Figure 2.11 shows a trailing read operation.

Figure 2.9

Logic for a main processing loop

```
Step 1  Begin   program
            LOOP a fixed number of times
               Input data
               Process data
               Output data
            END LOOP
         End program
```

Figure 2.10

Expanded pseudocode for a main processing loop

```
Step 1 Begin program
   LOOP a fixed number of times
      Step 2   Input data
      Step 3   IF status field is not W, process data
               Execute Calculate-Semester-GPA module
               Execute Calculate-Cumulate-GPA module
               END IF
               Step 4   Output data
   END LOOP
Step 5 End program
```

Figure 2.11

Pseudocode for a fixed loop

```
Step 1  Begin program
   Set counter to 1
   Input first record
   LOOP until counter = 350
      Step 2   IF status field is not W, process data
               Execute Calculate-Semester-GPA module
               Execute Calculate-Cumulative-GPA module
               END IF
               Step 3   Output data
               Step 4   Add 1 to counter
   Input Next Record
   END LOOP
Step 5   End program
```

In many cases it is not possible to know the exact number of records to be processed as part of a loop. For instance, many data files are considered *volatile*. This term means that the content and size of the file changes continually. In the student records example, new student records are added from time to time; other records are deleted when students drop out of school.

Variable Loops

In these kinds of cases, it is usually more efficient to design a *variable loop* to handle main processing. As this label suggests, a variable loop is one in which the exact number of passes through the loop is not known when the program is executed. In other words, the number of records in the file can vary from one processing session to the next.

Figure 2.12 illustrates the two types of variable loops used in program designs. The first is called a LOOP UNTIL structure; the second is called a LOOP WHILE structure. The difference lies in the minimum number of passes that will be made through the loop.

LOOP UNTIL. With a LOOP UNTIL structure, the program assumes that at least one pass will be made through the loop. In other words, at least one record will be processed before the loop is exited. So, the program inputs the first record and then loops until there are no more records.

LOOP WHILE. A LOOP WHILE structure ensures that the program will run correctly even if the file is empty. This looping structure does not assume any minimum number of passes through a file. The program inputs a record and then loops while there is a data record present. If the first input record is empty, the program exits the loop without performing any processing steps.

Figure 2.12

Two types of variable loops

LOOP UNTIL Structure
```
Step 1   Begin program
              LOOP UNTIL no more data
                 Step 2
                 Step 3
                 Step 4
              END LOOP
Step 5   End program
```

LOOP WHILE Structure
```
Step 1   Begin program
              LOOP WHILE more data
                 Step 2
                 Step 3
                 Step 4
              END LOOP
Step 5   End program
```

Variable Loop Design. A variable loop can be designed by including a trailer record, which is always placed in the last position in the file. This record contains dummy data in most fields. That is, alphanumeric fields contain blanks and amount fields contain 0s. The program uses this dummy record to detect the end of the file. In one field of the trailer record is a *sentinel value,* a value that a test searches for to identify a specific point. When the sentinel value is identified, the loop is terminated. The generic LOOP UNTIL and LOOP WHILE structures in Figure 2.13 include a test for a sentinel value.

Figure 2.14 shows the LOOP WHILE in the GPA program.

CASE STUDY: PAYROLL PROCESSING

The student records example in this chapter is sufficiently simple to illustrate basic control structures and their relationships to modules. However, in the real world, a program is rarely this simple. Consider a realistic business example: payroll processing.

Imagine that you have been hired by the Mickey's Hamburger Corporation to computerize the payroll process for hourly employees. You are told that the payroll program must contain the following fields:

Name
Employee number
Number of dependents
Rate of pay
Number of hours worked
Total earnings thus far this year

Figure 2.13

Structure for LOOP
UNTIL and LOOP WHILE

LOOP UNTIL Structure
```
Step 1 Begin program
            LOOP UNTIL sentinel value = 999
               Step 2
               Step 3
               Step 4
            END LOOP
Step 5 End program
```

LOOP WHILE Structure
```
Step 1 Begin program
            LOOP WHILE sentinel value < > 999
               Step 2
               Step 3
               Step 4
            END LOOP
Step 5 End program
```

Figure 2.14

LOOP WHILE used in the GPA program

```
Step 1 Begin program
   Input first record
        LOOP WHILE student number (sentinel value) = 999- 99-9999
             Step 2 IF status field is not W, process data
                      Execute Calculate-Semester-GPA module
                      Execute Calculate-Cumulative-GPA module
                   END IF
             Step 3  Output data
             Input next record
             Step 4
          END LOOP
     End program
```

You begin automating the payroll system by considering the wage summary report. The payroll manager for the Mickey's chain shows you the format in which manual reports are now being prepared. Each line on this report provides payroll data for a single employee. You are to duplicate the current format, which follows.

Weekly Wage Report

NAME	ID#	RATE	HRS	GROSS	FICA	TAX	HLTH	YTDNET
XXXXX	XXX	99.99	99	999.99	99.99	99.99	99.99	999.99
XXXXX	XXX	99.99	99	999.99	99.99	99.99	99.99	999.99
				.				
				.				
				.				
TOTALS				9999.99	9999.99	9999.99	9999.99	999999.99

To determine the pay for each employee, your program must:

- Define gross pay as pay for regular time plus pay for overtime. Define overtime pay as 1.5 times the regular rate for each hour after 40 hours.
- Define Social Security tax (FICA) as 6.45 percent of gross pay. Make FICA deductions until the employee's cumulative earnings are above $32,000. After cumulative earnings reach this amount, make no FICA deduction.
- Deduct income tax and group health plan contributions according to Table 2.1.
- Define net pay as gross pay less FICA deduction less income tax deduction less group health deduction.

Your program must print final totals for gross pay, deductions, and net pay for the year to date. A good way to transform these specifications into an initial program design is by creating an IPO chart. Recall that this type of design documentation lists general input, processing, and output requirements for the program. Later steps involve expanding this chart to identify and decompose individual modules.

Figure 2.15 shows an initial IPO chart for the payroll processing problem. Study this chart carefully before you continue reading.

Module Identification

In translating these specifications into modules, begin by considering the top five modules that are standard for all structured programs:

```
Begin payroll program (initialization)
    Do input procedure
    Do processing procedure
    Do output procedure
End program (termination)
```

Figure 2.16 shows a simple structure chart that portrays this arrangement of modules. All three of the procedures shown in pseudocode will include subordinate, or lower-level, modules. Within each procedure subordinate modules will carry out sets of specific processing operations.

Table 2.1

Dependents	Income Tax % of Gross	Group Health $ per Week
1	22	3.75
2	20	4.75
3	18	6.25
4 or more	13	7.75

Income tax and health plan deductions for payroll processing problem

Figure 2.15

IPO chart for the payroll processing problem

Requirements

Input	Processing	Output
ID#	GROSS = #HRS * PAYRATE	ID#
#HRS WORKED	TAXES = GROSS * PAYRATE FOR #DEPENDS	GROSS PAY
PAY RATE	HEALTH = HEALTH STATUS * RATE FOR #DEPENDS	TAX STATUS
# DEPENDS		TAXES
HEALTH STATUS	FICA = % UP TO AMOUNT	FICA
YTDPAY	NET = GROSS - DEDUCTIONS	NETPAY
YTDPAY	YEARTD = YEARTD + GROSS	YTDPAY

Case Study: Payroll Processing

Figure 2.16

The arrangement of
modules in the payroll
example

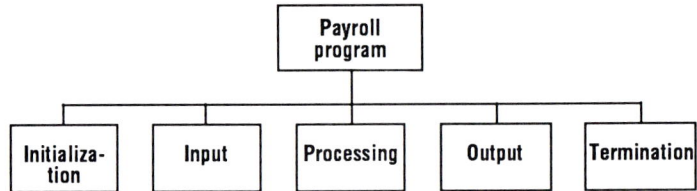

In Chapter 3 you will learn how control structures can be used to decompose each
of these general modules into submodules and, finally, into individual processing operations. Another point to keep in mind before continuing to Chapter 3: By organizing program design around this general modular structure, you can make changes to
the program relatively easily. For instance, federal tax tables change frequently. With
a modular program structure, you can make this kind of change within a single module. That is, you update the module that contains instructions for determining tax percentages, but it is not necessary to modify any other modules. By placing related
instructions within separate modules, this kind of program maintenance is easy.

Module Coding

This text will illustrate program design by using the BASIC and Pascal programming
languages. In Chapter 3 you will learn more about the structure and syntax of these
languages. For now, study the BASIC and Pascal program sections that follow. The
top-down approach to the problem in BASIC is:

    Initialization section
    Input section
    Processing section
    Output section
    Termination section

Also study this BASIC implementation:

```
GOSUB 100 ! INITIALIZE
GOSUB 200 ! INPUT
GOSUB 300 ! PROCESS
GOSUB 400 ! OUTPUT
GOSUB 500 ! TERMINATE
```

In the first approach, all low-level modules fall directly underneath each general-
level module heading, or section. The second approach uses a *control module*. The

control module calls, or executes, low-level modules, one section at a time. The first GOSUB (that is, GO to SUBROUTINE) instructs the program to branch to line 100, which contains all low-level modules for the INITIALIZE section of the program. This is the approach suggested by the pseudocode structure.

After all initialization modules have been executed, program control returns to the next line of the control module (GOSUB 200 ! INPUT). In response to this line of code, the program branches to line 200 of the program to execute all INPUT section modules. This structured approach continues until all modules within the TERMI-NATE section of the program have been executed.

The Pascal program looks like this:

```
PROCEDURE  INIT
PROCEDURE  ENTER
PROCEDURE  PROCESS
PROCEDURE  OUTPUT
PROCEDURE  TERMINATE
BEGIN {MAIN PROGRAM}
   INIT
   ENTER
   PROCESS
   OUTPUT
   TERMINATE
END {MAIN PROGRAM}
```

In this example all five general-level modules are defined at the head of the program. Then the BEGIN statement is used to instruct the program to execute modules within each section of the MAIN PROGRAM, section by section. After all modules within the TERMINATE section of the program have been executed, the program comes to a halt.

Module Differentiation

At this point the top-down approach allows you to specify and briefly describe separate modules within the general program structure. You can do this one module at a time, beginning with the initialization module.

Initialization Module. Recall that initialization includes setting variables to an initial value. Variables should be set to 0 if you expect the variable name to appear to the left of an assignment operation. This type of program statement establishes a value for a variable or constant. An assignment operation is indicated by an equals sign. Other variables will be used to make calculations and thus will not be assigned to a register as a result of processing.

Take a look at Figure 2.15, the IPO chart for this program. As you can see, six variables appear to the left of assignment statements. These are GROSS, TAXES, HEALTH, FICA, NET, and YEARTD. Each must be set to 0 during initialization. The pseudocode for this module is:

```
Begin initialization module
      Initialize variables to 0 (GROSS, TAXES, HEALTH, FICA, NET, YEARTD)
End initialization module
```

Input Module. Now the input module can be planned. The IPO chart shows that six fields must be read into the program in preparation for processing. These fields must be input for each record that is processed. Here is the pseudocode for this input procedure:

```
Begin input module
      Read In ID#,#HOURS WORKED,PAY RATE,#DEPENDS,HEALTH STATUS,YTDPAY
End input module
```

Processing Module. With variables defined and input fields specified, you can define the basic structure of the processing module. Figuring gross pay, tax, and health deduction involves a simple calculation for each variable. These calculations can be specified as separate instructions within the pseudocode for the processing module.

However, calculating FICA, net pay, and year to date pay requires two or more processing steps for each variable. For instance, FICA is calculated only if the employee's year-to-date pay is less than $32,000. This suggests the need to specify at least one condition test and one possible calculation. When you begin designing a program, you might not realize this need to decompose further. However, that is the purpose of modular decomposition. By beginning with the topmost, or most general, processing operations, you can add details for separate modules until you have a complete program.

To indicate the need to call a low-level module, use DO within pseudocode. The resulting pseudocode for the processing module is:

```
Begin process module
      Calculate gross (#HRS WORKED * PAY RATE)
      Calculate taxes (GROSS * #DEPENDS)
      Calculate deductions based on #DEPENDS and HEALTH STATUS
      DO FICA module
      DO NETPAY module
      DO YTDPAY module
End process module

Begin FICA module
      Calculate FICA Tax
End FICA module

Begin NETPAY module
      Calculate NETPAY = GROSS - TAXES - FICA - HEALTH
End NETPAY module

Begin YTDPAY module
      Calculate YTD PAY total = YTD PAY + GROSS
End YTDPAY module
```

Notice that the three submodules that will be part of the general processing module are set apart. Later, you can decompose these modules—as well as the processing module itself—to include individual processing instructions. To portray the structure of the processing module and its submodules, it helps to draw a structure chart. This is done in Figure 2.17. Figure 2.17 combines a structure chart with the high-level chart shown in Figure 2.16.

Figure 2.18 shows the pseudocode for the initialization, input, and processing modules.

Figure 2.19 implements the pseudocode in BASIC. Figure 2.20 implements the pseudocode in Pascal. At this point you are not expected to understand the syntax used to write code in these languages. Introductory information about these languages is discussed in Chapter 3. Chapter 3 also decomposes the payroll program further and includes explanations for the output module.

SUMMARY

This chapter introduces you to modular decomposition and structured programming techniques. Each is crucial to building programs that are easy to understand and maintain. By knowing how, why, and where to use the various looping, branching, and sequencing techniques, you will learn the process of solving a problem.

Branching is a particularly important topic because it forms the basis for top-down modules. Through branching you can go from one part of a problem-solving process to another.

Figure 2.17

The structure for the payroll program, showing top-down modular decomposition

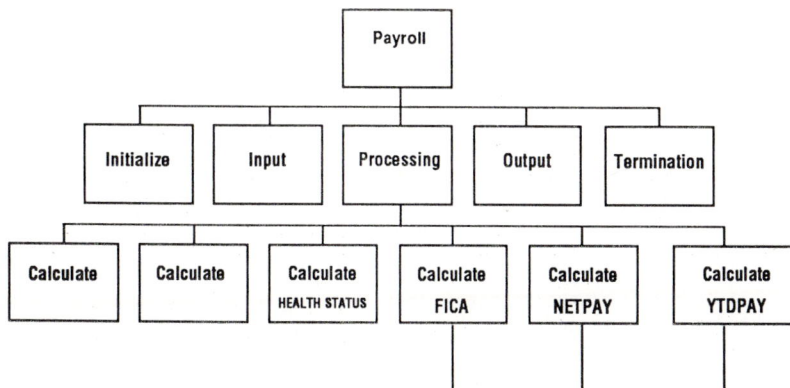

Figure 2.18

Psuedocode for initialization, input, and processing modules

```
A.PSEUDOCODE FOR SIMPLE PROGRAM
      BEGIN PAYROLL PROGRAM
            DO INITIALIZATION PROCEDURE
            DO INPUT PROCEDURE
            DO PROCESSING PROCEDURE
            DO OUTPUT PROCEDURE
      END PAYROLL PROGRAM

      BEGIN INITIALIZATION MODULE
            INITALIZE VARIABLES TO 0 (GROSS, TAXES, HEALTH STATUS, FICA, NETPAY)
      END INITIALIZATION MODULE

      BEGIN INPUT MODULE
            READ IN ID#, #HOURS WORKED, PAY RATE, #DEPENDS, HEALTH STATUS,
            YEAR TO DATE PAY
      END INPUT MODULE

      BEGIN PROCESS MODULE
            CALCULATE GROSS (#HOURS * PAY RATE)
            CALCULATE TAXES (GROSS * #DEPENDENTS %)
            CALCULATE HEALTH DEDUCTION BASED ON #DEPENDS AND HEALTH STATUS
            DO FICA MODULE
            DO NETPAY MODULE
            DO YEAR TO DATE PAY MODULE
      END PROCESS MODULE

      BEGIN FICA MODULE
            CALCULATE FICA TAX
      END FICA MODULE

      BEGIN NETPAY MODULE
            CALCULATE NETPAY = GROSS - TAXES - FICA - HEALTH
      END NETPAY MODULE

      BEGIN YEAR TO DATE PAY MODULE
            CALCULATE YEAR TO DATE PAY TOTAL = YEAR TO DATE + GROSS
      END YEAR TO DATE PAY MODULE
```

Figure 2.19

Psuedocode written in MS-DOS version 3.2 BASIC

```
10    REM PROGRAM TO SHOW MODULAR DECOMPOSITION
20    GOSUB 100  !  INITIALIZATION MODULE
30    GOSUB 200  !  INPUT MODULE
40    GOSUB 280  !  PROCESSING MODULE
50    GOSUB 400  !  OUTPUT MODULE
60    GOSUB 500  !  TERMINATION MODULE
100   REM INITIALIZATION MODULE
110   G=0
120   TX=0
130   H=0
140   F1=0
```

(continued)

Figure 2.19 (continued)

```
150   NP=0
160   YD=0
170   RETURN
200   REM INPUT MOUDLE
210   INPUT ID
220   INPUT HR
230   INPUT PR
240   INPUT DP
250   INPUT HS
260   INPUT YD
270   RETURN
280   REM PROCESSING MODULE
300   G=HR*PR
310   IF DP=1 AND HS=1 THEN TX=G*.2:H=50
320   IF DP=2 AND HS=1 THEN TX=G*.18:H=80
330   IF DP=3 AND HS=1 THEN TX=G*.16:H=100
340   IF DP>34 AND HS=1 THEN TX=G*.14:H=100
350   GOSUB 800
360   GOSUB 900
370   GOSUB 1000
380   RETURN
400   REM OUTPUT MODULE
410   PRINT ID,G,TX,F1,NP,YD
420   RETURN
500   REM TERMINATION MODULE
510   END
800   REM FICA MODULE
810   IF YD>32000 THEN F1=0 ELSE IF YD+G>32000 THEN F1=(32000-YD)*.2 ELSE F1=G*.2
820   RETURN
900   REM NET PAY MODULE
910   NP=G-F1-H-TX
920   RETURN
1000 REM YEAR TO DATE TOTAL MODULE
1010 YD=YD+G
1020 RETURN
```

Figure 2.20

```
PROGRAM MODULAR (INPUT,OUTPUT);
{PROGRAM TO SHOW MODULAR DECOMPOSITION}

VAR
  ID:INTEGER;
  DEPENDENTS:INTEGER;
  GROSS:REAL;
  TAXES:REAL;
  HEALTH:REAL;
  FICA1:REAL;
  NET PAY:REAL;
  HOURS:REAL;
  PAYRATE:REAL;
  HEALTHSTATUS:REAL;
  YEARTD:REAL;
```

**Pseudocode written
in Pascal**

(continued)

Figure 2.20 (continued)

```
PROCEDURE INIT;
  BEGIN
      GROSS:=0.0;
      TAXES:=0.0;
      HOURS:=0.0;
      FICA1:=0.0;
      NET_PAY:=0.0;
  END;

PROCEDURE DATAIN;
  BEGIN
      READLN(ID);
      READLN(HOURS);
      READLN(PAYRATE);
      READLN(DEPENDENTS);
      READLN(HEALTHSTATUS);
      READLN(YEARTD);
  END;

PROCEDURE FICA;
  BEGIN
      IF YEARTD = 32000   THEN FICA1:=0
      ELSE IF YEARTD+GROSS>32000    THEN
           FICA1:= (32000-YEARTD)*0.20
      ELSE FICA1:= GROSS*0.20
  END;

PROCEDURE NET;
  BEGIN
      NET_PAY:=GROSS-(FICA1+HEALTH+TAXES)
  END;

PROCEDURE YTDTOTAL;
BEGIN
      YEARTD:=YEARTD+GROSS
END;

PROCEDURE PROCESS;
  BEGIN
      GROSS:=HOURS*PAYRATE;
      IF(DEPENDENTS=1 AND HEATHSTATUS=1) THEN
              BEGIN
                TAXES:=GROSS*0.20;
                HEALTH:=50
              END;
           ELSE IF (DEPENDENTS=2 AND HEALTHSTATUS=1) THEN
              BEGIN
                TAXES:=GROSS*0.18;
                HEALTH:=100
              END;
           ELSE IF (DEPENDENTS=3 AND HEALTHSTATUS=1) THEN
              BEGIN
                TAXES:=GROSS*0.16;
```

(continued)

Figure 2.20 (continued)

```
              HEALTH:=100
           END;
      ELSE IF (DEPENDENTS>3 AND HEALTHSTATUS=1) THEN
           BEGIN
             TAXES:=GROSS*0.14;
             HEALTH:=100
           END;
      END;
      FICA;
      NET;
      YTDTOTAL;
  END;

PROCEDURE DATAOUT;
  BEGIN
      WRITELN(ID:7,GROSS:8:2,TAXES:8:2,FICA1:8:2,NET_PAY:8:2,YEARTD:8:2);
  END;

BEGIN{MAIN PROGRAM}
  INIT;
  DATAIN;
  PROCESS;
  DATAOUT
END. (MAIN PROGRAM)
```

Key Terms

Argument	Local argument
Argument list	LOOP UNTIL
Conditional branch structure	LOOP WHILE
Control module	Main processing loop
Counter	Passing
Declare	Passing by reference
DO	Scope
Dummy data	Sentinel value
Endless loop	Subroutine
External module	Termination value
Fixed loop	Trailer record
Global argument	Trailing read
Increment	Unconditional branch structure
Initial value	Variable loop
Internal module	Volatile

Review Questions

1. What are the types of control structures?

2. What is a module?

3. What is sequencing? How is it determined in BASIC and Pascal?

4. What is branching?

5. What are the similarities and differences between internal and external branching?

6. How can data be passed between subprograms?

7. What are the differences among variable, value, local, and global passes?

8. What is passing by reference?

9. What is looping?

10. What are the types of loops and how are they different?

11. What kind of loops are UNTIL and WHILE? How do they differ?

12. What is modular decomposition?

13. Match the terms that follow with the related concepts listed in this exercise. The terms can be used once, more than once, or not at all.

Argument	Local	UNTIL
Conditional	Numbered lines	Value argument
External	Sentinel	Variable argument
Fixed	Subprogram	Variable
Global	Unconditional	WHILE
Internal		

_____ Looping
_____ Branching
_____ Sequencing

14. Study the program that follows.

```
10 REM
20 REM
30 REM
40 READ A
50 IF A=999 THEN GOTO 160
60 ON A GOTO 70,90,110,130
70 PRINT "VALUE OF A IS 1 SO 1ST NUMBER BRANCH"
80 GOTO 140
90 PRINT "VALUE OF A IS 2 SO SECOND NUMBER BRANCH"
100 GOTO 140
110 PRINT "VALUE OF A IS 3 SO 3RD NUMBER BRANCH"
120 GOTO 140
130 PRINT "VALUE OF A IS 4 SO 4TH NUMBER BRANCH"
```

```
140 GOTO 40
150 DATA 1,4,2,3,999
160 END
```

What line number(s) form(s) a variable loop? What line number(s) form(s) a conditional branch? What line number(s) form(s) an unconditional branch? How is sequencing determined?

15. Study the following program:

```
10  REM
20  REM
30  REM
40  REM
50  COUNT=1
60  F=0
70  G=0
80  DIM A(100)
90  REM
100 REM
110 REM
120 READ A(COUNT)
130 IF A(COUNT)=999 THEN GOTO 160
131 REM
132 REM
133 REM
140 COUNT = COUNT + 1
150 GOTO 120
160 COUNT = COUNT - 1
170 REM
180 REM
190 REM
200 FOR I=1 TO COUNT
210      F=F+A(I)
220 NEXT I
230 G=F/COUNT
231 REM
232 REM
233 REM
240 PRINT "TOTAL     =";F
250 PRINT "AVE       =";G
260 PRINT "N =";COUNT
270 DATA 100,90,80,70,60,50,40,30,20,10,20,30,40,50,60,70,80,90,100,999
271 REM
272 REM
273 REM
280 END
```

a. What line number(s) form(s) a fixed loop? What line number(s) form(s) a variable loop? What line number(s) form(s) a conditional loop? What line number(s) form(s) an unconditional branch?

b. Given your understanding of modularization, what comment would you make at each of these lines: 20, 100, 132, 180, 232, and 272.

16. Study the following program:

```
PROGRAM TAXED(INPUT,OUTPUT);
{PROGRAM TO COMPUTE PROPERTY TAXES}

VAR
    CATEGORY:    INTEGER;
    VALUE:       INTEGER;
    RATE,
    TAX:            REAL;
BEGIN
    WRITELN('ENTER DOLLAR VALUE OF HOME   ');
    READLN(VALUE);
    WHILE(VALUE>0) DO
        BEGIN
            CATEGORY:= VALUE DIV 1000;
            IF CATEGORY > 6 THEN CATEGORY:=6;
            IF CATEGORY < 2 THEN RATE:=0.03
                ELSE IF CATEGORY < 3 THEN RATE:=0.04
                        ELSE IF CATEGORY < 6 THENRATE:=0.05
                                ELSE RATE:=0.06;
        TAX:= VALUE*RATE;
        WRITELN(' ASSESSED VALUE = $',VALUE);
        WRITELN(' TAX IS =           $',TAX:12:2);
        WRITELN;
        WRITELN('ENTER DOLLAR VALUE OF HOME—TO END ENTER -1');
        READLN(VALUE);
        END {WHILE}
END. {PROGRAM}
```

a. What line(s) form(s) a fixed loop? What line(s) form(s) a variable loop? What line(s) form(s) a conditional branch? What line(s) form(s) an unconditional branch? What line(s) form(s) a global variable?

b. List the first and last lines of the initialization, input, process, output, and termination modules of the program.

Problem-Solving Assignments

1. Modify the payroll program pseudocode presented in Figure 2.18 to show the following:

   a. Separate tax and health calculations
   b. Taxes, health, and gross pay moved into separate modules.
   c. Add a loop to process several records rather than one.
   d. Add a termination module to print totals for each category (year to date, gross pay, net pay, taxes, health, and FICA).

2. Modify the BASIC code of Figure 2.19 or the Pascal code of Figure 2.20 to reflect the pseudocode changes you have made for assignment 1.

3. Write pseudocode for the following problem:

Enter four numbers. Two are integers and two are real numbers. Add the two integers; add the two real numbers. Print out the results in the following format:

```
INTEGER 1  = X        INTEGER 2   = X        SUM  = XX
REAL 1     = X.XX      REAL 2      = X.XX     SUM  = XX.XX
```

4. Write pseudocode to

- Calculate annual, quarterly, and continuous interest

Sample input = $1000 at 12.4% for 3 years
$7700 at 11.7% for 7 years

- Prompt the user for input
- Include an error routine to catch bad data.
  The processing formulas are:

Annual   Principal *   (1 + rate) ^ number of years
Quarterly   Principal *   (1 + rate/4) ^ (4 * number of years)
Continuous   Principal *   Exponent of (rate * number of years)

The output should look like this:

The principal of XXXX.XX at XX.X% for X years will be worth:

     Annual $XXXXX.XX
    Quarterly $XXXXX.XX or
   Continuous $XXXXX.XX

3

Modular Details
of Problem Solving

Now that the concept of structured problem solving using the top-down approach has been presented, you can proceed with some practical aspects of software development.

INITIALIZATION MODULE

A computer program can be likened to someone who has just awakened from a blow on the head to discover that he or she is suffering from partial amnesia. Such a person may be able to speak the language but can't remember what he or she was doing an hour before. This comparison relates to program variables. A *variable* is a memory area or field that can contain more than one value during program processing.

Contrast variables with constants. A *constant* is a value that remains the same throughout program processing. For instance, if you know how many records will be processed by a program, you can establish a constant for this amount. You can instruct the computer to terminate its main processing loop after it has processed 150 records. In the payroll program example in Chapter 2, the minimum wage might be used as a constant, because this value remains stable for a relatively long period of time. On the other hand, other items processed by a program, such as a running total or a customer name, change for each record processed. These items represent variables.

To continue the example of the amnesiac: The values of counters and other data requirements are unknown at the time a program "wakes up" and begins processing. In the early days of programming, the contents of variables could be "garbage" if memory areas contained numeric values that had lingered from the previously executed program. Fortunately, most modern language compilers and interpreters initialize all variables to some safe state (such as 0s for numeric variables and null strings for character variables). However, it is still wise to initialize any variable that will be assigned a value as a result of processing.

Built-in safeguards do save the software developer some effort, but they do not take care of variables that have to be given some specific value before processing can begin. For example, imagine that the student GPA program discussed in Chapter 2 needs to access the student records file on a disk. When the program begins to execute, it must initialize a variable with the name of the file to be opened. This name specification allows the information to be passed by the program when it requests the operating system software to get the desired file. You can be certain that the program will not get much done if the requested file is filled with blank spaces. The same concept holds true for any variable that must be passed between a main program and its subprograms (modules). For this reason, experienced programmers take great care to define all variables before determining how these values will be processed. Initialization procedures include but are not limited to the following:

- Output headers
- First value assignments
- Documentation
- Environment definitions

Output Headers

One of the first things that a software package must do is to prepare input and output devices for use.

In general, when a program is initially invoked or when it begins a new section, it clears the screen. The program then displays information that identifies the particular program section that is being executed and what the section should accomplish. The screen also displays any additional information that is helpful or necessary to the user. This is done to eliminate old information and messages from a previous section that might confuse or mislead the user.

If the program generates printer output or editable output files, such output entities should also be initialized. This initialization, which is accomplished by *output headers,* might sound like a great deal of unnecessary work, done only for the sake of appearance. However, experience has proven that, as software becomes more powerful and complex and as inexperienced users are placed in front of the computer, these techniques become important. A user who does not understand what a program is doing at a given point in processing is probably uncomfortable with the software.

First Value Assignments

To assign initial values to all variables, most languages in use today require that the variable name to be initialized be placed on the left side of an assignment operator. The initial value for the variable is placed to the right of the operator. For example:

```
G  = 0
H1 = 1
```

Recall from Chapter 2 that an assignment operator is specified in pseudocode by using the equals sign. In programming languages different symbols may be required.

For instance, assignment operators include := for Pascal, = for BASIC and FOR-TRAN, and == for the programming language C.

For constants, the name of the constant appears to the left of the assignment operator. The constant value is placed on the right side of the assignment operator. As previously explained, constants should be defined only for quantities that will not change during the execution of the program.

Documentation

Documentation refers to all material that helps users and other programmers understand the intent and features of a program. Structure charts and pseudocode used to design a program are examples of documentation. Other examples include user's manuals, source code listings, and flowcharts.

One of the most beneficial types of documentation is the remark line. A remark line is a description, written in English, that can be embedded in pseudocode as well as the source code of a program. When source code is compiled or interpreted, remarks are ignored. In this way source listings can be printed that show coded modules as well as sentences that describe the processing activities that the modules perform.

Why include clear documentation when you design programs? The long-term success of your program depends on it. The costs for maintaining and debugging a program can be quite high when adequate documentation is not available. This fact holds true no matter how well a program is designed and partitioned. Also, users may refuse to accept a program that proves to be difficult to operate or understand.

The critical point to keep in mind: The primary function of documentation is to explain what a program can and cannot do. Many programs have failed to become accepted solely because program limitations are not explained to users. Maintenance programmers also need to know the extent of capabilities.

Many different techniques are available to document programs. Each approach has advantages and disadvantages. Use whatever appears best suited for the job at hand. Often a flowchart and structure chart are important. Other times, a prose explanation is helpful. In any case, the following items should be included in every program or module (as applicable):

- Program name and description
- Environment needed to run (what hardware, what operating system)
- Variable names
- Name of developer
- Date originally developed
- Name of maintenance programmer, date revised, and explanation of changes made
- List of all available external documents (including design documentation)

Environment Definitions

In programming terminology, an *environment* refers to the hardware and data resources that a program will use during processing. In most cases the operating system controls the use of hardware devices. However, data resources are the domain of an application program. For this reason, it is important to define all data that will be input, processed, and output by a program.

Consider an analogy: When you take notes, you separate information according to the different classes you are taking. For each class you might underline and define items that represent major topics. By doing so, you provide a method for identifying and grouping information when you study your notes later. Similar organizational methods are used in preparing a program for processing.

For instance, a program must allocate memory space for the fields of each input record. Memory space must also be defined for constants, values, and any new fields that result during processing. The program must "understand" the processing relationships for different fields. These relationships can be defined by specifying data types.

To understand the importance of defining the environment in which a program will operate, consider the different ways in which data can be stored and represented in memory.

DATA HIERARCHY

This section describes the hierarchy that programs use to organize, store, and process data. The hierarchy begins with the smallest component and works up; therefore, it is known as a bottom-up structure. Figure 3.1 shows the components in the structure.

Computers do not really understand any instructions written in English or even in a programming language. A completed program must be translated into sets of 0s and

Figure 3.1

Hierarchy data structure

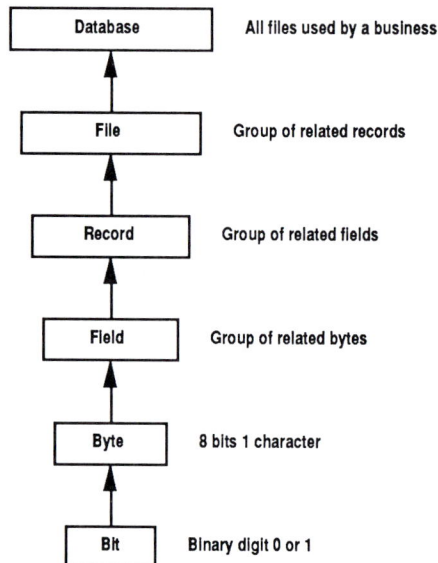

Database	All files used by a business
File	Group of related records
Record	Group of related fields
Field	Group of related bytes
Byte	8 bits 1 character
Bit	Binary digit 0 or 1

1s, a configuration called *machine language*. These digits direct the operations of computer circuits.

At this point you might wonder how this can be so. A computer is a bi-state device. This means that each circuit within a computer is either on or off. If a circuit is on, then current is allowed to pass through. If a circuit is off, current is prevented from passing through. By combining several thousand circuits, a computer can alternate the flow of current to represent separate instructions. Each instruction represents a way to input, process, output, or store data in some manner.

Computer circuits are controlled directly by machine language. System programmers develop sets of machine-language instructions that are coded entirely using 0s and 1s. These two digits form the *binary* system of instruction for a computer. Each 0 represents a circuit that is off. Each 1 represents a circuit that is on. This explanation is somewhat simplified, but it does suggest the basic operating states for all computers.

Bits

A single binary digit is called a *bit*. This is the smallest unit that a computer can use to process program instructions and data. All other data structures are built from this basic unit. Thus, data storage in digital computers is extremely well defined and is actually rather easy to understand.

Bytes

Bits are rather useless by themselves; they have to be grouped together to form useful structures. The next higher structure is called a *byte,* which typically consists of 8 bits. The rightmost bit is called the *least significant digit* or the units bit. The least significant digit is usually assigned the value of 2^0. The least significant digit represents only the value 0 or 1.

Moving from right to left are bits that represent growing powers of 2: 2^1, 2^2, . . . , 2^7. Remember, all computer operations are represented by combining 0s and 1s. The computer does not recognize, at the machine-language level, the values 3 through 9. This means that the normal base 10 numbering system that you use in daily life is useless in communicating directly with computer circuits. Computers use *base 2*. This simply means that all values are based upon the ordering of the values 0 and 1 in multiples of two.

The base 2 values correspond, in base 10, to 2, 4, 8, and so on up to 128. Figure 3.2 shows the available range of values in base 2. In the figure, the term *binary* means base 2; *decimal,* in this context, means base 10.

Figure 3.2

```
00000000 binary  =  0 decimal
11111111 binary  =  128 + 64 + 32 + 16 + 8 + 4 + 2 + 1 =225 decimal
```

Set of binary values with their decimal equivalents

At this point it is not necessary for you to understand these numbering systems thoroughly. However, it is helpful to familiarize yourself with the basic structures available for communicating directly with a computer. For instance, when bits are grouped into an individual byte, they typically represent one character of data, such as the letter C, the number 8, or the symbol *. This is often referred to as the symbolic level of computer representation.

In most cases you will work with individual characters (symbolic patterns) to create data structures and programming language instructions. You will use separate translation programs (called compilers or interpreters) to translate the symbolic instructions of a program into the machine-language instructions that a computer can execute directly.

Most computer data are organized in multiples of bytes. For instance, the letter *A* is represented as a single byte. Representing the word *Adams* takes 5 bytes or more. The main memory of a computer is usually defined in terms of kilobytes, or *Kbytes*. The letter *K* stands for *kilo,* or (in this context) approximately 1000 bytes. Specifically, 1 Kbyte of data is equal to 2^{10} or 1024 bytes.

Another quantity used to describe storage (especially nonvolatile storage on magnetic media such as floppy or hard disks) is *megabyte*. This term refers to approximately 1,000,000 bytes—specifically, 2^{20} or 1,048,576 bytes.

In the early days of computers, a megabyte of memory cost hundreds of thousands of dollars and required special power and cooling arrangements. Today, it is not uncommon to find a desktop personal computer with a megabyte of main memory and 20 megabytes or more of hard-disk storage. These capacities are available at a price well within the reach of an individual or small company. These large amounts of storage capacity have become necessary, since many of today's powerful programs require hundreds of Kbytes of memory for program and data.

Records

Related bytes of data, as you know, are organized to form individual fields. A field is the smallest unit of data that has meaning to users. For example, a customer's last and first names represent two different fields. A sales total represents another field. When fields are grouped to show relationships, they are said to be a record. For instance, a customer record might include a customer's last name, first name, street address, city, ZIP code, phone number, and so on. Recall from Chapter 2 that each iteration of a main processing loop typically inputs and processes fields for a single record. Thus, the record is a useful structure for organizing fields for input, processing, output, and storage.

Files

Just as related fields can be combined to form a record, so related records can be combined to form a file. In computer terms a file is a set of related records that are stored as a unit. Typical files within companies today may contain hundreds of Kbytes per file. In addition, powerful programs often process entire *databases,* or related collections of files, that can consume several megabytes of magnetic storage.

DATA TYPES

Now that you have learned the general physical structure of data within a digital computer, a detailed explanation of the basic data types is in order. As mentioned earlier, a data type indicates the basic use to which a field will be put. Data types are usually part of data definition activities that take place during or prior to initialization.

Because of the properties of binary arithmetic, bytes can comprise 256 separate representations. The bytes might represent letters of the alphabet, hair color, height, or weight. Most high-level languages reserve one 8-bit piece of memory for each variable type. The two types are character and Boolean.

Character Type

A *character* is a representation of an uppercase or lowercase letter, a numeric digit, a punctuation mark, or a symbol that is understandable to a programming language. Figure 3.3 shows the ASCII character equivalents for the numerals 1 through 9. ASCII is the most widely used coding standard for microcomputers.

A group of characters is called a *string*. A string could represent names of files, students, and other fields. Character strings can vary from a length of 0 (an empty string, also called a null string) to a maximum length defined by the programmer and/ or the language implementation.

Strings can be copied, compared, combined, concatenated, and parsed (extracted from a larger string). Later chapters will introduce the operators available for string manipulation.

Boolean Type

A *Boolean* type is used to represent a field that can have only two possible states: true or false. For instance, in a student records file, you might create a Boolean field to indicate whether a student has paid his or her registration fees. If the student has paid, the field is marked as true. If the student has not paid, the field is marked as false.

Figure 3.3

ASCII code for numerals 1 through 9

Numeric Character	ASCII Representation
1	49
2	50
3	51
4	52
5	53
6	54
7	55
8	56
9	57

Other Useful Data Types

As a programmer, you will encounter several other data types on a fairly regular basis. These types require more room to be reserved in memory. Two of the more common types are integers and reals.

Integer Type. An integer is almost always defined as a multiple number of bytes long. Most languages treat an integer as either 2 bytes or 4 bytes long. Because of the properties of binary arithmetic, an integer is always represented with the most significant bit being the sign bit. This means that a value is either positive or negative. The remaining bits represent the actual numeric value.

Thus, as Figure 3.4 shows, a 2-byte integer can represent numbers from 32767 to minus 32768. In many languages, if you repeatedly add the value 1 to an integer variable it will eventually wrap around, as shown in Figure 3.4. Thus, 2-byte integers are often inadequate to represent data associated with business applications that involve extremely large numbers, such as bank account processing. For such cases, larger integers are often available. Their size is usually language and machine specific.

Real Type. The real variable type is often used for applications that do not demand extreme precision. A real consists of two parts: a fraction part that holds digits and an exponent part that tells the machine where to put the decimal point. Conceptually, this is similar to scientific notation, in which exponents of 10 are used to represent very large or very small quantities.

Because of the limited bit length of a real, it is possible that the addition of a very small number to a very large number will not change the bit pattern associated with the large number. Thus, it is again important to select the appropriately sized real variable for the amount of precision required.

Information regarding the capabilities of the available data types can almost always be found in the language reference manuals provided by the compiler vendor; the professional programmer should always be familiar with these capabilities.

DATA CONVERSION

Keep in mind that the reason for providing data types to variables is to indicate to the computer how the variable is to be processed. For instance, an integer variable can be used in mathematic calculations, but a character variable cannot. However, situations often arise where it is necessary in a program to use a single variable for two or more types of processing. To solve this problem, almost all programming languages provide features for *data conversion*. For instance, many languages have provisions for moving numeric values from one data type (say, an integer) to another type (perhaps a real).

Consider: If you try to move the contents of a real variable that holds the number 1000000 into an integer variable that can hold a maximum positive value of 32767, something is going to go terribly wrong. In most cases the result of such an illegal operation is garbage.

Data conversions are programming language specific. That is, each programming language has its own rules and requirements for converting a value. However, knowing the general uses and limitations of different data types will enable you to accommodate data conversions when you design your programs.

CONSTANTS

So far, you have studied only the variables used in program design. *Constants* represent an equally important category of values. Program constants fall into two general categories: explicitly defined constants and implicit constants.

An *explicitly defined constant* receives a value at the outset of a program. It can then be used for a specific purpose during processing. For instance, you might want to specify that a main processing loop be repeated a specific number of times. You can establish a constant value for this purpose. When the loop counter matches the constant value, the program exits the loop.

An *implicit constant* is one that is used within a particular programming instruction, without having been defined. For instance, in the equation A = 3 * B, the value 3 remains constant, while the variables A and B may change. Note that the constant 3 in this equation is of unknown type and precision. Depending on the language used and other program factors, this constant might be treated as an integer or a real. The constant 3 could be any length—2 bytes, 4 bytes, etc.

Thus, the precautions stated for mixed variable-type computations apply to constants as well. For this reason many languages have facilities for the definition of explicitly typed constants. In Pascal, for example, the real constant PI might be defined as:

```
CONST
PI: REAL = 3.14159;
```

These two instructions tell the computer to reserve a location in the nonchanging part of memory and to store there a specific binary pattern that corresponds with the

Figure 3.4

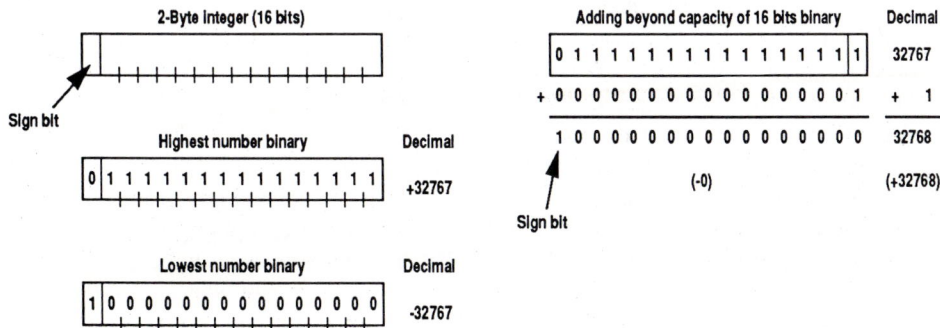

Range for 2-byte integers, and the wraparound effect

representation of the real value 3.14159. The second instruction states that the particular location for the constant will be called PI. Whenever the computer sees the name PI, it will refer to the contents of the constant defined in the CONST section of the program.

This feature points to another advantage of explicitly defined constants—the ability to conserve memory. Imagine that you are writing a program that uses the value 3.14159 many times. If you write 3.14159 within each instruction that uses it, the computer saves a separate copy of the numeric value in each instance. In complex programs this can be very wasteful of memory. Additionally, it is possible that you could mistype 3.14159 as 3.14195 and thus produce an incorrect computation. By explicitly defining a constant in only one place (usually at the beginning of the program), you can check the value carefully once and be confident that the computer will always use the correct value.

INTRODUCTION TO DATA STRUCTURES

In many applications it is useful to bind several pieces of data into a packet to simplify processing. Under this approach several data items are linked to form a single unit, called a *data structure*. Two such structures are used frequently in business programming: arrays and records.

Arrays

An *array*, in general, is a structure that can be referenced using a single data name. The structure can hold several data values in adjoining memory positions. Programmers use arrays in situations in which a clear, sequential relationship exists between the values. Think of an array as a multicolumn table. Separate *elements* within the table are organized into columns and rows. An index can then be set up to determine the position of each value stored in the array.

Single-Dimensional Arrays. Suppose a manager of a business has a program that interacts with a news retrieval service. The program samples the value of a particular stock every five minutes during hours in which the stock market is open. These samples are placed in a single-dimensional array. A dimension of an array is the number of data values that can be referenced for each position. The opening value is the first table element, and it has an index value of 1 or 0, depending on which language is used. Subsequent values are placed in the array in the order in which they are sampled. Figure 3.5 shows how this simple single-dimensional array could be viewed in table form.

With this array it is not necessary to define a separate field name for each stock value. Instead, the entire array of values can be accessed through a single table name. This approach saves time in defining fields and it also saves memory. In addition, you can take advantage of the table format in creating processing options for the manager. For instance, you could design a program that allows the manager to perform calculations based upon the content of the array. The manager might want to determine the fastest rate at which the stock rose or fell for any three samples.

Two-Dimensional Arrays. Now imagine that the manager wants to sample values for several commodities, in addition to the stock. Say that this manager wants to sample the price of gold, the price of petroleum, and the price of treasury bonds at the same moment that the stock price is sampled.

A *two-dimensional array* can be established for this purpose. In this case, the array contains two arguments, or data values, for each row in the array. Two indexes keep track of these arguments. One index identifies the desired commodity to be accessed. The index value 1 specifies the stock, the index value 2 specifies gold, the value 3 specifies petroleum, and the value 4 specifies treasury bonds.

The second index identifies the time slot at which the readings are taken. This allows the manager to compare the relationships among the four economic goods. To continue the example, imagine that the manager wants to sample the data over a long period of time (say, a year). This situation suggests the need for a *three-dimensional array*. In this case, a third table argument to the array indicates the day within the year.

The arrays described are considered *numeric arrays* because they contain numeric values that can be used to make computations. Most compilers allow arrays to be defined for each data type recognized by that particular language implementation. Thus, arrays can be defined of type BYTE, INTEGER, REAL, and so on. However, all elements of an array must be of the same type. Many languages also allow for the definition of character string arrays. These are useful for holding the names of students, products, or other values that are composed of characters.

Arrays are discussed in greater depth in Chapter 6. For now, just keep in mind that an array is a useful data structure that can simplify processing steps and save memory space.

Records

A record is generally considered a higher form of data structure than an array. The reason: Records usually allow for different types. A record is a meaningful collections of fields that describe a single entity—a person, place, event, transaction, or the like. A simple example of a record is the collection of fields that a school keeps in a file for each student. It contains both a name field of type character and a grade point average field of type real. The record structure allows for easy and reliable manipula-

Figure 3.5

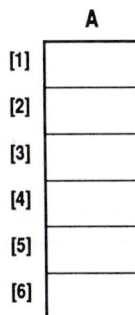

A

[1]
[2]
[3]
[4]
[5]
[6]

Single-dimensional array in table form

tion of information that naturally belongs together. The record is a powerful concept, and it is used in almost all business programs as a way of organizing data into a file.

CASE STUDY: PAYROLL PROGRAM, INITIALIZATION MODULE

A good way to view the details involved in initialization is through an example. Recall the payroll program developed in Chapter 2. The pseudocode developed so far for the initialization module looks like this:

```
Begin initialization procedure
      Initialize variables to 0 (GROSS, TAXES, HEALTH, FICA, NETPAY, YTDPAY)
End initialization module
```

It should be apparent that this pseudocode description is incomplete. For instance, no attempt has been made to document variables or to meet initialization requirements by defining data types or providing output headers. To plan for these initialization needs, begin by making a list of all variables and constants to be used by the program, as well as their data types and any required first value assignments:

NAME	TYPE	FIRST VALUE
GROSS	Numeric, real	0
TAXES	Numeric, real	0
FICA	Numeric, real	0
HEALTH	Numeric, real	0
HEALTH STATUS	String (Y or N)	
NETPAY	Numeric, real	
YTDPAY	Numeric, real	
NAME	String	
#DEPENDS	Numeric, integer	
#HRS WORKED	Numeric, real	
PAY RATE	Numeric, real	
DEDUCTIONS	Numeric, real	

Use this documentation as an aid in decomposing the pseudocode and in providing programming code later. Consider how you can account for these variable and constant values within an expanded pseudocode:

```
Begin initialization module
      Provide proper internal documentation
      Define data variables and constants
      Assign first values
      Define output formats (headers, etc.)
End initialization module
```

Figure 3.6 shows the expanded structure chart for this initialization module.

These pseudocode instructions can now be translated into code for the BASIC and Pascal languages.

BASIC Initialization Module

The BASIC code for the initialization module for the payroll program is shown in Figure 3.7. Notice how each of the pseudocode steps has been accounted for through the use of a REM statement, or remark line. Remember: Statements on REM lines will not be translated into machine language. A REM statement is for documentation purposes only.

Also notice the DEFINE OUTPUT section, in which a line of output is defined with the variable specification X$. In BASIC the dollar sign can be used with a variable to specify a string. A BASIC string is simply a sequence of characters that are processed as a single unit.

The string itself is marked, or delimited, through the use of quotation marks. The string appears to the right of the assignment operator. The pound sign (#) is used to indicate the format of each field to be output for each processed record. Notice that, within the string, dollar signs specify a currency (money) field. Decimal points are inserted within field formats.

Pascal Initialization Module

Figure 3.8 shows the Pascal code for the payroll initialization module. Pascal is a strongly typed language. That is, a data type must be specified for each variable and constant used in the program. Notice that the VAR and CONST statements are used to indicate these definitions to the Pascal compiler. For each line within the VAR and CONST portions of the program, a field name is provided along with a data type (for variables) or first value (for constants).

Note that first values for variables are assigned separately. The term BEGIN is used to indicate the start of actual program instructions to be executed. For each variable name that follows BEGIN, the program assigns a 0. The END term specifies that this block of instructions has come to an end. In Pascal, program code is organized into blocks of related instructions. This structured requirement of Pascal helps to enforce the modular concept of structured programming. In general, you may think of a Pascal block as a separate module, although this is not always true.

Figure 3.6

Structure chart for initialization module

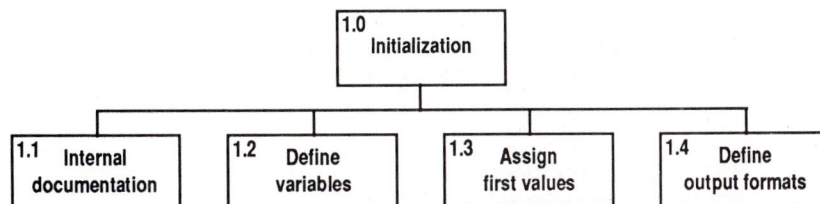

Case Study: Payroll Program, Initialization Module

Figure 3.7

BASIC code for the initialization of the payroll program

```
10       REM    PROGRAM TO SHOW PAYROLL EXPANSION IN A MODULAR FASHION
20       GOSUB 1000   !   INITIALIZATION PROCEDURE
30       GOSUB 2000   !   INPUT PROCEDURE
40       GOSUB 3000   !   PROCESSING PROCEDURE
50       GOSUB 4000   !   OUTPUT PROCEDURE
60       GOSUB 5000   !   TERMINATION PROCEDURE
1000     REM    INITIALIZATION PROCEDURE
1010     REM    PAYROLL PROGRAM FOR FUN FANTASIES
1020     REM    WRITTEN BY J. ADAIR          JULY 1988
1030     REM
1040     REM    PROGRAM DESIGN TO RUN ON MACHINE USING A STANDARD
1050     REM         BASIC (NO SPECIAL DEVICES NEEDED)
1060     REM
1070     REM    THIS PROGRAM IS A REVISON OF PROGRAM INTRODUCED IN
1080     REM         CHAPTER 2
1090     REM    REFER TO TEXT IN THIS CHAPTER FOR EXPLANATION
1100     REM
1110     REM    DEFINE VARIABLES
1120     REM
1130     REM    G  =  GROSS PAY
1140     REM    TX =  TAXES
1150     REM    H  =  HEALTH COSTS
1160     REM    FI =  FICA
1170     REM    NP =  NET PAY
1180     REM    ID =  PERSON ID
1190     REM    HR =  HOURS WORKED
1200     REM    PR =  PAY RATE/HR
1210     REM    DP =  # OF DEPENDENTS
1220     REM    HS =  HEALTH STATUS
1230     REM    YD =  YEAR TO DATE PAY
1240     REM    H1 =  RATE FOR 1 DEPENDENT HEALTH COST
1250     REM    H2 =  RATE FOR 2 DEPENDENT HEALTH COST
1260     REM    H3 =  RATE FOR 3 DEPENDENT HEALTH COST
1270     REM    M1 =  MINIMUM WAGE
1275     REM    MX =  MAXIMUM WAGE
1280     REM
1290     REM    ASSIGN FIRST VALUES
1300     REM
1301     REM    ASSIGN VALUES TO ALL VARIABLES THAT WILL APPEAR
1302     REM    LEFT OF AN ASSIGNMENT SIGN (=).  MAY HAVE TO
1303     REM    REINITIALIZE WITHIN PROGRAM
1310     G  = 0
1320     TX = 0
1330     H  = 0
1340     FI = 0
1350     NP = 0
1355     YD = 0
1360     REM
1370     REM    DEFINE CONSTANTS
1380     REM
1381     REM    USED TO SET VALUES THAT CAN CHANGE FROM YEAR TO
```

(continued)

Figure 3.7 (continued)

```
1382 REM        YEAR DUE TO CONTRACT NEGOTIATIONS AND GOVERNMENT
1383 REM        REGULATIONS
1390 H1 =  50
1400 H2 =  80
1410 H3 =  100
1420 MI =  5.50
1430 MX =  12.50
1440 REM
1450 REM     DEFINE OUTPUT
1460 REM
1470 X$ =      "#######    $######.##      ####.##   ###.##   ####.##
$######.##"
1480 RETURN
```

Figure 3.8

**Pascal code for the
initialization module of
the payroll program**

```
PROGRAM PAYROLL (INPUT, OUTPUT);

{PROGRAM TO SHOW PAYROLL EXPANSION IN A MODULAR FASHION}

PROCEDURE INIT;

{PAYROLL PROGRAM WRITTEN BY J. ADAIR          JULY 1988

PROGRAM DESIGNED TO RUN ON MACHINE USING A STANDARD Pascal
(NO SPECIAL DEVICES NEEDED)

THIS PROGRAM IS A REVISION OF PROGRAM INTRODUCED IN CHAPTER TWO.
REFER TO TEXT IN THIS CHAPTER FOR EXPLANATION

DEFINE VARIABLES}

VAR
   GROSS_PAY:   REAL;
   TAXES:       REAL;
   HEALTH_COSTS: REAL;
   FICA:        REAL;
   NET_PAY:     REAL;
   PERSON_ID:   INTEGER;
   HOURS:       REAL;
   PAY_RATE:    REAL;
   NUMDEPENDENTS:INTEGER;
   HEALTH_STATUS:CHAR;
   YEAR_TO_DATE: REAL;
 CONST    {DEFINE AND ASSIGN IN ONE STEP}
    ONEDEPENDEDNT=50;
    TWODEPENDENT=80;
    THREEPLUSDEPENDENT=100;
    MINWAGE=5.50;
    MAXWAGE=12.50;
```

(continued)

Case Study: Payroll Program, Initialization Module

Figure 3.8 (continued)

```
BEGIN
   GROSS_PAY     := 0.0;
   TAXES         := 0.0;
   HEALTH_COSTS := 0.0;
   FICA          := 0.0;
   NET_PAY       := 0.0;
END;
PROCEDURE DATAIN;
{TO BE DEFINED LATER}
BEGIN
END;
PROCEDURE PROCESS;
{TO BE DEFINED LATER}
BEGIN
END;
PROCEDURE DATAOUT;
{TO BE DEFINED LATER}
BEGIN
END;
BEGIN {MAIN PROCEDURE}
   INIT;
   DATAIN;
   PROCESS;
   DATAOUT;
END. {MAIN PROCEDURE}
```

Finally, notice that remark lines in Pascal are enclosed within braces ({}). When the Pascal compiler encounters an opening brace, it knows to ignore all entries until a closing brace is identified. The braces act like the REM statement of BASIC. Also observe that the main procedure is included and has not changed from the earlier example. The reason lies in the top-down structure of the program. Low-level modules change as they are expanded to include new details; however, the high-level modules that call the low-level blocks need not change.

THE OUTPUT MODULE

This book stresses the logical steps that a computer must follow to get results. At this point, you might ask a logical question: Why design details for an output module before designing an input module? The answer is logical.

Consider what happened to the early explorers during the fourteenth, fifteenth, and sixteenth centuries. Columbus, for instance, set sail with three fully stocked ships (input). However, he had only a vague idea of where he was going (output). The result: He stumbled onto some islands in the Caribbean. In programming, it is just as easy to become lost if you do not have a good idea where you are headed. So, you determine output details before you "stock your ship." With an output module well defined, you can return to your input module and expand it to reflect output needs.

The Purpose of Output

The output module of a program controls the presentation of information to end-users. In a strict sense, the end-user is the person viewing the screen or reviewing a printed report, or an output file that will later be used as input to another program. An end-user might even refer to specialized hardware that converts numbers and other commands to voltages or other physical quantities to control an external process such as an industrial robot or a chemical plant.

The first step in decomposing an output module is to identify the information that needs to be presented and its form. For example, the stock-monitoring array mentioned earlier in this chapter used an integer index to identify each five-minute slot of the business day. Unfortunately, knowing that the 20th sample was the highest of the day may not be of much use to the human user; what he really wants to know is that the peak occurred at 10:40 a.m. So, an algorithm needs to be developed to convert the index number to a human-usable form. The intelligent programmer should ask questions to determine what output should be presented and in what form. For instance:

- Should the information be presented in the form of a graph rather than as a jumble of numbers on a screen or on paper?
- Should data appear in tabular form on the screen?
- Should the data presentation rate be intentionally slow to allow the user an opportunity to evaluate numbers carefully?
- Should a "freeze" key be provided to allow the user to stop the data presentation when he or she spots something unusual?

Output Mechanisms

Generally, the most important consideration for the design of the output module is the output mechanism. The most common types are printers, screens, and data files. Sometimes the application requires output to more than one of these at the same time. For instance, many graphic design packages available for personal computers allow the screen to show a picture of the object being designed while the design data are being updated on the disk.

Printer Output. In the case of printer output, some considerations are:

- Page numbering and job title information
- Date and time
- Column header information
- Justification (alignment) of data output within a column
- Special control sequences for special effects—underlining, boldfacing, subscripting, and so on.
- Special processing for graphics data

Screen Output. For screen output, the main considerations focus on ease of use of the information and professional appearance and function. Anyone who has ever used a poorly written program can attest to the frustration and confusion that poor screen output can cause.

In designing screen output the first step is to lay out the appearance of the screen on paper. Begin by taking into account the maximum required width for each data field and the total number of columns and rows available on the screen. For example, most personal computers support a screen that is 80 characters wide and 25 lines high. One common workstation can support both 80- and 132-character screens.

Other considerations for screen output involve the selection of appropriate colors (where available) for various parts of the screen and the selection of options such as blinking and reverse video. However, a warning is in order here: Many programmers have become overly involved in the "artistry" of their screen displays. The result is often a display of characters in a distracting and confusing format. In general, it is best to use the simplest screen design possible to provide the most information.

File Output. File output formats are usually more limited than those available for printer and screen outputs. The chief concern for file output is the size of each record. Wasteful techniques in defining and storing records can "eat up" magnetic storage at an alarming rate. A balance must be struck between storage efficiency (how tightly you can package all the information that needs to be saved) and program execution time (if data are too tightly packed, they may need to be "expanded" before they can be used by a program).

Output Style

Another important consideration for program output is the level of sophistication and detail that the output requires. For example, a spreadsheet screen must usually show the values computed for each entry. (As you may know, a spreadsheet is a display of values in row and column format, and it is usually for making financial calculations.) The user must be able to see each entered or computed value to evaluate its accuracy or usefulness. On other displays, some values might need to be hidden. For instance, it is not necessary for the user of a word processing package to view all the processing options during a writing or editing session. Instead, some provision should be made to allow the user to call a menu of processing options when needed. Whatever the application, the software developer should always keep clearly in mind the needs of the intended user.

CASE STUDY: PAYROLL PROGRAM, OUTPUT MODULE

Return again to the payroll program example. The pseudocode for the output module looks like this:

```
Begin output procedure
      Print ID#, GROSS PAY, TAXES, FICA, NETPAY, YTDPAY
End output procedure
```

This is a simple declaration of the field values to be printed for each record. However, no mention has been made of the format in which these fields will be shown. Also missing is an indication of the device(s) to which records will be output. So, you might expand the pseudocode in this way:

```
Begin output procedure
      Print proper headings and provide labels for output
      Print, in readable form, data corresponding to headings (ID#...YTDPAY)
End output procedure
```

You are still not ready to code this module or even to elaborate upon input. A specific output format, or layout, must be described. The term *layout* refers to the general appearance of output. Layout considerations include titles, column headings, field descriptions and length, and any totals to be printed.

One formatting approach is to develop a *print chart*. This piece of documentation graphically shows all headings, field types and field lengths, and spacings for the required output. In other words, the print chart portrays the appearance of an output document. A print chart for this program is shown in Figure 3.9.

Notice that the character "b" is used whenever a blank line or blank space is indicated. This is a common approach to output specification. Also observe the similarity between print specifications for fields and the output format specified within the BASIC code of Figure 3.7. As you can see, the output format has already been provided in the initialization module of the BASIC version of the program.

The BASIC Output Module

At this point, you can write code that will provide the output results that you are seeking. The output module for the BASIC version of the payroll program appears in Figure 3.10. Notice that PRINT statements are used to specify data to be sent to a printer. *Literal strings,* the strings to be printed, are enclosed within quotation marks. In programming, a literal represents a value literally—that is, a literal value is composed of the letters, numerals, and symbols shown.

To illustrate, take a look at line 2070 in Figure 3.10. The PRINT statement in this line specifies that the literal string, ID#, be printed as a column heading. These are the same three characters shown in the print chart in Figure 3.9. However, the next speci-

Figure 3.9

Print chart for the payroll program

```
PAYROLL                                          JULY 1988
-----------------------------------------------------------
b
b
b
ID#bbbbbbbGROSS PAYbbTAXESbbbbbFICAbbbbbbbNETPAYbbbbYEAR TO DATE
b
xxxxxxx     $xxxxx.xx   xxxx.xx   xxx.xx     xxxx.xx   $xxxxxx.xx
b
b
```

Case Study: Payroll Program, Output Module

fier on this PRINT line is not a literal. This specifier, TAB(10), uses the TAB instruction to tell the printer to skip to column ten. The next item to be printed, GROSS PAY, is a literal. This is followed by another TAB instruction. The pattern repeats for all column headings to be printed.

Now turn your attention to line 2100. This line uses a PRINT USING statement to designate variables to be printed. The instruction

```
2100 PRINT USING X$
```

tells the printer to use the string format specified by X$, which is defined in the initialization module. Using this format, the program prints the values stored in the variable and constant names provided. In this case, values are printed for ID (person ID), G (gross pay), TX (taxes), FI (FICA), NP (net pay), and YD (year-to-date pay).

The Pascal Output Module

In standard Pascal, print formats are a bit more difficult to define than in BASIC. Standard Pascal does not provide a statement similar to the PRINT USING in BASIC. As a result, each printed field must be specified by using its variable or constant name, as well as its maximum length. Spaces between fields must be included within field lengths.

The Pascal output module for the payroll program is shown in Figure 3.11. Notice that the term WRITELN is used to specify output. Output destination is determined on the program header. Observe how the column heading line is specified as a literal string through the use of parentheses and single quotation marks. For each record to be output, the WRITELN statement must provide the field name, field length, optional number of decimal places, and optional dollar sign to specify currency.

Also notice the block structure used by the module. The module begins with a PROCEDURE name (DATAOUT). Instructions to be executed within this PROCEDURE are enclosed within the BEGIN and END terms.

Figure 3.10

BASIC code for the output module of the payroll program

```
2000     REM       OUTPUT  PROCEDURE
2010     REM
2020     PRINT     "PAYROLL  PROGRAM  JULY  1988"
2030     PRINT     "--------------------------------------------------"
2040     PRINT
2050     PRINT
2060
2070     PRINT     "ID#";TAB(10);"GROSS PAY";TAB(20);"TAXES";
TAB(30);"FICA";TAB(40);"NET PAY";TAB(50);"YEAR TO DATE PAY"
2090     PRINT
2100     PRINT USING X$;ID;G;TX;F1;NP;YD
2110     PRINT
2120     PRINT
2130     RETURN
```

Figure 3.11

Pascal code for the
output module of the
payroll program

```
PROCEDURE DATAOUT;
BEGIN {OUTPUT PROCEDURE}
   WRITELN('PAYROLL PROGRAM JULY 1988');
   WRITELN('------------------------------------------------------------------
----------------------------------------');
   WRITELN;
   WRITELN;
   WRITELN('ID GROSS PAY  TAXES FICA NETPAY YEAR TO DATE PAY')
   WRITELN(PERSON_ID:10;'$';GROSS_PAY:9:2;TAXES:10:2;FICA:10:2;NET_PAY:10:2;'$';
YEAR_TO_DATE:10:2);
   WRITELN;
   WRITELN;
END;          {OUTPUT PROCEDURE}
```

THE INPUT MODULE

Now turn your attention to expansion of the input module. Some programs, such as
the student GPA program, have rather straightforward input requirements: When invoked, the program reads data for student records and generates a summary. In
theory, the program could be run in the middle of the night, without the need for any
human intervention (in what is commonly called batch mode). Of course, the programmer must supply the computer with alternate courses of action if it cannot complete normal processing. In planning input the programmer might ask these questions:

- What should the program do if it can't get to the input file?
- What if the program reads an illegal value as part of the input phase?
- If a problem occurs, should the program quit, skip the particular student, or try
  to get the information for that student from a backup file?

Error Handling

These three questions address an area of program design called *error handling*. In
planning error-handling procedures the programmer expects that everything that can
go wrong will go wrong. Special routines are then coded to test for and to resolve
these problems. Error handling is a critical part of input. Many programs include
separate error-handling modules to test and resolve potential problems.

At any rate, the first step in planning input involves determining what input data are
required to support the desired output. This may seem trivial. However, you might be
amazed to learn how many multi-million-dollar projects get into serious trouble because the program design team overlooked this simple admonition: Not only must you
identify what data must be gathered, you must also identify the required type, range,
and precision of each input item.

For example, several years ago a company developed a world navigation system that used 2-byte integers to hold latitude and longitude data. Latitude values run from 90 degrees at the North Pole to 0 degrees at the equator, and minus 90 degrees at the South Pole; longitude is measured from the reference at Greenwich, England, in the range 180 degrees through minus 180 degrees. Unfortunately, the best resolution that the poor designer could hope to get for longitude was

180 degrees/32768 = 0.005493 degrees per INTEGER bit

At the equator, one degree of longitude is equivalent to approximately 60 nautical miles (N.M.), so the best resolution was

0.005493 degrees/bit * 60 N.M./degree = 0.330 N.M. per bit

This was terrible: The input processing and the internal resolution of the variables had to be redefined later to achieve greater precision.

Even when data precision is not critical, range almost always is. The range for a value specifies the maximum and minimum allowable values for a field. For instance, a range specification for the field AGE might be 1 TO 115. Certainly, a person cannot be 0 years old or less; an input age that contains the value 150 almost certainly signals an error. Thus, by specifying the range of values for an input field, you automatically build in an error-handling capability. Values that exceed the specified range can be processed accordingly.

Input Devices

The next consideration for data input is to determine and specify the device(s) that will provide the data. The traditional sources are the keyboard and magnetic storage files. Using these sources is reasonably straightforward. The biggest challenge usually involves presenting a useful human interface that is tolerant of human error.

For example, what should your program do if it detects a letter as part of an input stream that was supposed to be all numbers? What if the number is out of the acceptable range? The programmer must plan for these kinds of error-handling problems to avoid disaster. Some keyboard entry programs use a conversational approach in which the computer asks a question and then evaluates the response provided by the user. This is called an *interactive* approach.

Some specialized programs use a screen template, or set display, to provide the electronic equivalent of a fill-in-the-blank format. This is particularly useful when the system will be used by persons with limited knowledge of the internal workings of the program. Today, special presentation-management environments are commercially available that greatly simplify the development of professional-looking and user-friendly interfaces.

So far, you've considered input from keyboards and data files, but there are many other devices that must be considered. A *mouse*, or *trackball*, is a device that allows the user to point a cursor (such as an arrow or a plus sign) to any point on the screen. These devices are becoming increasingly popular, especially for use with microcomputers. When combined with pull-down menus, such technology provides a powerful and easy-to-learn environment. The mouse is especially well suited to nontechnical users. Other widely used input devices include optical scanners to read marks on paper, light pens to select locations on a screen, and digitizer interfaces to sample x,y input coordinates.

Computers today can read voltages, weights, speeds, accelerations, etc., directly from relatively inexpensive electronic sensors. Machine vision systems are being developed that can even analyze television images to recognize people and to figure out which object in the picture is closer, taller, and so forth. A discussion of programming techniques for all these input devices is far beyond the scope of this book, but they are worth learning about at a later date.

CASE STUDY: PAYROLL PROGRAM, INPUT MODULE

Now turn your attention to a practical illustration of the input concepts discussed. Recall that the input module for the payroll module was shown with these pseudocode entries:

```
Begin input module
      Read in ID#, #HRS WORKED, PAY RATE, #DEPENDS, HEALSHATUS, YTDPAY
End input module
```

These entries, of course, simply provide a list of fields to be input. At this point it is possible to expand these entries to include more practical input requirements:

```
Begin input module
      Use question and answer format to read in ID# (7 or 4 digits),
      #HOURS WORKED (0-80), PAY RATE (MIN-MAX), #DEPENDS (1-20),
      HEALTH STATUS (YES OR NO), AND YTDPAY  (0-1000000)
End Input Module
```

Note that this block of pseudocode includes acceptable ranges for all input fields. The sections that follow show how this module can be decomposed and coded in BASIC and Pascal.

The BASIC Input Module

The BASIC code for the expanded input module is shown in Figure 3.12. As you study this section of code, notice the IF...THEN statements. In BASIC (as well as Pascal and many other languages) the term IF indicates a condition test. A condition test, remember, is used to test two values to determine whether they meet some predetermined criteria. For instance, study line 3060:

```
3060 IF ID<1000000 OR ID>9999999 THEN PRINT "ERROR": GOTO 3050
```

This line provides a test to determine whether an input I.D. number fits within the acceptable range. The THEN term is used to specify the processing that should follow when the test returns a true result. In this case, the IF test is true if the I.D. number is outside the specified range. In response, the program prints an error message. The GOTO statement then instructs the program to return to line 3050 so that a new I.D. number can be input. Study the other IF condition tests and THEN responses for other input fields.

Also observe the use of the INPUT statement, which tells BASIC to enter data into main memory from an input device. The CLS statement in line 3170 instructs the program to clear the screen after all fields for a record have been input successfully.

The Pascal Input Module

The Pascal code for the input module, shown in Figure 3.13, bears many similarities to the BASIC code. However, there are two major differences. The first involves the I.D. number. In the BASIC program the I.D. number was seven digits long. In Pascal only four digits can be read for an integer, unless LONGINTEGER is specified. For this reason the I.D. number has been shortened to four digits in this example.

Also, to illustrate a different programming technique, the health-status variable has been changed to character (Y or N). In contrast, the BASIC code used 1 or 2 to indicate true or false.

As with BASIC, the IF term is used to specify a condition test. THEN indicates the action the program is to follow if the test result is true. In BASIC, GOTO statements are used to cause the program to branch to a previous statement in the event of true results.

Figure 3.12

BASIC code for the expanded input module of the payroll program

```
3000  REM       INPUT PROCEDURE
3010  CLS
3020  PRINT
3030  PRINT     "INPUT DATA"
3040  PRINT
3050  INPUT     "ENTER ID# FOR EMPLOYEE (IE 8888888): ";ID
3060  IF ID<1000000 OR ID>9999999 THEN PRINT "ERROR": GOTO 3050
3070  INPUT     "ENTER HOURS WORKED (IE. 40): ";HR
3080  IF HR<0 OR HR>80 THEN PRINT "ERROR": GOTO 3070
3090  INPUT     "ENTER PAY RATE (IE. 7.50): ";PR
3100  IF PR<MI OR PR>MX THEN PRINT "ERROR": GOTO 3090
3110  INPUT     "ENTER NUMBER OF DEPENDENTS (IE. 4): ";DP
3120  IF DP<0 OR DP>20 THEN PRINT "ERROR": GOTO 3110
3130  INPUT "ENTER HEALTH STATUS (1=YES 2=NO): ";HS
3140  IF HS<>1 OR HS<>2 THEN PRINT "ERROR":GOTO 3130
3150  INPUT "ENTER YEAR TO DATE EARNINGS (IE. 32000): ";YD
3160  IF YD<0 OR YD>100000 THEN PRINT "ERROR":GOTO 3150
3170  CLS
3180  RETURN
```

Figure 3.13

Pascal code for
expanded input module
of the payroll program

```
PROCEDURE DATAIN;
  BEGIN {INPUT PROCEDURE}
      CLRSCR;
      WRITELN;
      REPEAT
          WRITE('ENTER ID # FOR EMPLOYEE IE. 4444: ');
          READLN(PERSON_ID);
          IF PERSON_ID<1000 OR PERSON_ID>9999 THEN
              WRITELN('ERROR');
      UNTIL PERSON_ID>999 AND PERSON_ID<10000;
      REPEAT
          WRITE('ENTER HOURS WORKED IE. 40: ');
          READLN(HOURS);
          IF HOURS<0 OR HOURS>80 THEN WRITELN('ERROR');
      UNTIL HOURS>-.1 AND HOURS<80.
      REPEAT
          WRITE('ENTER PAY RATE IE. 7.70: ');
          READLN(PAY_RATE);
          IF PAY_RATE<MINWAGE OR PAY_RATE>MAXWAGE THEN
              WRITELN('ERROR');
      UNTIL PAY_RATE>=MINWAGE AND PAY_RATE<=MAXWAGE.
      REPEAT
          WRITE('ENTER # OF DEPENDENTS IE. 4: ');
          READLN(NUMDEPENDENTS);
          IF NUMDEPENDENTS<1 OR NUMDEPENDENTS>20 THEN
              WRITELN('ERROR');
      UNTIL NUMDEPENDENTS>0 AND NUMDEPENDENTS<21.
      REPEAT
          WRITE('ENTER HEALTH STATUS IE. Y FOR YES/N FOR NO');
          READLN(HEALTH_STATUS);
          IF HEALTH_STATUS<>'Y' OR HEALTH_STATUS<>'N' THEN
              WRITELN('ERROR');
      UNTIL HEALTH_STATUS='Y' OR HEALTH_STATUS='N';
      REPEAT
          WRITE('ENTER YEAR TO DATE EARNINGS IE. 32000: ');
          READLN(YEAR_TO_DATE);
          IF YEAR_TO_DATE<0 OR YEAR_TO_DATE>1000000 THEN
              WRITELN('ERROR');
      UNTIL YEAR_TO_DATE>-.1 AND YEAR_TO_DATE<1000000;
      CLRSCR;
  END; {INPUT PROCEDURE}
```

In Pascal, a more structured technique is available. Statements encoded within a REPEAT...UNTIL structure execute, over and over, all statements within it. This repetition control structure ends only when the UNTIL statement proves to be true. For instance, when the I.D. number is input and tested, the program repeats the input procedure until an I.D. number is found to fall within the accepted range. This same coding structure is used to test and respond to each input field.

CODING CHOICES

The input and output modules shown for BASIC and Pascal include several terms and syntax expressions that might seem unusual to you. Learning the rules for using these and other statements can be helpful. For this reason this section introduces some of the basic commands and operators used in BASIC and Pascal. Keep in mind that you should refer to the language reference manuals for details about particular language implementations.

Constructs in BASIC

Input/Output. In BASIC the fundamental input/output commands are READ, INKEY$, INPUT, PRINT, PUT, and WRITE. The READ command is of rather limited use, since it must obtain values from DATA statements and then assign them to variables. READ is most often used to initialize arrays to known states or processing expectations. Because of the data stream approach that it uses, the READ statement has fallen out of favor with demanding software developers.

INKEY$ detects whether a key has been pressed. This is often used when a program has paused for the operator to make a selection from a group of options. If no key is being pressed, a null (empty) string is returned; otherwise, a character or string is returned that identifies the key or key combination selected by the user.

INPUT obtains actual numbers, strings, and other values from the keyboard or from a disk file. It is by far the most versatile BASIC input command. In certain implementations, INPUT can even prompt the user by displaying a string that provides instructions for pressing specific keys or by supplying specific pieces of information.

PRINT is used to send output to the screen; LPRINT sends the data to the mechanical printer device. In combination with USING, both commands can control the precision, column assignments, and other assignment details for the output. When used in conjunction with the LOCATE command, the PRINT command is capable of placing a piece of data at any point on the screen. The variant PRINT # generates output for disk files.

The PUT command is used similarly to PRINT #, but PUT has the additional capability to randomly access the records in a disk file.

WRITE is used to place information on the screen, and it is similar to PRINT. The major difference between them is that WRITE separates data items with a comma. WRITE # behaves exactly like WRITE except that it sends output to a disk file. Since BASIC favors commas as delimiters between input items, WRITE is commonly used with files that will later be read by another BASIC program.

Data Definition. As previously discussed, the DATA statement is used to provide information for READ statements. Because it is easy to get READ statements out of sequence with DATA statements, this type of data initialization is not as popular as it once was. Today, software developers are more likely to use disk files to perform the same task.

Operators. The arithmetic and relational operators available in BASIC are +, -, *, and /. The symbols stand for addition, subtraction, multiplication, and division, respectively. A backslash (\) generates the result of integer division so that $13 \backslash 4 = 3$. The MOD statement provides the residue of the integer division operation. For example:

$$(13 \text{ MOD } 4) = 13 - ((13 \backslash 4) * 4) = 13 - 12 = 1$$

The operators <, >, <=, >=, =, and < > mean less than, greater than, less than or equal to, greater than or equal to, equals, and not equal to, respectively. Such relational operators can be used to compare both numbers and strings. The logical operators—AND, OR, and NOT—are used to evaluate Boolean expressions. The order of execution of these operators is different in different languages. The order of operations in BASIC is:

```
^
* , /
+, -
<, <=, =, < >, >, >=
NOT, AND, OR
```

Assignment. In BASIC the equals sign is used as both a relational operator and an assignment operator. Because of the simplicity of BASIC, the interpreter or compiler generally has no trouble distinguishing between the two uses. When used as a relational operator, the equals sign is part of a construct supporting flow-control statements such as IF, FOR, or WHILE. (These types of statements are illustrated in greater depth later.) Otherwise, the equals sign is usually within assignment statements.

Remarks. BASIC supports only one type of comment: the REM line. By interspersing such lines with the code, it is possible to do a fairly thorough job of documentation. Some BASICs do allow for end-of-line remarks using a symbol such as !.

Flow Control. The IF...THEN...ELSE is the fundamental flow-control statement in BASIC. It provides the ability to select the existence or the absence of a relationship. When the relationship identified is true, the statement following THEN is executed; otherwise, the statement following ELSE is activated. Note that the ELSE keyword is optional; there need not be an action if the relationship is false.

Loop Control. The FOR...NEXT and WHILE...WEND statement pairs control program looping in BASIC. Both types can be *nested,* so that one statement pair resides completely within the control span of another. This can be very useful for processing such things as multi-dimensional arrays.

You can understand the concept of nesting easily by considering this example: The United States is a working whole, a social structure. Within this structure, 50 separate states are nested. Each state has nested within it numerous counties. Each county, in turn, contains several cities.

Similarly, one program structure is nested, or embedded, within a larger structure. This embedded structure may also contain smaller, similar structures, and so on.

The FOR statement in BASIC uses a counter that is incremented by a specified value each time the NEXT statement is encountered. Incrementation continues until a terminal value is reached or exceeded.

The WHILE structure continues looping indefinitely until the specified condition is no longer true.

Constructs in Pascal

Input/Output. The fundamental commands available for input and output in Pascal are the READ, READLN, WRITE, and WRITELN commands. The READ and WRITE commands transfer data from variables to and from files. The READLN and WRITELN commands are almost identical to READ and WRITE except that, at the end of a READLN or WRITELN operation, the program skips to the next line.

Data Definition. Pascal supports two types of blocks for the definition of data: VAR and CONST. The VAR block is used to declare all program variables (integers, reals, etc.) that are expected to change during the course of execution. The CONST block performs the same duties for names that will be used to denote nonchanging quantities.

Operators. For the most part, the arithmetic, relational, and logical operators in Pascal function identically to those in BASIC. The main difference is that the backslash used to denote integer division in BASIC is replaced by the keyword DIV in Pascal. The order of operators in Pascal is shown below. The first minus sign represents unary negation; the second minus represents subtraction.

```
( )
- NOT
/ DIV, MOD, AND
+, -, OR
<, <=, =, < >, >, >=
```

Assignment. Pascal overcomes the structural sloppiness of BASIC by defining a slightly different operator for assignment than for comparison. The two characters := are used for the assignment operation.

Comments. Pascal is much more cooperative than BASIC where comment structures are concerned. Pascal treats all characters enclosed within sets of braces or within the two-character delimiter sets (* and *) as material to be ignored (comments). This allows the programmer to place comments anywhere on a line (although traditionally they are placed at the end of the line to improve code readability).

Flow Control. The IF...THEN...ELSE structure in Pascal is much more powerful than in BASIC, because in Pascal it can be coupled with the BEGIN...END terms. These two keywords can enclose large amounts of code to be executed as part of the THEN or ELSE clause. In addition, it is possible to nest additional IF structures within each of these code blocks. Traditionally, programmers indent each level of nested code by three or more spaces to visually reinforce the descent of control to lower levels.

An additional Pascal flow-control structure is the CASE statement. The CASE statement compares a control variable to various enumerated options and executes the particular code block associated with a match. If no match is found, an ELSE block is executed (if present).

Loop Control. Loop control in Pascal is performed by FOR, WHILE, and REPEAT structures. The FOR construct is similar to the FOR in BASIC. The Pascal WHILE and REPEAT loops both require that the test quantity evaluate to a Boolean (true or false) value. In a WHILE structure, the body of the loop is executed as long as the control Boolean value resolves true; if the value is false on entry to the WHILE, the code within the WHILE is never executed. The REPEAT structure, however, evaluates at the end of the code body. In this way, the REPEAT guarantees that the code within the REPEAT structure is executed at least once; looping continues as long as the control value remains false.

CASE STUDY: PAYROLL PROGRAM, PROCESSING MODULE

Now to return to the payroll example and expand the existing pseudocode for the processing module. So far, output and input modules have been fully decomposed. In other words, you know what results you want to achieve, and you have determined the data that have to be input to achieve those results. The processing module, then, is devoted to transforming input data into results—output information.

Recall that the general processing steps were described in pseudocode in this way:

```
Begin process module
      Calculate GROSS PAY (#HRS WORKED)
      Calculate TAXES (GROSS * #DEPENDS)
      Calculate DEDUCTIONS based on #DEPENDS
             and HEALTH STATUS
      Do FICA Module
      Do NETPAY Module
      Do YTDPAY Module
End process module
```

The three low-level modules were then blocked out through the use of BEGIN and END terms.

To begin the expansion, it is important to consider which control structures will be required to process a record successfully. For each tax calculation four dependent statuses are possible. Each status requires a separate tax calculation. Thus, separate tests are needed to account for each status. A similar testing procedure is required to determine an employee's health deduction. Recall that this deduction is determined by testing the values for dependents and for health status.

The BASIC Processing Module

The BASIC payroll processing module for this portion of code is shown in Figure 3.14. Notice in lines 4070 through 4110 that the program assigns a health-status constant, defined in the initialization module (page 73), after it determines the employee's health status. The FICA, net pay, and year-to-date modules are all handled by separate submodules. These three modules are shown in Figure 3.15.

The Pascal Processing Module

The gross pay and health status portions of the processing module are shown in Pascal in Figure 3.16. Notice the use of nested IF statements for the health-status calculations. The first IF statement tests to determine whether the employee's record contains a Y in the health-status field. If so, additional IF tests are conducted to determine the appropriate health costs. The tests are based upon the number of dependents for the employee.

In the Pascal program the separate FICA, NETPAY, and YEARTODATE modules actually appear before PROCEDURE PROCESS. In other words, they are defined first, then executed. The code for these three modules is shown in Figure 3.17.

THE TERMINATION MODULE

Program termination is like parking a car: If you don't turn off the engine, something is eventually going to get damaged. At the very least, a program should tell the operating system that it is done with all the disk files that have been opened so that they may be secured and made available to the next user.

It is important to remember that most computers will not allow a second person to write data into a file if a different user is already using it. In fact, on certain multiuser systems, it is possible to get into a situation where an abnormal termination leaves a file open even after the user logs off the system; sometimes it takes intervention by the system manager to remove such files.

In addition to gracefully closing out all disk files, the termination module may clear the screen and provide the user with status information such as number of records processed, numbers of errors encountered during operation, and so on.

If printer output has been generated, the termination module should advance the paper to the top of the next page to prevent the next print job from starting in the middle of a page. On large multiuser systems the termination module should deallocate system resources such as temporary disk space.

SUMMARY

This chapter introduces the details needed to complete the initialization, input, processing, output, and termination modules. These details include data types, input devices, and output devices. You also learn how to implement these different concepts in program code.

Figure 3.14

```
4000  REM       PROCESS PROCEDURE
4010  REM
4020  G=HR*PR
4030  IF DP=1 THEN TX=G*.20
4040  IF DP=2 THEN TX=G*.18
4050  IF DP=3 THEN TX=G*.16
4060  IF DP>3 THEN TX=G*.14
4070  IF DP=1 AND HS=1 THEN H=H1
4080  IF DP=2 AND HS=1 THEN H=H2
4090  IF DP=3 AND HS=1 THEN H=H3
4100  IF DP>3 AND HS=1 THEN H=H3
4110  GOSUB 6000
4120  GOSUB 7000
4130  GOSUB 8000
4140  RETURN
```

BASIC code for the processing module of payroll program

Figure 3.15

```
6000  REM    FICA PROCEDURE
6010  REM
6020  IF YD>32000 THEN F1=0
      ELSE IF  YD+G>32000 THEN F1=(32000-YD)*.20
            ELSE F1=G*.20
6030  RETURN
7000  REM    NET PAY PROCEDURE
7010  REM
7020  NP=G-(F1+H+TX)
7030  RETURN

8000  REM    YEAR TO DATE TOTAL PROCEDURE
8010  REM
8020  YD=YD+G
```

BASIC code for FICA, net pay, and year-to-date modules of the payroll program

Figure 3.16

```
PROCEDURE  PROCESS;
BEGIN  {PROCESS  PROCEDURE}
    GROSS_PAY:=HOURS*PAY_RATE;
    IF  NUMDEPENDENTS  =1  THEN  TAXES:=GROSS_PAY*0.20;
    IF  NUMDEPENDENTS  =2  THEN  TAXES:=GROSS_PAY*0.18;
    IF  NUMDEPENDENTS  =3  THEN  TAXES:=GROSS_PAY*0.16;
    IF  NUMDEPENDENTS  >3  THEN  TAXES:=GROSS_PAY*0.14;
    IF HEALTH_STATUS='Y' THEN IF NUMDEPENDENTS=1
                          THEN HEALTH_COSTS=ONEDEPENDENT;
                          ONEDEPENDENT
                    ELSE IF NUMDEPENDENTS=2
                        THEN HEALTH_COSTS=TWODEPENDENTS;
                        TWODEPENDENTS
                    ELSE IF NUMDEPENDENTS>2
                        THEN HEALTH_COSTS=THREEPLUSDEPENDENTS;
```

Pascal code for gross pay and health status portions of the payroll processing module

(continued)

Figure 3.16 (continued)

```
        FICA;
        NETPAY;
        YEARTODATE;
END;   {PROCESS PROCEDURE}
```

Figure 3.17

Pascal code for FICA, NETPAY, and YEARTO-DATE modules

```
PROCEDURE  FICA;
BEGIN  {FICA  CALCULATIONS  PROCEDURE}
       IF YEAR_TO_DATE > 32000 THEN
                                FICA:=0.0
            ELSE  IF  YEAR_TO_DATE+GROSS_PAY> 32000  THEN
                               FICA:= (32000-YEAR_TO_DATE)*0.20
            ELSE FICA:=YEAR_TO_DATE*0.20;


END;   {FICA PROCEDURE}

PROCEDURE NETPAY;
BEGIN {NETPAY PROCEDURE}
       NET_PAY:=GROSS_PAY-(FICA+HEALTH_COSTS+TAXES);
END;   {NETPAY PROCEDURE}

PROCEDURE  YEARTODATE;
BEGIN  {YEAR  TO  DATE  CACULATIONS}
       YEAR_TO_DATE=YEAR_TO_DATE+GROSS_PAY;
END;  {YEAR  TO  DATE  PROCEDURE}
```

Key Terms

Array	Error handling
Binary	Explicitly defined
Bit	FOR
Boolean	FOR...NEXT
Byte	IF...THEN...ELSE
CASE	Implicit constant
Character	INKEY$
CONST	INPUT
Constant	Integer
Database	Interactive
Data conversion	Kbyte
Data structure	Layout
Dimension	Least significant digit
Element	Literal string
Environment	LPRINT

Machine language
Megabyte
MOD
Mouse
Nested
Numeric array
Output header
PRINT
PRINT#
Print chart
PUT
READ
READLN

Real
REPEAT
Single-dimensional array
String
Three-dimensional array
Two-dimensional array
VAR
Variable
WHILE...WEND
WRITE
WRITE#
WRITELN

Review Questions

1. What is the initialization module and what should it contain?

2. What is the programming environment?

3. List the data hierarchy from smallest to largest unit.

4. What are the main data types? How much room in memory is typically required for each type mentioned above?

5. What is a Boolean value? Give an example of how it can be used.

6. The following Pascal program, BOOLS, demonstrates the use of Boolean variables. First sit down and predict the output. Then enter the program in your computer and use 5, 2, 6, 3, and 4 as input. Summarize which predictions did and did not come true.

```
PROGRAM BOOLS(INPUT,OUTPUT);

VAR
    I,J,K,L,M: INTEGER;
    ALPHA,BETA, GAMMA:BOOLEAN;
BEGIN
    READLN(I,J,K,L,M);
    IF (I<J) OR (M=K*3) AND NOT (L=M) THEN
                    WRITELN('TRUE')
                    ELSE WRITELN('FALSE');
    ALPHA:=NOT(L=M);
    BETA:=(M=K*3) AND ALPHA;
    GAMMA:= (I<J) OR BETA;
    WRITELN('NOT(L=M) ',ALPHA);
    WRITELN(' (M=K*3) AND NOT (L=M) ',BETA);
    WRITELN(GAMMA)
END. {OF PROGRAM}
```

7. Can the number 1 be directly compared to the character 1? Why or why not?

8. What are the differences between the number 27.00 and the number 27?

9. What is a constant? When is it used?

10. What are the differences and similarities between records and arrays?

11. What is the rule for assigning or not assigning initial values to variables?

12. What elements should be included in effective internal documentation?

13. What is the purpose of output?

14. What media choices do you have for output?

15. In planning input, what questions do you need to ask?

Problem-Solving Assignments

1. Modify the payroll pseudocode in Chapter 2 to provide separate modules for taxes and health costs. Then modify the code for each language.

2. Modify the error-handling pseudocode and code for the input module to make them more elaborate. For example, change the code to accommodate input for more than 20 dependents or create a new wage of more than $12.50 per hour.

3. Modify the payroll program pseudocode to allow for multiple employees. This requires the building of a termination module to print out summary results. The presence of a termination module suggests the need for counters and accumulators for information output. These variables must be defined and initialized within either the initialization module or the process module.

4. Take the interest program you planned in Chapter 2, assignment 4, and convert it to the program code of your instructor's choice.

4

Information Delivery:
Outputting

Output refers to information that has been converted from a computer-readable form to a form that can be understood by people. Output is critical to the success of any program. Computers exist solely to serve the information and processing needs of people. The ultimate goal for any program is to provide output to users in the most readable and effective form.

The emphasis in this chapter is on output and the output module. It discusses the devices, programming methods, and human factors that impact the output designs for your programs. As the program design process indicates, outputting begins by defining a problem, partitioning the problem into subproblems, and then proceeding to solve each subproblem by designing logical solutions. At all stages of problem solving for output requirements, your focus should be on people—the users of your program who expect results. This is the first step in good top-down problem-solving design.

PROBLEM DEFINITION

There is an old saying: You can't get there from here. What does this have to do with programming? Simple. If you don't begin program design by determining outputs (information requirements), you won't get results. Input procedures are designed specifically to provide data that lead to appropriate output. Processing procedures provide the steps that transform input data into information that can be output. Thus, in defining a programming problem, the place to begin is with output.

Information requirements can be identified by asking a series of questions. Each question is intended to narrow your focus in providing information outputs that satisfy users:

- What information do users expect?
- What device should present information, and in what format?
- For whom is the information to be provided?
- When is the information required and how often?

What Information Do Users Expect?

This question pinpoints the goal of the program. Users rarely care about the details involved in programming. Instead, they want results. The place to go to determine information needs is to users. That is, the programmer questions users to determine what information they need to perform their jobs.

Users can often provide existing forms, typewritten reports, and other documents that can aid the programmer in identifying information requirements. These documents, in addition to comments from users, allow the programmer to pinpoint the specific terminology, records, fields, and amounts that should be provided as part of output. Basic formats also might be suggested at this point.

What Device Should Present Information, and in What Format?

Computers provide some specific features for outputting information. However, they also possess some limitations in the way information can be delivered. For these reasons, take care to instruct users about hardware and software limitations. From this foundation a programming team can work with users to determine the way in which information should be delivered. Problem solving must take into account two basic requirements: available output devices, along with their features and limitations, and report formats. Information that results from processing can be delivered onto three basic types of devices: screens, printers, and magnetic storage media.

Screen Output. Although CRT screens can output information in many attractive formats, all screens have a size limitation. For programming purposes a screen can be divided into rows and columns. The blocks created by the intersections of rows and columns form individual character display positions, sometimes called *cells*.

Although some screens are capable of displaying 132 characters per row, most screens in use today are limited to displays of 80 characters per row and 25 characters per column. However, many professional reports require much more space than this. The solution, typically, is to use the scroll feature.

To understand scrolling, consider a brief explanation of the operations of a screen. The inside surface of a CRT screen is coated with a thin, clear layer of light-sensitive substance called phosphor. Behind the screen is an electron gun, which fires a highly focused beam of electrons. The electron gun performs three actions. First, it can move the beam of electrons across the screen, from left to right. Second, it can move downward, row by row. Third, it can pulse the beam.

These pulsations, in combination with the movement of the gun, illuminate phospor in different patterns. These patterns form individual picture elements, or *pixels*. Pixels combine to form characters. Each cell on the screen can hold a single character at a time. Under control of the operating system and an application program, the electron gun can change its pulsation pattern to eliminate the display on one row and replace it with the pulsation pattern on the preceding or succeeding line. This activity creates the effect of movement. In other words, the lines displayed on the screen appear to be scrolling, or moving, up or down.

Scrolling provides one method for displaying new text or redisplaying old text. Another method involves clearing the screen and replacing it with a new screen, or page, of information. To clear the screen, the electron gun shuts off long enough for all phospor to fade, causing the screen to go black. Then a new screen filled with information replaces the previous display.

Most of the details involved in manipulating an electron gun are handled by operating system functions. However, you can control these actions by spacing characters, fields, and headings on the screen. In this way you can determine the screen format of your report. When the screen is filled with information (all lines used), you can specify that a new line or new page be displayed.

You already know that, for character displays, a screen is divided into row and column positions. Some programming languages, including BASIC, also divide each line of display into *print zones*. A print zone is a specific subset of columns. The print zone has a fixed length, and it can be useful in aligning columns of data with only a few commands.

An 80-column screen could contain five print zones, each 14 to 16 columns wide. The size of print zones varies with different equipment and different language implementations. You will need to consult hardware and software user's manuals to determine correct zone widths.

Most languages also provide control characters and commands for formatting displayed items. Commands exist for specifying individual row and column positions, for moving immediately from one print zone to another, for controlling and clearing page displays, and for tabbing to a specified column number. These techniques are discussed later in the section on BASIC and Pascal implementations.

A final consideration involves different highlighting techniques available with monochrome (single-color) and RGB (red, green, blue—that is, full-color) monitors. With a monochrome monitor it is usually possible to use *reverse video* to highlight blocks of text. In reverse video the normally black area surrounding a block of text is illuminated. The pixels that make up the characters within the block are set to black. Capabilities for specifying color are highly device dependent and differ greatly with different languages and language implementations. For this reason the use of RGB monitors is not discussed in this text.

Printer Output. Printers produce a paper copy of an output. Printers share many output characteristics with screens. That is, printers divide a sheet of paper into columns and rows. Almost all printers use paper that is 11 inches long. However, some production printers allow paper that is 17 inches wide. Smaller-capacity printers allow paper that is 8 1/2 inches wide.

Consider that a common print *pitch* is 10 characters, or columns, per inch. This means that, for 17-inch wide paper, a total of 170 characters is possible, although this full width is rarely used. The maximum number of characters for 17-inch paper is usually 150 characters or less.

For an 8 1/2-inch sheet of paper, 90 columns are available with a print pitch of 10 characters per inch. It is rare for more than 80 columns to be used per line; the remaining space is required to establish left- and right-hand margins.

Formatting techniques for printed output are similar to techniques used for display output. That is, each line of print can be divided into separate print zones, if the programming language to be used allows this technique. The size of print zones, of course, depends on the type of printer and programming language implementation used.

As is true for screen output, most languages also provide control characters and commands for formatting printed items. Commands exist for specifying individual row and column positions, for moving immediately from one print zone to another, for controlling page displays, and for tabbing to a specified column number. These techniques are discussed later in the section on BASIC and Pascal implementations.

Printed output does present some special problems. Specifically, a printed document is permanent; therefore, it should be highly descriptive. Techniques for enhancing the descriptiveness of printed reports include printing page numbers at the top or bottom of each page, reprinting report headings for each new page, and avoiding unsightly page breaks.

For instance, consider that 100 records are to be printed on a report, with subtotals to be printed after each group of 20 records. Further, each record to be output represents a line of print. If care is not taken, it is possible that *widows* and *orphans* might occur. A widow is a single line, such as a subtotal, printed alone at the top of a page, separated from the records it represents. An orphan is a single line, such as the first record of a new group, printed alone at the bottom of a page.

To overcome these potential page-break problems, the programmer must take into account the structure of each page. Separate line counters can be established to keep track of the number of lines printed on each page. Additional condition tests can be designed to check for potential widows and orphans. These page-break processing techniques are discussed in a later chapter.

Magnetic Storage Media. Often, the results of processing have to be sent directly to a storage device to await output at a later time. To handle this situation, programmers should have some understanding of the formats under which information is stored on magnetic disk. Since this book is microcomputer-oriented, it does not discuss the specific storage requirements of magnetic tape. This chapter focuses on logical requirements related to disk storage. Chapter 5 provides information about the physical characteristics of disk devices and media.

Two basic types of disks are used with microcomputers: *floppy disks* and *hard disks*. The two types of media have similar data storage features. The chief differences between the two lie in their physical characteristics and storage capacities. These differences are discussed in Chapter 5.

During disk formatting, the operating system for IBM personal computers and compatibles assigns a separate area on the disk for use as a file *directory*. A directory is an index that can be used to look up individual files stored on that disk. The directory contains a list of *track locations*. Tracks are narrow, concentric rings marked off by *sectors*. Figure 4.1 shows the way a disk is organized.

Each file name on a disk is keyed to a specific track location, which represents the starting point for the file. The directory also stores the date and time when the file was created or updated. Typical microcomputer operating systems store files within *stor-*

age blocks. A standard storage block length is 512 bytes. Why are these logical specifications important to you as a programmer? In most programming languages you have at least two file organization approaches available: *random organization* and *sequential organization.*

Each method has its benefits and disadvantages. Random organization, for instance, provides ease of access among individual records. The operating system establishes a separate index that uses a unique *key field* to store and locate each record in the file.

However, this approach tends to waste storage space because records may be scattered across a disk, arranged in no particular order. Several blocks might be only partially filled with record content, with remaining space unused. The primary index, which is used to address and locate records, also takes up considerable space on disk.

In contrast, sequential organization uses disk storage space extremely efficiently. The entire file is treated as a single string, or stream of characters, by the operating system. As a result, records can be stored in *contiguous blocks,* or adjoining blocks. No space between adjoining blocks is wasted. To access a file, the directory simply refers to the starting address for the file and then reads or writes all records as a single unit.

The single most important disadvantage of sequential organization is the inability to access a specific record directly. In other words, the directory system has no way of locating individual records. Instead, each record must be read in the same order in which it was stored. The program examines each record until the desired records are located.

Storing records by random organization is a sensible approach if you need to access individual records immediately. Sequential organization may be efficient if the file is small or if all or most records in the file will be accessed for each processing run.

Figure 4.1

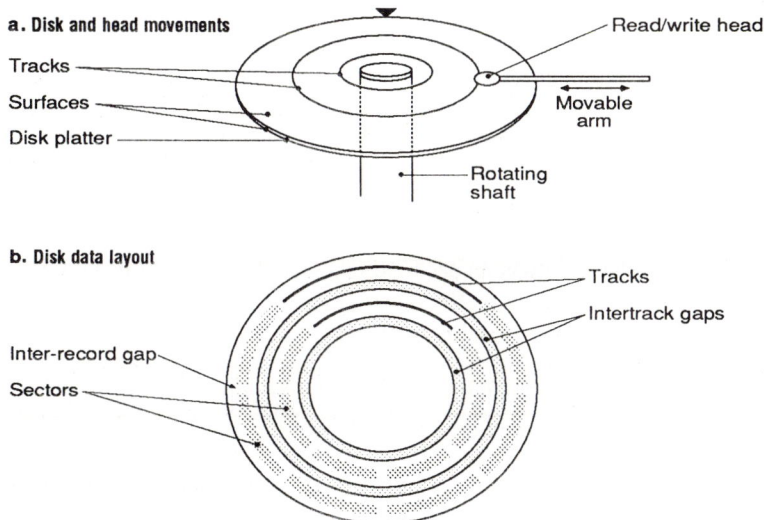

Parts of a magnetic disk

For Whom Is the Information to Be Provided?

Different users have different information needs and expectations. For instance, experienced businesspeople tend to prefer straightforward screen outputs that provide only the required information. People who do not use a system regularly tend to want information delivered in as "friendly" a format as possible—that is, with guidance.

For instance, consider the reports that a computer information system for a bank might output. The system has to provide checking account information for several user groups. Bank tellers and other bank personnel are used to entering *queries,* or programmed requests, through the keyboard and then receiving output in a recognizable format. When a customer calls to ask for a balance, the bank employee enters the query, waits a moment, then reads and interprets the amounts displayed on the screen.

However, the customer doesn't expect this kind of cryptic output on his or her monthly account statement. In this case, all information should be clearly categorized and labeled. A preprinted key should explain any codes that the customer does not understand immediately.

Now consider this same customer's expectations when he or she enters a balance inquiry at a local ATM. This person expects a card or paper slip that shows account information clearly, along with appropriate labels. In this case, records of individual transactions for the week or month are not desired. The user is looking for a single amount.

The point is that information contained in a file can be presented to users in almost limitless ways. To create each output application, the creative programmer has to evaluate the expectations and knowledge of different user groups.

It is also worth mentioning that effective presentation indicates professionalism. Sloppy output formats and lengthy response times usually lead to user complaints. As a programmer, you are in a service role. Users look to you, whether knowingly or not, to meet their information needs efficiently and professionally.

To drive home the point, consider a common programming problem: *rounding errors.* Most businesspeople do not want totals that are carried to four or five decimal places. They want totals that can be interpreted quickly. This involves rounding values to some nearest whole. Rounding requires a programmer to make a decision between two options: rounding subtotals and then generating a total or totaling the unrounded subtotals and then rounding the sum. Both approaches are valid. However, each method depends on an understanding of user expectations. Is it more important for users to be given a representative total based upon the sum of specific amounts? Or is it more important for users to view these specific amounts and then determine the importance each total plays in contributing to a final sum?

For salespeople, establishing rounding criteria is often important. The livelihood of individuals might depend upon an accurate representation of subtotals. For managers, the bottom line, the final total, is the most critical value. How does the programmer decide upon the appropriate rounding method? Usually, if subtotals have importance for users, these values should be calculated with precision. Rounding should be performed only after all calculations have been made. The urgency here is real: Someone's bread and butter can depend on the way in which a programmer interprets and processes the values.

When Is the Information Required and How Often?

Information is useful only if it is delivered within the time frame specified by the user. Thousands of formats have been developed to portray computer-produced output to people. When it comes to delivery, however, all these formats fall into two categories: scheduled and on demand.

Scheduled Reports. *Scheduled reports* occur at regular intervals, such as once a week, once a month, and so on. In each scheduled report it is important to specify the current reporting period to users. This often involves specifying a date on the report and providing variables to represent aspects that change from one reporting period to the next. For instance, quarterly reports should contain appropriate headings—"First Quarter," "Second Quarter," or the like. Monthly reports should specify the month the report describes.

On-Demand Outputs. *On-demand outputs* are required on a one-time basis. For on-demand outputs, response time is usually critical. A user often expects, with good reason, a response to a query within seconds. Such a one-time report probably does not require the detailed title and heading information expected for scheduled reports. However, some presentation details—such as date or time of inquiry, range of response, and other user-defined details—probably are required.

WHAT ARE THE CODING CHOICES?

This chapter has described the basic expectations surrounding output requests made by businesspeople. At this point you should be prepared to examine the BASIC and Pascal coding options for defining outputs.

BASIC Coding Structures

The BASIC programming language provides several coding structures that facilitate output. The five statements used widely within BASIC to manipulate output are:

- PRINT
- PRINT# or WRITE#
- LPRINT
- PRINT USING
- LPRINT USING

PRINT. In BASIC the PRINT statement is used in conjunction with other statements to position and display data on the screen. As you know, most microcomputer screens can hold 25 rows of text, with each row displaying a maximum of 80 characters of data. The PRINT statement can be used to format data items within this row-and-column structure.

When PRINT is used alone, it displays specified values within the first print zone of a line. The TAB statement can also be used to specify that a value be printed in a specified print position. The SPC instruction can be used to insert any number of spaces between two printed values.

The comma and semicolon are useful in specifying print positions in BASIC. When commas follow values to be printed, the program prints the values in consecutive print zones. When semicolons follow values to be printed, BASIC prints the values in adjoining locations. Figure 4.2 illustrates these BASIC statements.

WRITE#. PRINT# and WRITE# act like PRINT except that they send output to a magnetic file. Both are covered in a later chapter.

LPRINT. LPRINT is identical to PRINT except that LPRINT specifies that output be sent to a printer, rather than the screen. LPRINT can also use TAB and SPC to format values to be printed. In addition, the comma and semicolon function with LPRINT as they do with PRINT. Figure 4.3 illustrates the use of LPRINT and its assisting instructions.

PRINT USING. Use the PRINT USING statement to display numeric data in a specified form. With PRINT USING you can use commas, decimal places, and a preceding dollar sign to specify the format in which you want values to be printed. Figure 4.4 shows options available for implementing the PRINT USING statement to format and output values to the screen.

LPRINT USING. The LPRINT USING statement is identical to the PRINT USING statement, but LPRINT USING sends output to a printer, rather than to the screen. LPRINT USING also allows use of commas, decimal places, and a preceding dollar sign to format characters.

Figure 4.2

Example PRINT statements in BASIC

```
5     REM   ** DEMO 1 **
10    A = 10
20    B = 20.01
30    PRINT A
40    PRINT B
50    PRINT A,B
60    PRINT A;B
70    PRINT A,
80    PRINT B
90    PRINT
100    PRINT A;TAB(40);B
110    PRINT A;SPC(40);B
120    END
```

Figure 4.3

```
5      REM   ** DEMO 2 **
10     A = 10
20     B = 20.01
30     LPRINT A
40     LPRINT B
50     LPRINT A, B
60     LPRINT A; B
70     LPRINT A,
80     LPRINT B
90     LPRINT
100    LPRINT A;TAB(40);B
110    LPRINT A;SPC(40);B
```

Example LPRINT statements in BASIC

Figure 4.4

```
100    REM PROGRAM TO DEMONSTRATE PRINT USING ** DEMO 51 **
110    REM THE # SIGN
120    REM
130    A(1)=123456!
140    A(2)=12345
150    A(3)=1234
160    A(4)=123.5
170    A(5)=123.4
180    REM
190    FOR I=1 TO 5
200        PRINT USING "#####";A(I)
210    NEXT I
220    END
```

Options for implementing the PRINT USING statement

a. Using the pound symbol

```
100    REM PROGRAM TO DEMONSTRATE PRINT USING ** DEMO 53 **
110    REM THE PERIOD (.) SYMBOL
120    REM
130    A(1)=123.456
140    A(2)=123.4
150    A(3)=123.4567
160    A(4)=123
170    A(5)=1234.123
180    REM
190    FOR I=1 TO 5
200        PRINT USING "#####";A(I)
210    NEXT I
220    END
```

b. Using the decimal point

(continued)

Figure 4.4 (continued)

c. Using a dollar sign

```
100    REM PROGRAM TO DEMONSTRATE PRINT USING ** DEMO 56 **
110    REM THE DOLLAR ($) SYMBOL
120    REM
130    A(1)=123.456
140    A(2)=12.3456
150    A(3)=1.23456
160    A(4)=.123456
170    A(5)=.0123456
180    REM
185    PRINT "$ IS FIXED TO LEFT MOST SPOT"
190    FOR I=1 TO 5
200               PRINT USING "###.##";A(I)
210    NEXT I
211    PRINT
212    PRINT
213    PRINT "$ FLOATS NEXT TO NUMBER"
214    PRINT
220    FOR I=1 TO 5
230       PRINT USING "$$$$.##";A(I)
240    NEXT I
241    PRINT
242    PRINT
243    PRINT "PARTIAL FLOATS ?"
244    PRINT
250    FOR I=1 TO 5
260       PRINT USING "$$##.##    $$$$.$$";A(I);A(I)
270    NEXT I
280    END
```

d. Using backslashes

```
100    REM PROGRAM TO DEMONSTRATE PRINT USING ** DEMO 58 **
110    REM STRING FORMATS
120    REM THE BACKSLASH(\)
130    REM
140    REM
150    A$(1)="BEOGRAD"
160    A$(2)="SHREMSKA MITROVICA"
170    A$(3)="DUBROVNIK"
180    A$(4)="SPLIT"
190    A$(5)="ZAGREB"
200    REM
210    FOR I=1 TO 5
220       PRINT USING "\    \";A$(I)
230    NEXT I
240    PRINT
250    PRINT "COMBO IN PRINT USING"
260    PRINT
270    B$="YUGOSLAVIAN CITY VISITED WAS \      \"
280    FOR I=1 TO 5
290       PRINT USING B$;A$(I)
300    NEXT I
999    END
```

Pascal Coding Structures

The Pascal language is far more limited than BASIC in terms of the structures available for outputting information. Two basic statements are available for outputting information:

- WRITE
- WRITELN

WRITE. The WRITE instruction simply causes information that follows to be output, either to a screen or printer, depending on the device that has been specified. Information to be output by these statements is specified within a pair of parentheses. Any string constants to be output are usually placed within single quotation marks. Figure 4.5 illustrates the use of the WRITE statement.

WRITELN. The WRITELN statement is similar to WRITE, but WRITELN provides a bit of flexibility. When WRITELN is used, the display or printer device advances to the next writing line after it has written specified data. With WRITE, in contrast, several WRITE statements can be specified in sequence, with all items printed on the same line. Figure 4.6 demonstrates the use of WRITELN.

CASE STUDY: PAYROLL PROGRAM, OUTPUT MODULE

The previous chapter described within a separate module output for the payroll program. The pseudocode developed thus far looks like this:

```
Begin output procedure
      Print proper headings and provide labels for output
      Print, in a readable form, data corresponding to headings (ID#...YTDPAY)
End output procedure
```

The BASIC Expansion

As you may recall, a PRINT USING statement in the initialization module provides output. The one additional feature to be added at this point is the date function. This

Figure 4.5

Using the WRITE
statement in Pascal

```
PROGRAM RESULTS1(OUTPUT);
   PROGRAM TO DEMONSTRATE WRITE AND WRITELN

BEGIN
  WRITE(1,2);WRITE(3);WRITE(4,5);WRITELN;
  WRITE(1,2);
  WRITE(3);
  WRITE(4,5);
END
```

Figure 4.6

**Using the WRITELN
statement in Pascal**

```
PROGRAM RESULT3(OUTPUT);
VAR
      ALPHA:BOOLEAN;
BEGIN
 WRITELN(6)         DEFAULT
 WRITELN(6:6);      6 COLS WIDE
 WRITELN(127.3468);DEFAULT
 WRITELN(127.3468:10); 10 COLS WIDE
 WRITELN(9127.3468:3:2); 10 COLS, 2 DECIMALS
 WRITELN('J','A','M','E','S');
 WRITELN('JAMES');
 WRITELN('J':2,'A':2,'M':2,'E':2,'S':2);
 IF 10<10THEN ALPHA:=FALSE
        ELSE ALPHA:=TRUE;
 WRITELN(ALPHA)
END.
```

function is used to print the date on which the program prints. Thus, if your BASIC implementation allows, you can modify line 2020 to read:

```
2020 PRINT "PAYROLL PROGRAM";TAB(50);DATE$
```

In addition, the processing procedure needs to be changed to ensure that proper rounding takes place. Add the lines that follow to handle rounding.

```
4025 G=(INT(G*100+.5))/100
4065 TX=(INT(TX*100+.5))/100
6025 F1=(INT(F1*100+.5))/100
7025 NP=(INT(NP*100+.500))/100
8025 YD=(INT(YD*100+.500))/100
```

The Pascal Expansion

If Turbo Pascal is available, it is possible to add a function to automatically place a date in the output. First, add YEAR, MONTH, DAY, and DAYOFWEEK to the VAR declaration list in the initialization section. Each of these is of type WORD.

Next add the procedure GETDATE prior to the DATAOUT procedure. Then simply change the processing procedure to include a call to this new subroutine. The call should be at the end of the procedure.

```
    .
    .
    .
 NETPAY;
 YEARTODATE;
 GETDATE;
END; {PROCESS PROCEDURE}
```

At this point the output procedure can also be changed to make use of the data gathered by the call to GETDATE.

```
PROCEDURE DATAOUT;
BEGIN {OUTPUT PROCEDURE}
WRITELN('PAYROLL PROGRAM
    ',MONTH, YEAR);
```

Turbo Pascal includes an integer function, which can be used to round the results of a calculation prior to printing. To implement this approach, add these lines after GETDATE and before ending:

```
GETDATE;
GROSS_PAY:=(INT(GROSS_PAY*100.0+0.50))0/100.0;
TAXES:=(INT(TAXES*100.0+0.500))/100.0;
FICA:=(INT(FICA*100.0+0.5))/100.0;
NETPAY:=(INT(NETPAY*100.0+0.5))/100.0;
YEARTODATE:=(INT(YEARTODATE*100.0+0.5))/100.0;
END; {PROCESS PROCEDURE}
```

SUMMARY

Top-down design begins with an understanding of the problem. This chapter discusses that aspect of problem solving most crucial to the user: output. It discusses various aspects of output, such as the type of report required and the media to which output is sent. In addition, the chapter introduces various coding options for output.

Key Terms

Cell
Contiguous blocks
Directory
Floppy disk
Hard disk
Key field
LPRINT USING
On-demand output
Orphan
Sector
Sequential organization
Storage block

Pitch
Pixel
Print zone
Query
Random organization
Reverse video
Rounding error
Scheduled report
Scroll
Track
Widow

Review Questions

1. What questions identify output requirements?

2. What kinds of output media are there? List the characteristics of each.

3. What types of magnetic file organization are available to you? Explain how each works.

4. What types of magnetic file access are available to you? Explain how each works.

5. What must you consider when designing numeric output?

6. For what kinds of reports might you be called upon to build output formats? How should the formats differ?

7. Look at the following output segment of a BASIC program:

```
100 A=10
120 B=20.01
140 PRINT A
160 LPRINT B
180 PRINT #1,A,B
```

What is printed to magnetic disk? What is printed to paper? What is printed to the screen?

8. Look at the Pascal program RESULTS1. Predict the output.

```
PROGRAM RESULTS 1(OUTPUT);
  BEGIN
     WRITE(1,2);WRITE(3);WRITE(4,5);WRITELN;
     WRITE(1,2);
     WRITE(3);
     WRITE(4,5);
     WRITELN;
     WRITELN(1,2);
     WRITELN(3);
     WRITELN(4,5)
  END. {MAIN PROGRAM}
```

9. Look at the following BASIC program segment:

```
100 A1=123456
110 A2=12345
120 A3=1234
130 A4=123.5
140 A5=123.4
150 PRINT USING "#####";A1
```

```
160 PRINT USING "#### ####";A2,A3
170 PRINT #1 USING "### ###";A4,A5
180 END
```

What is printed to the printer? What is printed to magnetic disk? What is printed to the screen?

1. The pseudocode that follows describes rounding.

```
Value = 198.8549
Begin rounding module
        Two decimal places = (int(value * 100))/100
        Three decimal places = (int(value * 1000))/100
        Whole = (int(value * 1))/1
End rounding module
```

Expand the pseudocode to include rounding to one decimal place and to the nearest 10 (for example, 198.8549 = 200.00).

2. Convert the pseudocode in assignment 1 to Pascal and/or BASIC.

3. Design pseudocode for the following output:

TOTALS FOR ARON H

MON	TUE	WED	THU	FRI	SAT	SUN
*******	******	*******	********	*******	*******	*****
235.30	72.78	47.07	48.19	132.89	60.00	24.50

TRAVEL	MEALS	LODGING	ENTERTMT	MISC	TOTAL
*******	******	*******	********	********	*******
204.50	161.36	98.22	100.00	32.15	596.23

4. Write a program in Pascal and/or BASIC that encodes the pseudocode you wrote in assignment 3.

5. Write the pseudocode for the following problem: You have been hired by Jim's, a restaurant in Center City, Pennsylvania, that specializes in gourmet wild-mushroom dining. Joe must classify mushrooms according to the main dish they accompany. He wants to make sure he has a good supply of mushrooms on hand. Your assignment is to write pseudocode that will generate four lists extracted from the following information:

Mushroom	Amt in Stock (oz)	Beef Dish	Chicken Dish	Vegetable Dish
Common store	1000	Yes	Yes	Yes
King Bolete	500	Yes	Yes	Yes
Chicken	1200	No	Yes	Yes
Inky Cap	0	No	No	Yes
Morel	50	Yes	Yes	No
Black	400	Yes	Yes	No
Chanterelles	500	No	Yes	No
Caesar's	8	No	No	Yes

a. Write pseudocode to list all mushrooms in stock.
b. Write pseudocode to list all mushrooms for chicken dishes.
c. Write pseudocode to list all mushrooms for beef and vegetable dishes.
d. Write pseudocode to list all mushrooms for beef and chicken and vegetable dishes.
e. Design a proper output format.

6. Convert the pseudocode you wrote in assignment 5 into Pascal and/or BASIC.

5

Data Accumulation: Inputting

Inputting is the transformation of human communications into a form usable by a computer. This chapter investigates the different techniques and devices employed in inputting. These techniques will help you in the detailed decomposition of input modules.

INPUT REQUIREMENTS

Three major factors must be considered when evaluating the input requirements of a program:

- Data requirements
- Data media
- Data style

Data Requirements

The job to be accomplished determines data requirements. For example, the student GPA program in Chapter 2 needed two types of data: the sum of the individual GPA values of all the students and a count of the number of students whose GPA values were included in the sum. Thus, two separate forms of input data were associated with the small example—a direct data input (the GPA scores) and an indirect input item (the count of the number of GPA values used to compute the sum). Notice that the complexity of the algorithm is unimportant in identifying the data inputs. For example, imagine that the school administrator believes that a better measure of the average student GPA is obtained by taking each GPA value, multiplying it by itself (to get the square of the value), and adding the product to a sum variable to accumulate a sum of the squares of the individual GPAs.

This revised program still keeps track of how many values are read into it. When the last value is processed, the program divides this sum by the number of students used in the calculation. Then it takes the square root of the result of the division (a square root finds the number that, when multiplied by itself, results in the original value).

Notice that, in the original program and the revised program, the input is identical—even though the formula used to calculate the answer is definitely more complicated in the revised program.

Data Media

Another major concern for the software developer involves decisions about data input media. The developer must ask two major questions: How and where are the required data stored? How does the program read the data?

To understand data input media and their storage requirements, consider a bit of history. In the late 1940s and into the 1950s, the first form of data entry for computers consisted of rows of toggle switches on the front of the machines. The user set these switches to specific patterns that represented each individual bit position—a painfully slow approach by today's standards.

The next approach to data input involved separate media for storing data representations. These media included punched paper tape and the Hollerith punched card. Each medium could be input through one or a set of input devices such as paper tape drives or card readers.

These methods used holes punched in cardboard cards or on long pieces of thick paper to represent data. The problems with these data forms were that they were difficult to modify, tended to wear out with repeated use, and (in the case of punched cards) could be extremely heavy. For instance, a file drawer containing 4000 cards was as much as most adults could carry at one time.

Storage technology continued to improve with the advent of multitrack magnetic tapes and high-density magnetic disk storage. Unfortunately, like cards, these early devices were large, expensive, and often had special requirements. For example, the range of temperature in which they could operate effectively was narrow. Today, programmers enjoy a wide variety of affordable and durable devices. These include such media as floppy disks, rigid-case microfloppy disks, miniature hard disks, optical disks, streaming-tape systems (for mass storage backup), and so on.

In addition, the human interface changed with the advent of the extended keyboard, which contains more than the usual typewriter keys. The extended keyboard includes programmable function keys, cursor-control keys, and other special-use keys. Other user-friendly input devices include the light pen (which allows a user to select a specific word or symbol on a screen by simply pressing an electronic pen to the screen) and the mouse. The computer mouse has proven especially versatile. It minimizes typing and makes certain operations more intuitive.

Data Style

The third major factor to be considered when evaluating program input requirements is data style. The most common forms of data input are numeric (groups of digits used to represent specific quantities) and text (such as the letters on this page). If a pointing device such as a mouse or a light pen is used, the input consists of vertical and horizontal distances on the screen; the program converts the position data to a more useful data form, such as yes/no, up/down, and so on.

Thanks to today's microelectronic technology, it is now affordable to connect many different types of sensors directly to a computer. For example, it is now commonplace for a computer to receive position data from a robot arm or temperature data at some point in a chemical plant in the form of a voltage signal. The voltage input is converted to a number by an inexpensive analog-to-digital converter. The computer then uses a conversion algorithm to determine the actual temperature or position. The input possibilities are endless.

INPUT MEDIA FEATURES

The sections that follow examine features and programming techniques for several widely used input media and devices.

Keyboards and Screens

Thanks to the worldwide proliferation of personal computers and video terminals, the keyboard is probably the most prevalent means of data entry today. The keyboard is used to type in, or enter, numeric or text data. The screen echoes each entered character by displaying it.

Screen display allows "conversation" between inputter and computer, since the computer typically prompts the user for required data. The user responds by entering the data. Figure 5.1 illustrates this kind of question-and-answer session. The computer gets the rest of the data it needs from mass storage (such as disk).

Figure 5.2 shows the pseudocode to generate the display in Figure 5.1. Figures 5.3 and 5.4 show how such pseudocode could be implemented in BASIC and Pascal, respectively.

Several problems can arise with the *question-and-answer method.* If the user is experienced in using the software package and the questions asked are routine and predictable, the user may get impatient while waiting for each prompt. Sometimes a user answers several questions before discovering that the program needs a specific

Figure 5.1

```
Enter ID# 3413590
Enter # hrs worked: 16
Enter pay rate:_____
Enter # of dependents:_____
Enter health status:_____
Enter year-to-date pay:_____
```

A "conversation" between computer and inputter

piece of data that is unavailable. Such a situation either causes a delay while the user tries to find the data or forces the cancellation of the session. When the user begins again, he or she must reanswer questions from the canceled session. This can be frustrating.

A more desirable and coordinated use of the screen and keyboard implements the *fill-in-the-blank approach.* Spreadsheet programs used for business and scientific applications embody this concept. In this approach the program creator designs elec-

Figure 5.2

Pseudocode to generate the display of Figure 5.1

```
Do input procedure
    Input id#
    Enter # hrs worked
    Enter pay rate
    Enter # of dependents
    Enter health status
    Enter year-to-date pay
End input procedure
```

Figure 5.3

BASIC code that creates the display of Figure 5.1

```
1000    REM     INPUT PROCEDURE
1010    REM
1020    INPUT   "ENTER ID#: ":ID
1030    INPUT   "ENTER # HRS WORKED: ":HR
1040    INPUT   "ENTER PAYRATE: ":PY
1050    INPUT   "ENTER # OF DEPENDENTS: ":DP
1060    INPUT   "ENTER HEALTH STATUS: ":HS
1070    INPUT   "ENTER YEAR TO DATE PAY: ":YD
1080    RETURN
```

Figure 5.4

Pascal code that creates the display of Figure 5.1

```
PROCEDURE DATAIN:

{DATA INPUT PROCEDURE FOR PAYROLL PROGRAM}

BEGIN
    WRITE('ENTER ID#: ');
    READLN(ID);
    WRITE('ENTER # HRS WORKED: ');
    READLN(HR);
    WRITE ('ENTER PAYRATE: ');
    READLN (PY);
    WRITE ('ENTER # OF DEPENDENTS: ');
    READLN (DP);
    WRITE ('ENTER HEALTH STATUS: ');
    READLN (HS);
    WRITE ('ENTER YEAR TO DATE PAY: ');
    READLN (YD);
END;
```

tronic images of forms, or formats, that the user can follow in filling in the images with data. There are several advantages to this approach:

- A quick glance at the form allows the user to identify information not currently available.
- The form may seem unintimidating to users who are not accustomed to working with computers.
- An experienced user does not need to wait for prompting.

The disadvantages of the fill-in-the-blank method include:

- Increased software complexity
- Possible distortion of the software design to accommodate missing or conflicting data on the forms
- Possible user inefficiency in cases in which the user prepares unnecessary data

Physical Configuration. So far, this book has discussed some of the common data entry approaches while refraining from descriptions of the actual physical devices involved. For the sake of simplicity, the IBM Personal Computer and compatibles are described in the sections that follow. These computers are among the most common. However, keep in mind that this situation could change. Technology is rapidly advancing and, with it, the equipment available.

The IBM PC screen can be thought of as a grid 80 columns wide by 25 rows high; each cell in the grid can hold one character. The cursor (the underline or rectangle that indicates where the next character will appear on the screen) can be positioned by software that specifies column and row. It is also possible for the program to determine where the cursor is currently located.

The original IBM PC keyboard consisted of three areas: the typewriter keys; the function keys; and the numeric keypad, or cursor-control keys. The *typewriter keys* are configured in the traditional *QWERTY format*. The term *QWERTY* comes from the first six letters of the first row of alphabetic keys on a typewriter. The *function keys* are 10 keys labeled F1 through F10. These keys have no predefined function or meaning. Their function is determined by the program in use. Many programs take advantage of these keys to specify shortcuts for complicated commands.

For example, MS-DOS (the disk operating system developed by Microsoft Corportion) uses the F3 key to recall a previously issued command. Using this key can save the user a great deal of retyping if a command is repeated many times.

The *numeric keypad*, or *cursor-control keypad*, looks like an adding machine key set. A key along the top of the keypad area selects whether the output of the keypad is numeric or cursor control. For example, pressing one key produces an 8 in numeric mode; in the cursor-control mode, pressing the same key moves the cursor up. Certain of these keys are defined in particular ways by specialized programs. For example, many editors use the 3 and 9 keys on the numeric keypad to scroll through the document a page at a time.

Human Factors in Keyboard Use. Some manufacturers place the function keys in two columns along the left side of the keyboard. Others place them in a single row along the top. Each placement has advantages. For those who are left-handed and for applications in which most responses are simple multiple-choice selections, the left-side design seems best. For those who must alternate between typing and pressing function keys, the top-row design is preferred. Fortunately, inexpensive replacement keyboards are available. These keyboards allow the user to customize the system hardware to personal preference.

BASIC Keyboard Commands. The most widely used command for accessing the keyboard from BASIC programs is INPUT. For example, the instruction INPUT A$ prints a question mark in column 1 of the next available line on the screen. Obviously, a simple question mark in column 1 is not very helpful to the user, since it does not identify what information should be provided or whether the information should be numeric or text. Fortunately, the INPUT command allows descriptive information to be placed on the same line with the question mark prompt. The instruction

```
INPUT "What is your name",A$
```

would print on the screen as

```
What is your name?
```

Notice that BASIC automatically prints a question mark as a prompt after the message. The cursor is then positioned immediately to the right of the question mark to await user input.

Imagine an extremely simple program to calculate the hypotenuse of a right triangle. A right triangle is one in which one of the corners is 90 degrees; the hypotenuse is the longest side, and is always opposite the 90-degree corner. The program looks like this:

```
100 INPUT "Enter the length of the sides (separate with comma)",A,B
200 C = A^2 + B^2
300 C = SQR(C)
400 PRINT "The hypotenuse is ";C
```

Notice in this simple example that another feature of INPUT has been used to allow the user to request more than one piece of information at a time. That is, a prompt instructs the user to type in the length of the two sides and to separate the two numbers with a comma. BASIC uses the comma to identify where one number ends and the next begins.

Line 200 takes the first length and multiplies it by itself, then performs the same operation for the second length. Then, it adds these two results and places the result in the variable C.

In reality, the two lines could be combined in a single line:

```
200  C  =  SQR(A^2  +  B^2)
```

Another BASIC input command that accepts data from the keyboard is INKEY$. INKEY$ provides the program with a null string (if no key is pressed), a single character (if an alphanumeric key is pressed), or a two-character string (if special keys are pressed).

To illustrate the use of INKEY$, consider a simple educational game for children in which the Left Arrow and Right Arrow keys (the 4 and 6 keys on the numeric keypad) cause a "bug" to move left or right, respectively. The program samples the keyboard by using the INKEY$ command to change the position of the bug. Movement of the bug stops whenever the keys are released.

Other Devices

Many affordable peripheral devices can be employed for data acquisition. One device that has become widely used in recent years is the *optical scanner*. This device consists of a stable light source, a timing circuit, and a photoelectric sensor that can sense dark bands. The bands are called a *bar code*.

As the bar code moves past the sensor, the amount of light reflected by the bars varies. The electronic timing circuit can figure out the relative proportion of dark and light and, from this, extract the numeric information.

A scanner can be connected to a computer in several ways: as a card that is inserted in one of the expansion slots inside a PC, as a stand-alone unit that is connected to the serial or parallel I/O ports of the machine, or through a device called a *wedge*. A wedge is a box that converts the data being received from the peripheral to impulses like those that come from the keyboard. The wedge is connected to the keyboard input of the machine and "fools" the computer into sensing that someone is actually pressing the keys on the keyboard.

These kinds of "smart" peripherals perform an important function, since they allow large amounts of data to be collected in an efficient and highly reliable manner. They also reduce overall operating costs by minimizing the data entry effort of humans. So, you can expect to see these peripherals in use in increasing numbers. Today, a typical peripheral device costs only the equivalent of a few weeks salary, does not get fatigued, and is usually less error prone than a person performing the same function.

STORAGE MEDIA

With the explosion in the number of computer databases, the most common input form is probably the mass storage file. Mass storage devices fall into three predominant categories: hard disks, floppy disks, and magnetic tape.

Hard Disks

Most computer systems targeted for serious data processing have at least one hard disk, or rigid disk, for data storage. Large mainframe computers often have hundreds, or even thousands, of hard disks organized into packs and stored within disk units. Each large hard disk holds hundreds of megabytes, or 1,048,576 bytes, of data.

The chief advantages of a hard disk over floppy disks and tape include:

- Large storage capacity
- High access speed (the time required to find and retrieve a specific data item or record)
- Reliability

The chief disadvantages of hard disks include sensitivity to mechanical shock (being dropped, for example) and a relatively high cost per bit of storage.

Hard disks are usually made from a metal or other suitably rigid platter that is coated with special compounds. The compounds can be magnetized to represent 1s and 0s. Recall that this machine-language representation is the basis for almost all operations within digital computers.

The magnetic heads that read and write the data on the disk are designed to "fly" at a very small distance above the surface of the magnetic coating. Thus, no mechanical wear occurs at the disk surfaces, which implies an almost unlimited disk life under ideal conditions.

One of the greatest dangers to hard disks is smoke. The particles in smoke are small enough to pass into the computer but big enough to span the distance between the head and the disk. If enough particles are present, they may cause the head to crash into the disk surface, ruining both and causing loss of all data on the disk.

Floppy Disks

Floppy disks are an almost universal data storage form today. A disk is made from a circular piece of Mylar plastic film that has been coated with special iron-oxide coatings. The first floppies were eight inches in diameter and held around 200 Kbytes. The technology soon advanced to allow a reduced size of 5 1/4 inches and an increased storage capacity of 360 Kbytes.

Present technology allows both the 5 1/4 inch floppy disk and the 3 1/2 inch microfloppy to hold over one megabyte of storage. Since the magnetic heads that read and write data actually touch the disk surface, floppy disks are subject to eventual wear. For this reason, floppy disks are not as reliable as hard disks.

Magnetic Tape

Magnetic tape is one of the earliest data storage media for computer systems. This medium has by far the lowest cost per bit and can hold extremely large amounts of data. The main disadvantage of tape is relatively slow access time. It can take as long as a minute to find a particular file or record on a large tape.

Tape storage comes in two basic types: *open-reel storage* and *cartridge storage*. The open-reel system consists of a spool that holds the tape and a second, empty spool on which the tape is wound after it is read. The tape is approximately 1/2 inch wide and holds several tracks parallel to each other. This allows for high data density per line inch of tape. Cartridge tapes do not generally hold as much data as open-reel tapes. However, cartridge tapes do provide easier handling and storage then reel tapes.

STORAGE MEDIA ACCESS

Now that you've studied the basics of storage media, you can learn about methods for accessing data from these devices. The fundamental command in BASIC to access either floppy or hard-disk files is INPUT #. This command consists of three parts: INPUT #, an integer number placed immediately following the pound sign (#), and a list of variables that are to be read from the file. The number that follows the pound sign identifies which file is to be read. (In complex applications a program might open and use several files for processing.)

The computer expects data in a disk file to be similar to what a human would provide through a keyboard. It expects commas between data items, for example. Thus, the statement INPUT #1, A\$ reads a string into the variable A\$ from the data file allocated to logical file number 1. Remember that, for the string to be read properly, it should contain quotation marks to delimit it.

Another command for reading a disk file is INPUT \$. This command works in a manner similar to INPUT #. However, INPUT \$ allows a specified number of characters to be read directly from the input device. This technique allows an ambitious programmer to use such file values as control codes, which are normally stripped off by the BASIC input routines. Reading directly from the input device could implement a word processing program that includes special characters. For instance, special text processing characters might indicate hidden carriage returns, line feeds, and so on. The command takes this form:

```
A$ = INPUT $(N,#F)
```

Here N is an integer that identifies the number of characters to be read from the file at one time; F indicates the logical file number that identifies which file is to be read.

A final form of data input available in BASIC is the READ command. For example, the statement READ A\$ reads information from a DATA statement contained within the program and then assigns the data to the string A\$.

Each time a READ statement is encountered, BASIC assigns the value of the next available item in the DATA statement group to the first variable of the READ statement. If the number of variables in the READ statement exceeds the number of data items remaining on the DATA line, the variables are assigned from information available on subsequent DATA lines. Consider this program:

```
100   FOR   J=1 to 3
200     READ A, B, C
300   NEXT  J
```

```
400    DATA  5, 6, 7, 8
500    DATA  9, 10, 11, 12
600    DATA  13, 14
```

To see how these instructions assign values to the input variables, read the sequence that follows from left to right.

A = 5	B = 6	C = 7
A = 8	B = 9	C = 10
A = 11	B = 12	C = 13

Notice that the assignments "wrap around" the DATA statements. The value 14 in the last DATA statement is ignored unless there is a subsequent READ statement to retrieve it.

DATA STYLE CHOICES

The final input solution for a problem definition is to design an input style that is compatible with the person expected to provide the input. As mentioned in the discussion of the keyboard-screen interface, programs aimed at clerical personnel often use the simple question-and-answer format or the fill-in-the-form approach. These techniques trade off flexibility and creativity for ease of use. Programs that are more difficult to use may be capable of doing more than the easy programs.

For example, imagine that an architect wants to calculate the heat loss of a new house design. Given standard construction techniques and the dimensions of the house, an easy-to-use program could calculate the heat lost through the walls, windows, and ceilings of the building. A program that is a little harder to use could accept the dimensions and a target heat loss, then calculate backward to determine how much insulation would have to be present in the walls and ceilings to meet the target values.

Another technique often employed for data entry is the *menu* screen. On startup the screen appears mostly blank except for headings. With a pointing device (usually a mouse), the user can select one of the headings. When the heading is selected, a group of subcategories appears, usually enclosed in a box or highlighted with reverse video. If the user then selects a subcategory, an additional menu may appear or the machine might perform some action. Examples of actions are printing a file or asking the user to enter some required data item. Menu-driven screens were pioneered by researchers at the Xerox research center in Palo Alto, California, and at other locations in government and academia. Today, menu-driven programs are commonplace in personal computer applications.

Writing software to control the multiple levels of subcategories used to take a great deal of work. However, programmers today are able to purchase *window packages* that extend the normal I/O capabilities of programming languages. Windowing software allows a programmer to produce professional-looking menu screen systems with limited effort.

Figure 5.5 illustrates the screen display for a simple menu interface. Figure 5.6 contains the pseudocode needed to implement this menu interface. Figures 5.7 and 5.8 illustrate how such pseudocode might be implemented in BASIC and Pascal, respectively.

Figure 5.5

```
Payroll System for Fun Fantasies

What do you want to do?

     1. Input data
     2. Process payroll
     3. Output payroll reports
     4. Quit

Enter choice:
```

Figure 5.6

```
Do initialization procedure
Display options for Fun Fantasies payroll system
Choose Option
If option is 1, do input procedure
If option is 2, do process procedure
If option is 3, do output procedure
If option is 4, do quit system
Do termination procedure
```

Figure 5.7

```
10    PRINT "Payroll System for Fun Fantasies"
20    PRINT
30    PRINT
40    PRINT "What do you want to do?"
50    PRINT
60    PRINT
70    PRINT "    1. Input data"
80    PRINT "    2. Process payroll"
90    PRINT "    3. Output payroll reports"
100   PRINT "    4. Quit"
110   PRINT
120   INPUT "ENTER CHOICE:";C
130   ON C GOSUB 1000,2000,3000,4000
140   GOTO 10
1000  REM INPUT PROCEDURE *******************
         .
         .
         .
1999  RETURN
```

Figure 5.8

The Pascal implementation of Figure 5.6

```
BEGIN
    REPEAT
        WRITELN ('Payroll System for Fun Fantasies');
        WRITELN;
        WRITELN;
        WRITELN ('What do you want to do?');
        WRITELN;
        WRITELN;
        WRITELN ('    1. Input data');
        WRITELN ('    2. Process data');
        WRITELN ('    3. Output payroll reports');
        WRITELN ('    4. Quit');
        WRITELN;
        WRITELN ('ENTER CHOICE:');
        READLN C;
        CASE C OF
            1: INDATA; {PROCEDURE}
            2: PROCESS;{PROCEDURE}
            3: OUTDATA;{PROCEDURE}
            4: TERMINATE;{PROCEDURE}
        END; {CASE}
    UNTIL C=4;
END.
```

Notice line 130 of the BASIC program; it introduces a software construct:

```
ON C GOSUB XXX,YYY,ZZZ
```

If the value of the control variable (in this case, C) is 1, a subroutine call is made to the first line number (XXX). If the value of C is 2, a GOSUB is performed to the second line number listed (YYY), and so on. When the called routine completes its work, a RETURN statement transfers execution to the line following the ON...GOSUB block of code. If the value of C is 0 or greater than the number of arguments in the ON...GOSUB statement, control is passed immediately to the next line in sequence.

A variant of the ON...GOSUB command is ON...GOTO. This structure operates identically to GOSUB except that a software branch instruction is implemented. However, after the branch has been made, no easy method exists for returning to the code that caused the branch.

ERROR CHECKING

One of the key features of successful input processing is detection of errors in incoming data. One of the simplest forms of error checking is the *range check*. To illustrate, imagine that the value associated with a month of the year is to be entered into an inventory program. You know that the entered value must be within the range of 1 through 12. Any other value must be an error. If a range error is detected, the simplest response is the immediate request for entry of the correct value. Figure 5.9 is a simple BASIC program that implements range checking of input data.

A related test is a *value check*. If an input must be true/false, male/female, or some other Boolean value, the input can be checked to verify that it is of the proper type. The program requests correction of the improper value. Figure 5.10 illustrates how a value check of input data could be implemented in BASIC.

Another error-detection technique uses the *check digit*. For example, an identification number can be defined so that the last digit is the result of adding all previous digits. This provides a simple method for verifying long strings of data. Figure 5.11 implements this type of checking algorithm in BASIC.

A variation of the check digit is the *digit check*. Here a specific digit in a field— say, the first digit—is expected to contain a specific value. If not, an error exists and must be handled. Figure 5.12 illustrates this principle with a BASIC program.

Another checking technique involves the program user. This technique is called *visual verification*. This approach is used for question-and-answer and other interactive data entry approaches. The idea is to display an entered value on the screen and prompt for verification.

A widely used visual error-checking approach involves database verification. For

Figure 5.9

BASIC implementation of range checking

```
10    INPUT "Enter month (i.e., 1-12)",M
20    IF M<1 OR M>12 THEN WRITE "Wrong; please try again":GOTO 10
```

Figure 5.10

BASIC implementation of a value check

```
10    INPUT "Enter gender (i.e., M OR F)";G$
20    IF G$='F' OR G$='M' THEN GOTO 30 ELSE WRITE "Fallen asleep again?":GOTO 10
30    REM
```

Figure 5.11

BASIC implementation using a check digit

```
10    INPUT "Enter ID# ";I
20    A=I DIV 100
30    A1=I-A*100
40    B=A1 DIV 10
50    B1=A1-B*10
60    IF (A+B**2)=B1 THEN PRINT "Entered correctly" ELSE PRINT "ERROR":GOTO 10
```

Figure 5.12

BASIC implementation of a digit check

```
10    INPUT "Enter ID# ";I
20    A=I DIV 100
30    IF A <> 2 THEN PRINT "Entered incorrectly":GOTO 10
```

example, as items are scanned in a supermarket by an optical scanner, an item description and price are displayed at the cash register. This allows immediate feedback because the shopper usually recognizes immediately if an item is identified or priced incorrectly. Many inventory programs in use today display detailed information about a part when a part number has been entered. This allows the user to verify the information to determine whether the correct part has been chosen. Figure 5.13 shows a BASIC implementation of visual verification.

In another form of input verification, all data are entered twice. The program points out discrepancies between the two sets of data. The programmer can correct the set in which the error occurs. This technique is called the *double-entry method*. It was developed for use with punched cards and is still in use as a means of checking screen input.

CONTROL FIELDS

At some point in the execution of an interactive program, the user has to be able to indicate that all available data have been provided. This signals the computer to stop collecting data and to begin processing activities. The simplest way to perform this signaling function is through use of a *control field*.

For example, the pseudocode in Figure 5.14 describes a program that collects values until the ID field changes to a terminating value. At that point a grand total is printed.

A careful comparison of Figure 5.14 and the BASIC code that implements it in Figure 5.15 shows how close the final code can be to the pseudocode version. Lines 2 through 6 of the pseudocode are initialization, 8 and 9 are processing, 10 inputting, 12 outputting, 13 and 14 are additional processing, and 16 is termination. Thus, two processing modules exist within the pseudocode. If the different phases (input, processing, and output) were more complex, each would be placed in separate procedures in the BASIC program. The exercises at the end of the chapter require you to do this.

Figure 5.16 shows a Pascal version of the control program described in Figure 5.14. Note the differences in code structure brought about by the structured coding techniques enforced by Pascal.

Figure 5.13

BASIC implementation of visual verification

```
10    INPUT "Enter ID#" ;I
20    PRINT "You have just entered ";I
30    INPUT "Is this correct? (Y or N) ";R$
40    IF A$='Y' OR A$='YES' OR A$='y' OR A$='yes' THEN PRINT "OK"
              ELSE PRINT 'Enter again':GOTO 10
```

Figure 5.14

```
1     BEGIN PROGRAM
2     INITIALIZE GRANDTOTAL. GRANDCOUNT = 0
3     ENTER ID NUMBER. SALES
4     WHILE ID NOT EQUAL TO PROGRAM ENDING SENTINEL
5         SET CONTROL FIELD SENTINEL TO ID NUMBER
6         INITIALIZE TOTAL. COUNT TO 0
7         WHILE ID NUMBER EQUALS CONTROL FIELD VALUE DO
8             TOTAL=TOTAL + SALES
9             COUNT=COUNT + 1
10            ENTER ID, SALES
11        END WHILE
12        PRINT TOTAL. COUNT
13        GRANDTOTAL=GRANDTOTAL + TOTAL
14        GRANDCOUNT=GRANDCOUNT + COUNT
15    END WHILE
16    PRINT GRANDTOTAL, GRANDCOUNT
17    END PROGRAM
```

Figure 5.15

```
10  REM CONTROL BREAK CONCEPT
20  REM
30  REM **********INITIALIZATION **********
40  REM
50  GT=0
60  GC=0
70  INPUT "Enter ID #: ".ID
80  INPUT "Enter sale: ":S
90  WHILE ID <> -1
100 ST=ID
110    T=O
120    C=0
130    WHILE ID=ST
140       T=T+SALES
150       C=C+1
160       INPUT "Enter ID #: ":ID
170       INPUT "Enter sale: ":S
180    WEND
190    PRINT T,C
200    GT=GT+T
210    GC=GC+C
220 WEND
230 PRINT GT, GC
240 END
```

Figure 5.16

Pascal implementation of the pseudocode of Figure 5.14

```
PROGRAM CONTROLBREAKS (INPUT. OUTPUT):

VAR
      ID: INTEGER: {ID NUMBER}
      S : REAL:     {SALE IN DOLLARS}
      C : INTEGER: {NUMBER OF SALES FOR PERSON}
      T : REAL:     {TOTAL SALES FOR PERSON}
      GC: INTEGER: {TOTAL NUMBER OF SALES ALL PERSONS}
      GT: REAL:     {TOTAL SALES ALL PERSONS}
      ST: INTEGER: {SENTINEL SIGNALING CONTROL BREAK}
BEGIN
      GT:=0.0;
      GC:=0;
      WRITE('Enter ID # :');
      READLN(ID);
      WRITE('Enter sale: ');
      READLN(S);
      WHILE ID<>-1 DO
            BEGIN
                ST:=ID;
                C:=0;
                T:=0.0;
                WHILE ID=ST DO
                      BEGIN
                            T:=T+S;
                            C:=C+1;
                            WRITE('Enter ID #: ');
                            READLN(ID);
                            WRITE('Enter sale: ');
                            READLN(S);
                      END;
                WRITELN(T:5:2,C:5);
                GT:=GT+T;
                GC:=GC+C;
            END;
        WRITELN(GT:6:2,GC:5);
    END.
```

SUMMARY

This chapter concentrates on the inputting module in a top-down design. It discusses data requirements, data media, and data style as the main focus of a programmer when considering input requirements. It asks you to first consider input needs as a function of output. It asks you to consider the sources of input and their characteristics. It also asks you to focus on the person doing the inputting. Together, these considerations will help you build an effective input interface between the end-user and the machine.

Bar code
Cartridge storage
Check digit
Control field
Cursor-control keypad
Digit check
Double-entry method
Fill-in-the-blank approach
Function keys
INPUT #
INPUT $
Menu
Numerical keypad

Open-reel storage
Optical scanner
ON...GOSUB
ON...GOTO
QWERTY format
Question-and-answer method
Range check
Typewriter keys
Value check
Visual verification
Wedge
Window package

Review Questions

1. What factors should be considered in determining input requirements?

2. How are data requirements determined?

3. What questions do you ask in determining input media?

4. What are the advantages and disadvantages of fill-in-the-blank input forms?

5. What keyboard characteristics must you be aware of in designing your input module?

6. What screen characteristics should you be aware of when you are designing your input module?

7. What input style choices do you have?

8. What are the different error-checking schemes? Give an example of each.

9. What is a control field and why is it used?

10. The program that follows inputs data from within a BASIC program. Predict the output.

```
10 REM DEMO 7
20 REM
30 READ A1,A2,A3,B,C,X
40 D=A1,+A2+A3
50 E=B+C
```

```
55 F=(D+E)/X
60 PRINT "PARTIAL SUM1= ";D
70 PRINT "PARTIAL SUM2= ";E
80 PRINT "AVERAGE=      ";F
90 DATA 5,10,15,10,2,5,7
100 END
```

11. The BASIC that follows inputs data by using what kind of input style? Predict the output if you enter 100,90, minus 1. Write a pseudocode subprogram to prevent an error of this type. Code the pseudocode in BASIC.

```
10 REM DEMO 11
20 REM
30 REM
40 PRINT "ENTER THREE GRADES"
50 PRINT "(I.E., 100,90,80)"
60 PRINT "TO END PROGRAM TYPE -1,-1,-1"
70 INPUT "GRADE 1 ";A
80 INPUT "GRADE 2 =";B
90 INPUT "GRADE 3 IS";C
100 D=(A+B+C)/3
110 PRINT "THE AVERAGE IS ";D
120 END
```

12. The BASIC program that follows inputs data by using what kind of input style?

```
100 REM DEMO PROGRAM 60
110 REM
120 PRINT "SORT ALPHABETICALLY = 1"
130 PRINT "SORT BY ASSETS      = 2"
140 PRINT "SORT BY PROFITS     = 3"
150 PRINT "SORT BY EMPLOYEES   = 4"
160 PRINT "TO END PROGRAM      = 5"
170 PRINT
180 PRINT "ENTER NUMBER OF CHOICE NOW"
190 INPUT A
200 IF A<1 OR A>5 THEN GOSUB 5000
210 ON A GOSUB 1000,2000,3000,4000,6000
220 GOTO 110
1000 REM ALPHABETIC SORT ROUTINE
1010 REM
1020 PRINT "SORTING ALPHABETICALLY"
1999 RETURN
2000 REM ASSET SORT ROUTINE
2010 REM
2020 PRINT "SORTING BY ASSETS"
2999 RETURN
3000 REM PROFIT SORT ROUTINE
3010 REM
3020 PRINT "SORTING BY PROFITS"
3999 RETURN
4000 REM EMPLOYEE SORT ROUTINE
4010 REM
4020 PRINT "SORTING BY NUMBER OF EMPLOYEES"
```

```
4999 RETURN
5000 REM ERROR ROUTINE
5010 REM
5020 PRINT "YOUVE MADE AN ERROR, TRY AGAIN"
5999 RETURN
6000 REM WRAPUP ROUTINE
6010 REM
6020 PRINT "THATS ALL FOLKS"
6999 END
```

13. From what sources do the BASIC statements that follow retrieve data?

```
INPUT
INPUT #
READ
```

14. Look at the Pascal program ENTER:

```
PROGRAM ENTER(INPUT,OUTPUT);
VAR
C1,C2,C3:CHAR;
WORKING: BOOLEAN;
    BEGIN
        WORKING=TRUE;
        WHILE WORKING
            BEGIN
                READLN(C1,C2);
                WRITELN(C1,C2," IS THIS CORRECT? Y OR N"
                READLN(C3);
                IF C3="Y" THEN WORKING:=TRUE
                    ELSE WORKING:=FALSE;
            END;
        PRINTLN(C1,C2,C3,WORKING);
END. {PROGRAM}
```

What type of error routine is used? What input style is used?

15. Look at the BASIC program that follows. What kind of error routine is it performing?

```
10 REM DEMO 45
20 REM
30 REM
40 INPUT "ENTER A WORD";A$
50 FOR I=1 TO LEN(A$)
60     B$=MID(A$,I,1)
80     IF (B$<"A" OR B$>"Z") AND B$<>"." THEN GOTO 100
90 NEXT I
95 GOTO 150
100 PRINT "YOU HAVE MADE AN INPUT ERROR"
110 PRINT "THE STRING ";A$;"CONTAINS AN ERROR"
120 PRINT "THE BAD CHARACTER IS ";B$;" IT IS IN COLUMN ";I
```

```
130 PRINT "REENTER YOUR DATA OR YOU ARE FIRED"
140 GOTO 40
150 PRINT "YOU HAVE MADE AN ERROR FREE ENTRY!!!!!!!";A$
160 END
```

16. Explain the differences between keyboard, optical scanner, and disk input in terms of program pseudocode and BASIC code. Give a BASIC example of the code to input from each device.

Problem-Solving Assignments

1. Now that you have seen the basic structure for data input, modify the payroll program to include error checks. First, modify the pseudocode. Then modify either the BASIC or the Pascal code. Include a menu and use question-and-answer style.

2. Modify the control field program to include error checks. First, modify the pseudocode. Then modify the BASIC and/or the Pascal code.

3. Modify the payroll program so that all work is done within subprograms.

4. Modify the control-field program so that all work is done within subprograms.

5. Create a subroutine for ID# in the payroll program. The I.D. number is a six-digit number. The first five digits should be regular numbers; the sixth digit should be a check digit. Use the check digit example in the text as a starting point. The scheme is:

   First digit
   Second digit is second digit minus first digit
   Third digit is third digit squared
   Fourth digit is fourth digit doubled
   Fifth digit is fifth digit minus fourth digit doubled
   Sixth digit is the check digit

   Add the results of the first five digits. The last digit of the total should equal the sixth digit. Remember to write the pseudocode first.

6. Create pseudocode for the programs in review questions 10, 12, 14, and 15 in this chapter.

Table and Array Processing

The first five chapters in this text presented programming concepts that fit within the problem-solving approach. This chapter is the first of the processing module chapters. It discusses arrays and their characteristics. Near the end of this chapter, a practical application of arrays is demonstrated through use of the payroll problem developed in earlier chapters.

An array is a set of contiguous memory locations that can be identified through use of a single variable name. The term *contiguous* means that all memory areas used by an array are next to each other. Because locations are contiguous, the program can associate the array name with the starting position of the array. Individual positions, or elements, within the array can be identified through use of an index. The index is basically a counter that points to a particular memory position, or table element. Each memory location must be of the same data type.

Chapter 3 briefly introduced you to the concept of arrays. You learned that it helps to think of an array as a table, or collection of columns and rows. This approach makes sense because an array may have several sets of elements. Each set of elements is called a dimension. Think of a dimension as a column. Elements that align across multiple columns form a row. Each dimension of an array requires its own index.

Figure 6.1 shows a single-dimensional array of numbers. In this example the array contains ten elements, or consecutive memory locations. Each element can store one table value. This table contains a list of product numbers available through a single manufacturer. This table contains one column (dimension) with ten rows. Each row has only one position. Each row position is identified through use of an index value.

A two-dimensional array contains two columns, one for each dimension. Consider how Figure 6.1 can be extended to represent two manufacturers. Each manufacturer sells ten nearly identical products. In this case one index is established to locate the position of a product number (this index moves downward through each column). The second index, for the second dimension of the array, keeps track of the manufacturer and moves along the row positions. Thus, ten index values are possible for the first dimension, and two index values are possible for the second dimension. This array is illustrated in Figure 6.2.

Keep in mind that the terms *table* and *array* can be used interchangeably. Some programming languages use one; some use the other. Whatever the structure is called, its potential is the same: A collection of contiguous memory areas, called a table or array, can be established to store related values, all of which can be referenced by a single variable name. Different elements within this structure can be located through use of index values, one index value per dimension.

Arrays are extremely useful whenever relationships or dependencies exist between various pieces of data. For instance, in Figure 6.2 the manufacturers are related because they sell the same type of products. The product numbers are related because they are used by a single manufacturer.

In general, two types of arrays are used by professional programmers: numeric arrays and character arrays. Each type of array can have multiple dimensions.

Figure 6.1

A single-dimensional array of numbers

Table name, or variable name:	Array, or table element	Index value
	80347	1
	80351	2
	80472	3
	80596	4
PROD - TAB	80602	5
	80713	6
	80813	7
	90010	8
	90022	9
	90034	10

Figure 6.2

A two-dimensional array of numbers

Table name, or variable name:	Array, or table element	Index values	Array, or table element	Index values
	80347	(1, 1)	40756	(2, 1)
	80351	(1, 2)	40787	(2, 2)
	80472	(1, 3)	41010	(2, 3)
	80596	(1, 4)	41310	(2, 4)
	80602	(1, 5)	41425	(2, 5)
PROD - TAB	80713	(1, 6)	41618	(2, 6)
	80813	(1, 7)	41725	(2, 7)
	90010	(1, 8)	41800	(2, 8)
	90022	(1, 9)	41887	(2, 9)
	90034	(1, 10)	42200	(2, 10)

NUMERIC ARRAYS

You have already learned about three kinds of numeric arrays: one-dimensional, two-dimensional, and three-dimensional. Look again at these three varieties.

One-Dimensional Numeric Arrays

The simplest array type is the single-dimensional numeric array. As you recall from Chapter 3, this type of array usually has a specific size (number of elements) and consists of two parts: the array name and the index value. For example, if you want to find the value contained by the third element of an array called CURVE, use

```
A = CURVE(3)
```

CURVE specifies the name of the array, and (3) specifies the index position, or table element, in which the desired value can be found. As the name suggests, a numeric array stores a collection of numeric values.

Obviously, the statement A = CURVE(3) is satisfactory if the information you seek is always in the third element. However, it is not of much use if the data move around within the array or if you wish to access each element in sequence. Consider how you might generate an array containing the squares of the index value for the first ten integers. The first array element contains 1^2, the second contains 2^2, and so on. The pseudocode looks like this:

```
Do for I = 1 to 10
  Squares(I) = I * I
Doend
```

After the code is executed, the contents of this single-dimensional array are:

```
SQUARES(1)    =      1
SQUARES(2)    =      4
SQUARES(3)    =      9
SQUARES(4)    =     16
SQUARES(5)    =     25
SQUARES(6)    =     36
SQUARES(7)    =     49
SQUARES(8)    =     64
SQUARES(9)    =     81
SQUARES(10)   =    100
```

Two-Dimensional Numeric Arrays

Another interesting and frequently used type of numeric array is the two-dimensional variant. Imagine that a student wants to create a budget for the coming year. Since tuition and other expenses are not due every month, cash expenditures vary over time.

The simplest way to lay out such a budget is to draw 12 columns on a sheet of paper, with each column representing a month of the year. The rows perpendicular to the columns itemize the various expenses, as shown in Figure 6.3. As you can see, the student identifies different expense categories (food, tuition, and so on) and then places the numbers in the appropriate location on the sheet.

Think of the balance sheet as a two-dimensional array. The first index represents the row corresponding to a type of expense. The second index represents the specific month. Notice that there is nothing magical about the assignment of the first index to the item and the second to the month; assignment could just as easily have been the other way around, with the month as the first index and the item as the second index. Once relationships of dimensions have been assigned, however, they must be maintained for the remainder of the program.

Three-Dimensional Numeric Arrays

Now imagine that the student has sufficiently accurate information to project expenses and income for several years in the future. A separate sheet of paper could now be created for each year of school and labeled numerically by year (1 for the first year, 2 for the second year, and so on). The student now, without knowledge of programming concepts, has created a three-dimensional array. The first two dimensions are still month and expense; the third index identifies the school year. Figure 6.4 shows the setup of this three-dimensional array.

Four-Dimensional Numeric Arrays

As you might realize, arrays of more that three dimensions become rather difficult to visualize. A meaningful fourth dimension could be added to this example if the stu-

Figure 6.3

Student budget sheet

Figure 6.4

Illustration of a three-dimensional array

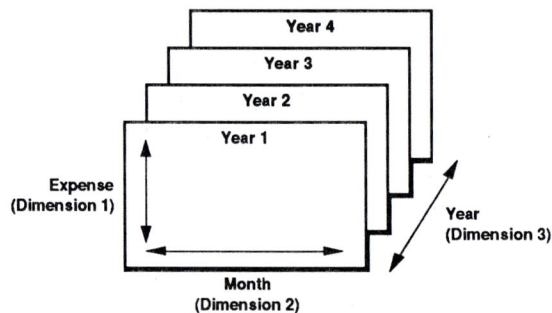

Chapter 6: Table and Array Processing

133

dent has a brother or sister. In this scenario two stacks of papers are created, one for each student. This arrangement is shown in Figure 6.5. The fourth index identifies the projections for each student.

CHARACTER ARRAYS

A second type of array is often used in software applications today: *the character array* or *string*. The simplest of this form is a single-dimensional character array in which each position in the array holds only one alphanumeric character, as shown in Figure 6.6. A two-dimensional character array is also straightforward, as shown in Figure 6.7.

A third form of character array is called an *array of strings*. Such arrays are useful for holding lists of names, such as the days of the week. This type of array is portrayed in Figure 6.8. Many languages permit the use of multidimensional string and character arrays, but they define certain limitations that are either language specific or machine specific. A competent software designer should always know the limitations of his or her tools and attempt to understand the trade-offs associated with the use of sophisticated features.

ARRAY IMPLEMENTATION

Now that you have been introduced to the fundamentals of arrays, consider several real-world problems to illustrate array use in BASIC and Pascal. Imagine this scenario. You have been hired as a programmer for a mail-order business that sold five types of items in the year 1987. You want to calculate total annual sales for the business by using this simple tabulation approach:

Figure 6.5

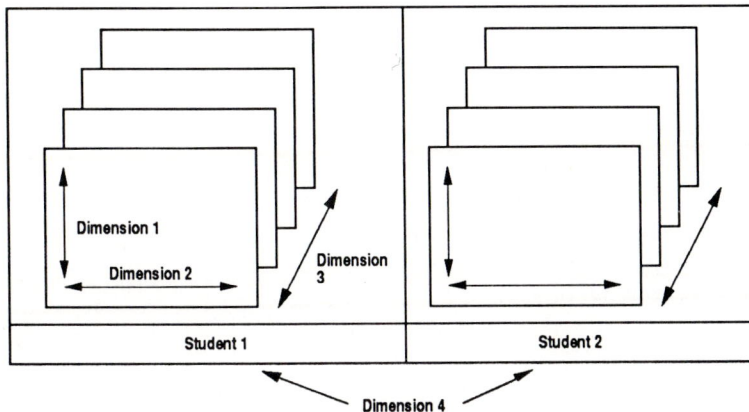

Illustration of a four-dimensional array

Array Implementation

Figure 6.6

A one-dimensional
character array of
length 10

| A | B | C | D | E | | | | | |

Figure 6.7

A two-dimensional
character array of
length 5 x 10

	[1]	[2]	[3]	[4]	[5]	[6]	[7]	[8]	[9]	[10]
[1]	R	E	D							
[2]	B	L	U	E						
[3]	G	R	E	E	N					
[4]	O	R	A	N	G	E				
[5]	Y	E	L	L	O	W				

Figure 6.8

A one-dimensional
string array of length 5

A

[1]	Monday
[2]	Tuesday
[3]	Wednesday
[4]	Thursday
[5]	Friday

```
Sales 1
Sales 2
Sales 3
Sales 4
Sales 5
------
Total_87
```

In pseudocode, the problem can be outlined as:

```
Begin processing procedure
    Initialize total to 0
    Add sales for each item to total
End processing procedure
```

Now let's consider several alternative strategies for organizing the data to solve this problem.

Strategy A

Under this approach all sales items are considered as separate variables. This can be expressed as

```
Total_87 = Sales1 + Sales2 + Sales3 + Sales4 + Sales5
```

This strategy suffers from a fundamental flaw: Every sales item must be assigned a unique name. If 1000 items had been sold rather than 5, the source code for this operation would take up several pages. Additionally, languages such as Pascal and C require the explicit definition of all variables. In these languages you might use several pages to define these items and many additional pages to specify processing for each variable. Obviously, this strategy can be extremely wasteful of memory space and programming time.

Strategy B

Under this approach, define a variable called SALES, which identifies a single-dimensional array of five elements. The total is calculated by this tabulation:

```
Total_87 = sales(1) + sales(2) + sales(3) + sales(4) + sales(5)
```

This can be implemented in standard BASIC as

```
T=S(1)+S(2)+S(3)+S(4)+S(5)
```

In Pascal the code is

```
TOTAL:=SALES[1]+SALES[2]+SALES[3]+SALES[4]+SALES[5];
```

Remember that, in Pascal, the symbol := stands for "Assign the value evaluated from the expression on the right to the variable on the left."

Strategy C

Strategies A and B are useful for a small number of items. However, they are not practical for large groups of items. Fortunately, the properties of an array allow the same algorithm implemented in strategy B to be performed within a loop. This approach gives you the power to attack large problems in a reasonable and efficient manner.

For example, another way to represent the processing in pseudocode looks like this:

```
ROW = 1
TOTAL = 0
Loop until row = 5
```

```
        TOTAL = TOTAL + SALES(ROW)
        ROW = ROW + 1
   End loop
```

In BASIC, this becomes

```
100  T=0
200  FOR R=1 TO 5
300     T=T+S(R)
400  NEXT R
```

In Pascal, the pseudocode becomes

```
TOTAL:= 0;
FOR ROW:=1 TO 5 DO
   TOTAL:=TOTAL+SALES[ROW];
```

Notice that, for both of these language implementations, you could easily expand the loop counter to 1000 without making any other major modifications to the program.

ARRAY PROCESSING: CODING CHOICES

Consider expanding the sales-totaling program by adding a set of data for 1988. Consider that the same number of item types (five) were sold in both years. Also consider developing independent totals for each year, as well as totals for each item sold over the two years.

The pseudocode for this problem is

```
Begin process module
     Add total sales for 1987
     Add total sales for 1988
     Add total for each item over both years
End process module
```

There are several strategies for implementing the solution to this problem.

Strategy 1

The first strategy treats all items as separate variables, which results in the following calculations:

```
Total_87 = S1_87 + S2_87 + S3_87 + S4_87 + S5+87
Total_88 = S1_88 + S2_88 + S3_88 + S4_88 + S5+88
Total_I1 = S1_87 + S1_88
Total_I2 = S2_87 + S2_88
Total_I3 = S3_87 + S3_88
Total_I4 = S4_87 + S4_88
Total_I5 = S5_87 + S5_88
```

In BASIC, this is coded as

```
T87=S187+S287+S387+S487+S587
T88=S188+S288+S388+S488+S588
I1=S187+S188
I2=S287+S288
I3=S387+S388
I4=S487+S488
I5=S587+S588
```

In Pascal, the calculations are

```
TOTAL87:=SALES1_87+SALES2_87+SALES3_87+SALES4_87+SALES5_87;
TOTAL88:=SALES1_88+SALES2_88+SALES3_88+SALES4_88+SALES5_88;
ITEM1:=SALES1_87+SALES1_88;
ITEM2:=SALES2_87+SALES2_88;
ITEM3:=SALES3_87+SALES3_88;
ITEM4:=SALES4_87+SALES4_88;
ITEM5:=SALES5_87+SALES5_88;
```

Again, for a large number of items, this approach becomes tedious and somewhat wasteful of memory space.

Strategy 2

Strategy 2 treats each year as a separate array. Obviously, you could use the arrays in the same manner as in the first part of strategy B earlier in this chapter. However, you have already learned that listing each array element individually is not much better than using individually named variables, the approach in strategy A.

As an improvement over individually named variables, strategy 2 uses loops to increase efficiency and readability. The BASIC code for this implementation is

```
100  T87=0
200  T88=0
300  FOR R=1 TO 5 DO
400     T87=T87+S87(R)
500     T88=T88+S88(R)
600     I(R)=S87(R)+S88(R)
700  NEXT R
```

Only lines 300 through 600 are executed for each pass—it does not matter whether you have five items or 1000 items. In Pascal, the implementation is

```
TOTAL_87:=0;
TOTAL_88:=0;
FOR ROW:=1 TO 5 DO
  BEGIN
    TOTAL_87:=TOTAL_87+SALES87[ROW];
    TOTAL_88:=TOTAL_88+SALES88[ROW];
    ITEM_TOTAL[ROW]:=SALES87[ROW]+SALES88[ROW];
  END
```

Strategy 3

Strategy 3 consolidates the data even further by specifying that all sales data be contained in a two-dimensional array. In this case one index relates to the item number, and the second index relates to the year in which the sales occurred.

By making each dimension of the array one element larger than what is needed to hold the sales data, you can hold the yearly and sales totals in the same array. If you visualize the yearly data as the total of those items in rows 1 and 2, then the sales totals are in the corresponding positions in row 3. The yearly totals can be in column 6, as Figure 6.9 shows. In BASIC, this is implemented as

```
100  S(6,1)=0
200  S(6,2)=0
300  FOR R=1 TO 5 DO
400     S(6,1)=S(6,1)+S(R,1)
500     S(6,2)=S(6,2)+S(R,2)
600     S(R,3)=S(R,1)+S(R,2)
700  NEXT R
```

In Pascal, the code is

```
SALES[6,1]:=0;
SALES[6,2]:=0;
  FOR ROW:=1 TO 5 DO
    BEGIN
      SALES[6,1]:=SALES[6,1]+SALES[ROW,1];
      SALES[6,2]:=SALES[6,2]+SALES[ROW,2];
      SALES[ROW,3]:=SALES[ROW,1]+SALES[ROW,2];
    END
```

These examples demonstrate the power of using numeric arrays in problem solving. Many computations in science and business depend on the ability to process large amounts of related data in an efficient form. Often, such computations can be handled most efficiently through the use of numeric arrays.

Figure 6.9

Sales data, sales totals, and yearly totals in a two-dimensional array

	Sales 1	Sales 2	Sales 3	Sales 4	Sales 5	Yearly Total
1987	S(1,1)	S(1,2)	S(1,3)	S(1,4)	S(1,5)	S(1,6)
1988	S(2,1)	S(2,2)	S(2,3)	S(2,4)	S(2,5)	S(2,6)
Sales total	S(3,1)	S(3,2)	S(3,3)	S(3,4)	S(3,5)	

STRING ARRAYS

As previously mentioned, string arrays are used a great deal in professional software. Imagine that you want to develop an extremely simple word processor for an IBM Personal Computer. The standard character display on a PC is 80 characters wide and 25 lines high. Thus, each line can be held in a one-dimensional character array that is 80 characters long. The index to the array defines the position (column) at which the character appears on the screen.

For example, if the first line on the screen contains the standard greeting "Dear sir:", then the contents of the array are

```
C(1) = "D"    C(2) = "e"    C(3) = "a"    C(4) = "r"
C(5) = " "    C(6) = "S"    C(7) = "i"    C(8) = "r"
C(9) = ":"    C(10)= " "    C(11)= " "
```

The quotation marks around each letter denote that the ASCII value for the letter is assigned to that particular array element. For example, C(1) actually contains the decimal number 68, which, in ASCII code, represents the uppercase letter D.

Obviously, if you use a separate array for each line, the code is clumsy. Instead, define the letters as a two-dimensional array. In this array one index defines the column number (1 through 80), and the second index defines the row or line on the screen (1 through 25). To move the contents of the array around, use loop techniques similar to those in strategy 2.

Now assume that you do not need to move individual letters around. Instead, suppose you want to be able to retrieve a word or group of words based on an index value. This can be done with an array of strings. Think of an array of strings as a two-dimensional character array in which only one index is actually used. For example, this line of BASIC defines a string array that contains five elements:

```
100 DIM B$(5)
```

The Pascal version is

```
STRING=ARRAY[1..10] OF CHAR
B=ARRAY[1..5] OF STRING
```

In Pascal, as you can see, it is necessary to define the maximum length of all strings. The maximum length is 10. To arrive at the maximum length, you must consider the length of each string in list B. The Pascal code also defines each type in the array.

The length of each string of characters within the array can vary, but the length must not exceed the maximum allowed by a language. For instance, the BASIC code that follows initializes (allocates memory for) a string array to hold the names of days of the week. The names vary in length.

```
100 DIM DAYS$(7)
200 DAYS$(1)="Monday"
300 DAYS$(2)="Tuesday"
400 DAYS$(3)="Wednesday"
```

```
500 DAYS$(4)="Thursday"
600 DAYS$(5)="Friday"
700 DAYS$(6)="Saturday"
800 DAYS$(7)="Sunday"
```

The Pascal version is

```
VAR
  STRING=ARRAY[1..9] OF CHAR;
  DAY=ARRAY[1..7] OF STRING;
BEGIN
  DAY[1]='MONDAY    ';
  DAY[2]='TUESDAY   ';
  .
  .
  .
  DAY[7]='SUNDAY    ';
```

After the array is initialized, it can be used anywhere in the program to provide the name of a day.

To continue the example, consider how to use arrays to return a date expressed in English. For example, you want the values 10-07 to be converted to the expression "October seventh."

Begin by defining and initializing a BASIC array of 12 elements. Call the array MON$. The elements of MON$ are the names of the months. Then define a second array of 31 items. Call the array DAY$. The values in DAY$ are "first," "second," and so on. With these arrays in place, you can easily convert a numeric date to an equivalent in English.

If the variable for the month IM is 2 and the variable for the day ID is 14, then

```
DATE$=MON$(IM)+" "+DAY$(ID)
```

Suppose the preceding code yields the string "February fourteenth." The " " between the two arrays inserts a space between the month string and the day string. In other words, the space prevents the display "Februaryfourteenth."

One of the useful properties of string arrays is the ability to perform numerous string-manipulation operations on the arrays. In other words, the structure of strings can be manipulated through the use of *string processing commands* available within a programming language.

For example, imagine that you want to extract the first three letters of the fourth element in the MON$ array. Such an extraction allows printing of the month abbreviation rather than the full name. For this application, use the following statement in BASIC:

```
1000 ABR$=LEFT$(MON$(4),3)
```

ABR$ now contains the string "Apr." (The Pascal equivalent of line 1000 is unwieldy; therefore, it is not discussed here.)

The function LEN, like ABR$, is often used with BASIC arrays. Suppose you want to count the number of letters in the sixth array entry (June) and assign the number 4 to the variable I. The code that follows does the job.

```
1000 I=LEN(MON$(6))
```

(As before, the Pascal equivalent is unwieldy, so it is not presented here.)

Some languages do not allow the definition of arrays of variable-length strings, however. In such circumstances the software developer has no choice but to define a two-dimensional array that is wide enough to handle the largest number of characters expected per single entry.

For example, Pascal allows the definition of a variable of type STRING, but the user must define the maximum length that this variable type will hold. Arrays to hold letters can be defined as type CHAR only, which again means that the user must define the largest string expected. All rows in the array will end up with the same amount of memory allocated to them—even though only one long string and dozens of short ones are used. Figure 6.10 shows this use of memory.

Languages that do not support variable-length strings, including the original forms of FORTRAN, tend to be difficult to use.

CASE STUDY: PAYROLL PROGRAM

This section focuses on the processing module of the payroll program developed in previous chapters. To transform each input record into output, you must add the ability to read, process, and output payroll fields. For identification purposes, the program should be able to read in the name for each employee record. For output, the program must print the total gross pay, taxes, health costs, FICA, and net pay as well as the number of employee records processed.

As the program is developed, notice how arrays are used to process and conserve memory.

The Initialization Module

The initialization module must be expanded to declare and initialize the arrays needed for this program. You must also declare new variables to support the printing of final totals for all employees. The general specifications for these declarations have already been set forth within the pseudocode. The task is now to implement the declarations as comprehensively as possible.

The BASIC Expansion. In the BASIC program additions begin at line 1276. The additions are remarks lines.

```
1275  REM  N  = NUMBER OF EMPLOYEES
1276  REM  TG = TOTAL GROSS ALL EMPLOYEES
1277  REM  TT = TOTAL TAXES ALL EMPLOYEES
```

Figure 6.10

Illustration of wasted
memory in fixed-
dimension character
strings

o	n	e								
t	w	o								
t	h	r	e	e						
f	o	u	r							
f	i	v	e							
s	i	x								
			.							
			.							
			.							
o	n	e	-	t	h	o	u	s	a	n	d

```
1278  REM  TH = TOTAL HEALTH COSTS ALL EMPLOYEES
1279  REM  TF = TOTAL FICA ALL EMPLOYEES
1280  REM  TN = TOTAL NET PAY ALL EMPLOYEES
1281  REM  N$ = NAME OF EMPLOYEE
1282  REM
```

Now you are ready to define the structure of arrays to be initialized prior to processing. The goal is to allocate memory space for each array. In BASIC this is done with the DIM (for dimension) statement.

```
1283 REM DECLARE ARRAYS FOR PAYROLL
1284 DIM  G(25), TX(25),  H(25), FI(25), NP(25), ID(25), HR(25)
1285 DIM PR(25), DP(25), HS(25), YD(25)
1286 REM
```

You must assign index values to several of these arrays. Do this with FOR...NEXT. The FOR command causes a variable (in this case I for Index) to be assigned values within a specified range (in this case 1 to 25). In this program variables to be indexed are initialized to 0. Elements within the array are then assigned consecutive index values from 1 to 25. These values can be used later, during processing, to identify corresponding data values stored within the array. Lines 1309 through 1352 comprise the FOR...NEXT structure. Notice that a string array is established to store employee names (N$):

```
1309 FOR I=1 TO 25
1310      G(I)=0
1320      TX(I)=0
1330      H(I)=0
1340      FI(I)=0
1350      NP(I)=0
1351      N$(I)=' '
1352 NEXT I
```

At this point, variables to be used to store totals are initialized to 0.

```
1353 TG = 0
1354 TT = 0
1355 TH = 0
1356 TF = 0
1357 TN = 0
1358 N  = 0
```

The Pascal Expansion. In Pascal new variables (including those to calculate final totals) and arrays are defined within the declaration section of the program. Note that arrays are dimensioned and typed as part of the declaration.

```
VAR
        GROSS,
        TAXES,
        HEALTH,
        FICA,
        NET PAY,
        HR,
        YTD,
        PAYRATE:ARRAY [1..25] OF REAL;
        ID,
        DEPENDENTS,
        HEALTH STATUS:ARRAY[1..25] OF INTEGER;
        NAMES:ARRAY[1..20] OF CHAR;
        EMPLOYEES:ARRAY[1..25] OF NAMES;
        NUM_EMPLOY:INTEGER;
        TOT_GROSS,
        TOT_TAXES,
        TOT_HEALTH,
        TOT_FICA,
        TOT_NET:REAL;
```

Variables and arrays are initialized as part of the initialization module. A FOR...DO loop is used to increment an index from 1 to 25 for each array to be initialized.

```
FOR INDEX:=1 TO 25 DO
      BEGIN
            GROSS[INDEX]:=0.0;
            TAXES[INDEX]:=0.0;
            HEALTH[INDEX]:=0.0;
            FICA[INDEX]:=0.0;
            NET PAY[INDEX]:=0.0;
            EMPLOYEES[INDEX]:=" ";
      END
```

The Input Module

The input module can now be modified to enter up to 25 employees. The input module must prompt the user to enter fields for a payroll record. The module should use looping structures to store fields for each record and to increment index values.

The BASIC Expansion. In BASIC the modified input module is

```
2000 REM INPUT PROCEDURE
2010 REM
2020 N=1    ! INITIALIZE NUMBER OF EMPLOYEES TO 1
2030 INPUT "ENTER ID # (TO END ENTER -99): ";ID(N)
2040 WHILE ID<>-99
2050       INPUT "ENTER EMPLOYEE NAME: ";N$(I)
2060       INPUT "ENTER HOURS WORKED: ";HR(N)
2070       INPUT "ENTER PAYRATE: ";PY(N)
2080       INPUT "ENTER # OF DEPENDENTS: ";DP(N)
2090       INPUT "ENTER HEALTH STATUS: ";HS(N)
2100       INPUT "ENTER YEAR TO DATE PAY: ";YD(N)
2110       PRINT
2020       N=N+1
2130       INPUT "ENTER ID # (TO END ENTER -99): ";ID(N)
2140 WEND
2150 N=N-1
2160 RETURN
```

The Pascal Expansion. In Pascal the expanded input module is

```
PROCEDURE DATAIN:

BEGIN
    NUM EMP:=0;
    WRITE('ENTER ID # [TO END ENTER -99]: ');
    READLN(ID[NUM_EMP]);
    WHILE ID[NUM_EMP] <> -99 DO
        BEGIN
            FOR INDEX:=1 TO 20 DO
                NAMES[INDEX]:=' ';
            WRITE('ENTER EMPLOYEE NAME: ');
            INDEX:=1;
            READ(LETTER);
            WHILE (LETTER <> ' ') AND (INDEX <= 20) DO
                BEGIN
                    NAMES[INDEX]:=LETTER;
                    READ(LETTER);
                END:
            READLN:
            EMPLOYEES[NUM_EMP]:=NAMES;
            WRITE('ENTER HOURS WORKED: ');
            READLN(HR[NUM_EMP]);
            WRITE('ENTER # OF DEPENDENTS: ');
            READLN(HR[NUM_EMP]);
            WRITE('ENTER HEALTH STATUS: ');
            READLN(HEALTH-STATUS[NUM_EMP];
            WRITE('ENTER YEAR TO DATE PAY: ');
            READLN(YTD[NUM_EMP]);
            WRITELN;
            WRITELN;
            WRITE('ENTER ID # [TO END ENTER -99]: ');
            READLN(ID[NUM_EMP]);
    END:
```

The Processing Module

At this point in program expansion, processing operations can be specified in detail. For each record, calculations must determine gross pay, taxes, health status, FICA, net pay, and year-to-date pay. A looping structure should control the number of records processed. To determine the correct element to be referenced for processing, use index values to look up values in appropriate tables.

The BASIC Expansion. In BASIC the main processing loop is formed by coding a FOR...NEXT structure. Thus, the processing module changes to

```
4000 REM PROCESSING PROCEDURE
4010 REM
4020 FOR I=1 TO N
4030     G(I)=HR(I)*PR(I)
4040     IF DP(I)=1 THEN TX(I)=G(I)*0.20
4050     IF DP(I)=2 THEN TX(I)=G(I)*0.18
4060     IF DP(I)=3 THEN TX(I)=G(I)*0.16
4070     IF DP(I)>3 THEN TX(I)=G(I)*0.14
4080     IF DP(I)=1 AND HS(I)=1 THEN H(I)=H1
4090     IF DP(I)=2 AND HS(I)=1 THEN H(I)=H2
4100     IF DP(I)=3 AND HS(I)=1 THEN H(I)=H3
4110     IF DP(I)>3 AND HS(I)=1 THEN H(I)=H3
4120     GOSUB 6000
4130     GOSUB 7000
4140     GOSUB 8000
4150     GOSUB 9000
4160 NEXT I
4170 RETURN
```

The GOSUB statements in lines 4120, 4130, and 4140 cause the program to branch to low-level subroutines to calculate FICA, net pay, and year-to-date pay. The module that begins at line 9000 has been added to develop final totals that reflect processing for all employees.

The FICA module becomes

```
6000 REM FICA PROCEDURE
6010 REM
6020 IF YD(I)>32000 THEN F1(I)=0
6021     ELSE IF YD(I)+G(I)>3200 THEN F1(I)=(32000-YD(I))*0.20
6022             ELSE F1(I)=G(I)*0.20
6030 RETURN
```

The net pay module becomes

```
7000 REM NET PAY PROCEDURE
7010 REM
7020 NP(I)=G(I)-(F1(I)+H(I)+TX(I))
7030 RETURN
```

The year-to-date module becomes

```
8000 REM YEAR TO DATE PROCEDURE
8010 REM
8020 YD(I)=YD(I)+G(I)
8030 RETURN
```

The new module used to calculate payroll totals for all employees becomes

```
9000 REM TOTAL FOR EMPLOYEES PROCEDURE
9010 REM
9020 TG=TG+G(I)
9030 TT=TT+TX(I)
9040 TH=TH+H(I)
9050 TF=TF+F1(I)
9060 TN=TN+NP(I)
9070 RETURN
```

The Pascal Expansion. In Pascal a FOR...DO loop controls the number of iterations of the module. Notice the use of nested IF statements to test for the appropriate status for gross pay and health calculations.

```
PROCEDURE PAYPROCESS;

BEGIN {PAYPROCESS PROCEDURE}
    FOR INDEX:=1 TO NUM EMP DO
        BEGIN
            GROSS[INDEX]:=HR[INDEX]*PAYRATE[INDEX];
            IF DEPENDENTS[INDEX]=1 THEN
                TAXES[INDEX]:=GROSS[INDEX]*.20
        ELSE IF DEPENDENTS[INDEX]=2 THEN
                TAXES[INDEX]:=GROSS[INDEX]*.18
            ELSE IF DEPENDENTS[INDEX]:=3 THEN
                    TAXES[INDEX]:=GROSS[INDEX]*.16;
            IF HEALTH STATUS[INDEX]=1 THEN
                IF DEPENDENTS[INDEX]=1 THEN
                    HEALTH[INDEX]:=H1
                ELSE IF DEPENDENTS[INDEX]=2 THEN
                            HEALTH[INDEX]:=H2
                ELSE IF DEPENDENTS[INDEX]>=3 THEN
                            HEALTH[INDEX]:=H3;
            FICA;
            NET;
            YEARTODATE;
            GRAND;
        END;
END: {PAYPROCESS PROCEDURE}
```

The FICA submodule becomes

```
PROCEDURE FICA;

BEGIN {FICA PROCEDURE}
    IF YTD[INDEX]>32000.00 THEN
            FICA[INDEX]:=0.0
        ELSE IF YTD[INDEX]+GROSS[INDEX]>32000 THEN
                FICA[INDEX]:=32000-YTD[INDEX]*.20
            ELSE
                FICA[INDEX]:=GROSS[INDEX]*.20;
END; {FICA PROCEDURE}
```

The net pay submodule becomes

```
PROCEDURE NET;

BEGIN {NET PROCEDURE}
  NETPAY[INDEX]:=GROSS[INDEX] - FICA[INDEX] + HEALTH[INDEX] + TAXES[INDEX];
END; {NET PROCEDURE}
```

The year-to-date module becomes

```
PROCEDURE YEARTODATE;

BEGIN {YEARTODATE PROCEDURE}
    YTD[INDEX] := YTD[INDEX] + GROSS[INDEX];
END; {YEARTODATE PROCEDURE}
```

The new module to calculate grand totals is

```
BEGIN {GRAND TOTAL PROCEDURE}
    TOT_GROSS  := TOT_GROSS + GROSS[INDEX];
    TOT_TAXES  := TOT_TAXES + TAXES[INDEX];
    TOT_HEALTH:= TOT_HEALTH + HEALTH[INDEX];
    TOT_FICA   := TOT_FICA + FICA[INDEX];
    TOT_NET    := TOT_NET + NETPAY[INDEX];
END; {GRAND TOTAL PROCEDURE}
```

The Output Module

You must now expand the output module to direct the printing of all fields required for each output record.

The BASIC Expansion. In BASIC the output module changes to

```
9095 FOR I=1 TO N
9100    PRINT USINGX$;NAME(I),ID(I),G(I),TX(I),F1(I),NP(I),YD(I)
9105 NEXT I
```

The PRINT USING statement in line 9100 suggests the need to change line 2070, which formats output for each report line. This line should be

```
2070 PRINT "NAME";TAB(15);"NAME";TAB(25);"GROSS PAY";TAB(35);
"TAXES";TAB(45);"FICA";TAB(55);"NET PAY";TAB(65);"YEAR TO DATE"
```

This causes line 1470 of the initialization procedure to change to

```
1470 X$="\              \ #######   $######.## ####.##   ###.##
    ####.##   $######.##"
```

The Pascal Expansion. In Pascal the output module is

```
PROCEDURE DATAOUT;

BEGIN {DATAOUT PROCEDURE}
  WRITELN('NAME':15:'ID':10:'GROSSPAY':10:'TAXES':10:'FICA':10;
      'NETPAY':10:'YEAR TO DATE');
  FOR INDEX := 1 TO NUM EMP DO
      WRITELN( EMPLOYEE[INDEX]:10: ID[INDEX]:10: GROSS[INDEX]:10:
              TAXES[INDEX]:10: FICA[INDEX]:10: NETPAY[INDEX]:10:
      YTD[INDEX]:10);
END; {DATAOUT PROCEDURE}
```

The Termination Module

At this point, you have established the variables required to print totals at the bottom of the report page. Calculations for these variables are included in the processing module.

Of course, report totals are printed after all processing for input records has been completed. Thus, the printing of totals is part of the termination module.

The BASIC Expansion. The new termination module appears in BASIC as follows:

```
5000 REM TERMINATION PROCEDURE
5010 REM PRINT OUT TOTALS AND END
5020 REM
5030 PRINT
5040 PRINT "TOTAL GROSS PAY WAS $";TG
5050 PRINT "TOTAL TAXES PAID WERE $";TT
5060 PRINT "TOTAL HEALTH DEDUCTIONS WERE $";TH
5070 PRINT "TOTAL FICA PAID WAS $";TF
5080 PRINT "TOTAL NET PAY WAS $";TN
5090 END
```

The Pascal Expansion. In Pascal the termination module is

```
PROCEDURE TERMINATE;

BEGIN {TERMINATION PROCEDURE}
    WRITELN('TOTAL GROSS PAY WAS        $':TOT GROSS:7:2);
```

```
    WRITELN('TOTAL TAXES PAID WAS          $':TOT TAXES:7:2);
    WRITELN('TOTAL HEALTH DEDUCTIONS WERE  $':TOT GROSS:7:2);
    WRITELN('TOTAL FICA PAID WAS           $':TOT FICA:7:2);
    WRITELN('TOTAL NET PAY WAS             $':TOT NET:7:2);
END; {TERMINATION PROCEDURE}
```

CASE STUDY: PROBLEM SOLVING, FUN FANTASIES

Almost all successful businesses have systems in place to control expenses. Consider the problem of tracking money spent by salespeople for business purposes. The purpose of expense account monitoring is to keep salespeople from spending lavishly on meals, accommodations, and other items. For this reason, most businesses require salespeople to provide receipts that describe all business expenses.

To simplify this reporting and monitoring, the Fun Fantasies recreational products company wants to automate expense account tracking. The pseudocode that follows describes input, processing, and output modules for this programming problem.

```
Begin expense account for Fun Fantasies sales personnel
    Do initialization module
    While more employees to process
        Do inputting module
        Do processing module
        Do outputting module
    End while
    Do termination module
End expense account program
Begin initialization module
   Define variables:One-dimensional NAME array parallel to
                    One-dimensional TOTAL array
                    Two-dimensional array for expenses
                    One-dimensional DAYOFWEEK and CATEGORY array
                    Grand total DAYOFWEEK and CATEGORY arrays
   Assign first values: Initialize grand total arrays to 0 as
                            well as PERSON TOTAL array
        Define constants: any range checks get constants
        Define output formats: Set up print formats to get
                    output as outlined in problem stated
        Print proper output headings
End initialization module

Begin input module
   Initialize EXPENSE array, DAYOFWEEK and CATEGORY array to 0
   Do NAME input module (separate if Pascal)
   Read in EXPENSES for each of 7 days in each of 5
        categories—requires nested DO loops for entering into
        two-dimensional expense array
End input module

Begin processing module
   Calculate DAYOFWEEK totals and CATEGORY totals—AGAIN
   Requires nested DO loops to calculate totals and place in
```

```
      DAYOFWEEK and CATEGORY totals
      Add DAYOFWEEK or CATEGORY totals to get PERSON TOTAL
      Add DAYOFWEEK totals to grand totals for all employees
      Add CATEGORY totals to grand totals for all employees
End processing module

Begin outputting module
   Print NAME, DAYOFWEEK totals and CATEGORY totals for employee
End outputting module

Begin termination module
   Print proper headings
   Print summary totals minus salesperson by total expenses
   Print proper headings according to specifications
   Print DAYOFWEEK grand totals
   Print proper headings
   Print CATEGORY grand totals
End termination module
```

Figure 6.11 shows input and output for the expense account program.

CASE STUDY: PROBLEM SOLVING, MAGAZINE LABELS

Most nationally circulated magazines use computer systems for dozens of applications from word processing and typesetting, to accounts receivable and payroll. One application that most magazines do not try to tackle is mailing. For most magazines, too many headaches are involved in making sure that magazines are sent to subscribers in an efficient manner.

Most magazines hire fulfillment companies to handle this problem. A fulfillment company devotes its attention to techniques for marketing and distributing publications. A fulfillment house needs efficient printing of mailing labels. Typically, mailing labels are generated by accessing name, address, and other fields from a file of subscribers.

A typical magazine mailing label includes information besides name and address. Typically, the label includes a special code that identifies the subscriber and includes the expiration date for that subscription. This code may contain both characters and numbers. Consider a situation in which the code is stored and printed as a single string. The code is in the first line and the name and address follow.

```
JA0391
James H. Adair
1564 Chiswick Court
El Cajon, CA XXXXX
```

When the subscription is updated, the code must also be updated. Thus, the task is to write an algorithm to update this code. Pseudocode for the command module for this problem follows.

```
Begin address label update program
   Do initialization module
   While more labels to update
      Do input module
      Do processing module
      Do outputting module
   End while
   Do termination module
End address label update module
```

Suppose that all data for all subscribers are in a disk file. The data entry clerk must access the proper subscriber's file whenever a subscription code must be updated.

Figure 6.11

a. Data to be input

Input and output for the
expense account
program

NAME	CATEGORY	MON	TUES	WED	THURS	FRI	SAT	SUN
				DAY OF WEEK				
Aron H	Travel	180.00	0	0	0	0	0	0
	Meals	22.56	25.78	14.33	28.69	70.00	0	0
	Lodging	32.74	32.74	32.74	0	0	0	0
	Entertainment	0	0	0	0	40.00	60.00	0
	Misc.	0	14.26	0	5.00	12.89	0	0
Burton B	Travel	0	326.00	15.60	0	0	0	61.00
	Meals	18.43	19.54	20.67	19.51	28.88	0	35.00
	Lodging	0	25.54	25.54	25.54	25.54	25.54	0
	Entertainment	0	30.00	30.00	30.00	0	0	0
	Misc.	0	10.00	14.63	0	6.51	0	14.00
Tenor C	Travel	25.08	51.66	14.23	0	0	0	0
	Meals	8.24	6.56	7.27	14.11	11.43	0	0
	Lodging	15.88	15.88	16.27	16.27	16.27	0	0
	Entertainment	40.00	0	0	0	0	0	30.00
	Misc.	2.35	4.81	3.73	5.25	6.15	0	0

b. Final output

TOTALS FOR ARON H

MON	TUES	WED	THURS	FRI	SAT-SUN
********	********	********	********	********	*******
235.30	72.78	47.07	33.69	123.89	60.00

Travel	Meals	Lodging	Entertainment	Misc.	Total
********	********	*********	*************	********	*******
180.00	161.36	98.22	100.00	32.15	571.73

Updating requires the clerk to modify the data and output the results to the screen or on an update report. The pseudocode that follows shows how the command module can be expanded somewhat. In the initialization and input modules, note the use of arrays to load related data for each label.

```
Begin initialization module
   Define variables
   Initialize variables
   Define constants
   Define output formats
   Print proper headings
End initialization module


Begin input module
   Read in CODE (6 digits)
   Read in NAME
   Read in ADDRESS
   Read in NUMBER OF YEARS TO EXTEND SUBSCRIPTION
End input module

Begin processing module
   Split the CODE into three parts
      INITIALS, MONTH, and YEAR
   Add the proper number of months for which the
      subscription is to be extended (Update MONTH and YEAR)
   Reassemble the code
   Count the number of codes processed
End processing module

Begin output module
   Print proper headings
   Print NAME, OLD CODE, NEW CODE, and NUMBER OF YEARS
   EXTENDED
   (this is to be reviewed by the proper supervisor)
End output module

Begin termination module
   Print out number of codes processed
End termination module
```

SUMMARY

An array (a set of contiguous storage and processing locations) contains data of the same type. Thus, the same array can contain numbers or characters, but not both. Numbers must be integers or all floating-point numbers, but not both.

Processing must often be done on several fields of different types. The array structure requires that parallel arrays be used in these situations. For example, the first element of the character array contains a person's name; the first element of the numeric array contains that person's salary to date. The second element in each array refers to a second person and so forth. When many fields contain similar data for many persons, multidimensional arrays are used.

ABR$ DIM
Array of strings   LEN
Character array   String-processing command

1. Look at the following diagram:

A

[1]	70
[2]	145
[3]	16
[4]	999

What is the array name? What is the array index? List the array element(s).

2. Look at the BASIC program that follows.

```
10 REM
20 REM
30 REM
40 DIM A(5)
50 F=0
60 G=0
70 FOR I = 1 TO 5
80      READ A(I)
90 NEXT I
100 FOR I = 1 TO 5
110     PRINT "A(";I;")";A(I)
120 NEXT I
130 PRINT
140 PRINT
150 FOR I = 1 TO 5
160     F = F + A(I)
170 NEXT I
180 G = F/5
190 PRINT "TOTAL =";F
200 PRINT "AVE   =";G
210 DATA 100, 90, 80, 70, 60
220 END
```

Predict the output of this program, then enter and run the program to confirm your prediction.

3. Look at this BASIC program:

```
10  REM
20  REM
30  REM
40  DIM A$(10), A(10), B(10), C(10), D(10), E(10)
50  COUNT=1
60  READ A$(COUNT), A(COUNT), B(COUNT), C(COUNT), D(COUNT), E(COUNT)
70  IF A$(COUNT) = "EOD" THEN GOTO 100
80  COUNT = COUNT + 1
90  GOTO 60
100 COUNT = COUNT - 1
105 PRINT COUNT
110 PRINT "DEADLY MUSHROOMS"
120 PRINT
130 FOR I = 1 TO COUNT
140      IF A(I) = 1 THEN PRINT A$(I)
150 NEXT I
160 PRINT
170 PRINT
180 PRINT "EDIBLE MUSHROOMS"
190 PRINT
200 FOR I = 1 TO COUNT
210      IF A(I) = 3 THEN PRINT A$(I)
220 NEXT I
230 DATA "AMANITA MUSCARIA",2,0,1,0,0
240 DATA "AMANITA VERNA",1,0,1,0,0
250 DATA "AMANITA VIROSA",1,0,0,1,0
260 DATA "AMANITA BRUNESCENCE",3,0,0,1,1
270 DATA "AMANITA CAESARIA",3,0,0,1,0
280 DATA "AMANITA RUBESCENCE",1,1,0,0,1
290 DATA "EOD",0,0,0,0,0
300 END
```

a. What kind of arrays are illustrated by this program? What is "EOD"?

b. Predict the output of this program. Enter and run the program to confirm your prediction.

4. Look at this BASIC program:

```
10  REM
20  REM
30  REM
40  REM
50  DIM PART$(10), PART#(10), QUANTITY(10)
60  REM
70  READ IN PARTS AND PART # TO CREATE INVENTORY
80  REM      ALSO READ IN NUMBER OF PARTS AVAILABLE
```

```
90  REM
100 FOR I = 1 TO 10
110      READ PART$(I), PART#(I), QUANTITY(I)
120 NEXT I
130 REM
140 REM
150 REM SEARCH FOR PART NUMBER AND QUANTITY
160 REM
170 REM
180 PRINT "WHAT ITEM # DO YOU WANT?"
190 PRINT "TO STOP ENTER 0"
200 INPUT ITEM
210 IF ITEM = 0 GOTO 400
215 FOUND$="FALSE"
220 FOR I = 1 TO 10
230  IF ITEM = PART#(I) THEN PRINT "PARTNUMBER:";PART#(I);"CALLED ":PART$(I)
240  IF ITEM = PART#(I) THEN FOUND$="TRUE"
250 NEXT I
260 IF FOUND$<>"TRUE" THEN PRINT "ITEM IS NOT IN INVENTORY"
270 DATA "HP110",1,1000
280 DATA "HP150",2,50
290 DATA "IBMPC",3,2500
300 DATA "TRASH-81",4,300000
310 DATA "LEMON",5,400000
320 DATA "DEC SUNBOW",6,1000000
330 DATA "DG1A",7,1000
340 DATA "APRICOT",8,30
350 DATA "PC LIMITED",9,2000
360 DATA "COMPAQUE",10,500
370 END
```

a. What is happening in lines 100 through 120? What kind of variable is on line 215?

b. Predict the output of this program. Enter and run the program to confirm your prediction.

5. Look at the BASIC program that follows.

```
10  REM
20  REM
30  REM
40  DIM A$(10), A(10,5)
50  COUNT=1
60  READ A$(COUNT)
70  IF A$(COUNT) = "EOD" THEN 200
72  FOR COL = 1 to 5
74       READ A(COUNT, COL)
76  NEXT COL
80  COUNT = COUNT + 1
90  GOTO 60
100 COUNT = COUNT - 1
```

```
110 PRINT "DEADLY MUSHROOMS"
120 PRINT
130 FOR I = 1 TO COUNT
140     IF A(I,1) = 1 THEN PRINT A$(I)
150 NEXT I
160 PRINT
170 PRINT
180 PRINT "EDIBLE MUSHROOMS"
190 PRINT
200 FOR I = 1 TO COUNT
210     IF A(I,1) = 3 THEN PRINT A$(I)
220 NEXT I
230 DATA "AMANITA MUSCARIA",2,0,1,0,0
240 DATA "AMANITA VERNA",1,0,1,0,0
250 DATA "AMANITA VIROSA",1,0,0,1,0
260 DATA "AMANITA BRUNESCENCE",3,0,0,1,1
280 DATA "AMANITA RUBESCENCE",1,1,0,0,1
290 DATA "EOD",0,0,0,0,0
300 END
```

a. What happens in lines 40 to 70? How do the arrays in this program differ from those in question 3? How are the arrays the same?

b. Predict the output of this program and then enter and run it to confirm your prediction.

c. How are numeric and character arrays different? How are they the same? Declare an array of each kind in BASIC and Pascal.

7. Look at the Pascal program that follows.

```
PROGRAM MATRICES

CONST
  ROWMAX=3;
  COLUMNMAX=4;
TYPE ROW:=1..ROWMAX;
  COLUMN=1..COLUMNMAX;
VAR
  A:ARRAY[ROW,COLUMN] OF INTEGER;
  B:ARRAY[ROW] OF INTEGER;
  C:ARRAY[COLUMN] OF INTEGER;
  I:ROW;
  J:COLUMN;
  SUM:INTEGER;
BEGIN {MAIN PROGRAM}
FOR I:= 1 TO ROWMAX DO
    FOR J:= 1 TO COLUMNMAX DO
        READ (A[I,J]);
    FOR I:=1 TO ROWMAX DO
        BEGIN
        SUM:=0;
```

```
            FOR J:=1 TO COLUMNMAX DO
          SUM:=SUM+A[I,J];
                B[I]:=SUM;
        END;
      FOR J:= 1 TO COLUMNMAX DO
        BEGIN
             SUM:=0;
             FOR I:=1 TO ROWMAX DO
                 SUM:=SUM+A[I,J];
             C[J]:=SUM;
        END;
      FOR I:=1 TO ROWMAX DO
        BEGIN
             FOR J:=1 TO COLUMNMAX DO
                 WRITE(A[I,J]);
                 WRITELN(B[I]:15);
        END;
      WRITELN;WRITELN;
      FOR J:=1 TO COLUMNMAX DO
          WRITE(C[J]);
END. {MAIN PROGRAM}
```

a. Where do the following sections begin and end?

   Initialization
   Input
   Processing
   Output
   Termination

b. What kind of arrays are used in this program?

c. Predict the output of this program. Enter and run the program to confirm your prediction.

d. Modularize this program so that all sections are in their own procedures.

8. Look at this Pascal program:

```
PROGRAM SALES(INPUT,OUTPUT);

CONST
  NUMBEROFSALESPERSONS=5;
VAR
  SALES:ARRAY[1..NUMBEROFSALESPERSONS] OF REAL;
  INDEX: 1..NUMBEROFSALESPERSONS;
  SUM,COMMISSIONLEVEL:REAL;
BEGIN
  SUM:=0.0;
  FOR INDEX:=1 TO NUMBEROFSALESPERSONS DO
```

```
      BEGIN
          WRITELN('ENTER SALES FOR 5 PERSONS');
          READ(SALES[INDEX]);
          SUM:=SUM+SALES[INDEX]
      END;
    COMMISSIONLEVEL:=(SUM*.70)/NUMBEROFSALESPERSONS;
    WRITELN;
    WRITELN('SALESPERSONS WHO QUALIFY FOR COMMISSION');
    WRITELN('SALESPERSON      TOTAL SALES');
    FOR INDEX:=1 TO NUMBEROFSALESPERSONS DO
        IF SALES[INDEX] > COMMISSIONLEVEL THEN
            WRITELN(INDEX:6, SALES[INDEX]:22:20);
  END. {MAIN PROGRAM}
```

a. Where do each of the following sections begin and end?

    Initialization
    Inputting
    Processing
    Outputting
    Termination

b. What kind of arrays are used in this program?

c. Predict the output of this program. Enter and run the program to confirm your prediction.

d. Modularize this program by placing each segment into a separate procedural module.

Problem-Solving Assignments

1. Place all calculation segments of the payroll program pseudocode within separate modules so that each module performs no more than one calculation. Then code the revised pseudocode.

2. Build or modify the error-checking modules of the payroll pseudocode to guard against input errors. Then code the revised pseudocode.

3. Code the expense account pseudocode provided in the chapter.

4. Expand the address label pseudocode to produce the sample output shown in Figure 6.11b. Then code the pseudocode.

5. Find the statements in this chapter that use ABR$ or LEN for string processing. Translate each into Pascal code.

6. Modify the code in questions 7 and 8 to create separate input, processing, and output modules called by the main program.

7. Expand the pseudocode and code the mailing label case study provided in this chapter.

Searches

A search routine is a processing module common to many programs. Searches are used to locate an item or name within a list of items or names. Typical uses include searching a customer file for a particular name or an inventory file for a specific item. The searching technique used depends on the organization of the file.

SEQUENTIAL SEARCHES

Basically, there are two methods of searching a list: a sequential search and a binary search. The easier of the two to implement in your programs is the *sequential search*. To illustrate a sequential search, imagine that you know a phone number but not the name that goes with it. You look through the phone numbers in an ordinary telephone directory, trying to find whose number you have. If you are doing a sequential search, you start on page one and leaf through the directory until you reach the number and find the name. If you run out of pages without finding the number, you report that it is not in the directory. A sequential search can work on any list, whether ordered or not.

The pseudocode for several versions of the sequential searching routine follows. The first example uses a Pascal WHILE loop. A copy of the searched-for item is stored at the end of the list to ensure success in the search.

```
Begin sequential search procedure
    Define LIST as an array of type numeric, string, etc.
    Set ELEMENT to number of items in LIST
    Initialize INDEX [0]
    Set FOUND = FALSE
    Read in searched-for item
    Place searched-for item in LIST as ITEM [ELEMENT + 1]
    Search WHILE not found
        INDEX = INDEX + 1
        If LIST [INDEX] = Searched-for ITEM then
            FOUND = TRUE
```

```
      End WHILE
      If INDEX <= ELEMENT then ITEM is found
                            else ITEM is not found
End sequential search procedure
```

If the item is found (FOUND = TRUE), then you need to eliminate the duplicate you stored at [ELEMENT + 1]. In other cases you might or might not leave the item at the end of the list, depending on the program and the reason for the search. An UNTIL loop could replace the WHILE loop, as illustrated in the next example.

```
Begin sequential search procedure
      Define LIST as an array of type numeric, string, etc.
      Set ELEMENT to number of items in list
      Initialize INDEX to 0
      Set FOUND = FALSE
      Read in searched-for ITEM
      Place searched-for item in LIST as ITEM [ELEMENT + 1]
      Repeat search
            INDEX = INDEX + 1
            If LIST [INDEX] = searched-for ITEM then
            FOUND = TRUE
      Until FOUND
      If INDEX <= ELEMENT then ITEM is FOUND
                            else ITEM is not FOUND
End sequential search procedure
```

Sequential searches are not very efficient. On the average, half the list must be read during each search effort. However, if the list is short, a sequential search works just fine. Just how short is short enough depends on the implementation of the language you are using and the speed of the computer. If the program needs to search the list only once, perhaps during the program's initialization, a sequential search might be practical for a longer list.

The coded examples that follow include a routine to load an array so the program has a list to search. The WHILE loop version in BASIC is presented first. In this segment E represents the element, I represents the index, and F represents FOUND.

```
10   DIM LI(100)
20   E = 0
30   I = 0
40   F = 0
50   REM LOAD THE ARRAY
60   PRINT "ITEM FOR LIST (USE 9999 TO FINISH)";
70   I = I + 1
80   INPUT LI(I)
90   IF LI(I) <> 9999 AND I <> 100 GOTO 60
100  E = I - 1
110  REM SEARCH
120  PRINT "ITEM FOR SEARCH";
130  INPUT IT
140  LI(E + 1) = IT
150  I = 0
```

```
160 WHILE F = 0
170    I = I + 1
180       IF LI(I) = IT THEN F = 1
190 WEND
200 IF I <= E THEN PRINT "ITEM ";LI(I);" WAS FOUND IN THE ";
    I;" POSITION OF THE LIST"
210 IF I > E THEN PRINT "ITEM ";LI(E + 1);" WAS NOT FOUND"
```

Line 100 is provided to get rid of the 9999 used to complete the array-loading sequence. If your version of BASIC includes the IF...THEN...ELSE structure, lines 200 and 210 could be combined.

Most versions of BASIC do not include the UNTIL structure; therefore, the next segment illustrates an alternate structure. You can also use this method if your version of BASIC does not include the WHILE...WEND structure.

```
10   DIM LI(100)
20   E = 0
30   I = 0
40   F = 0
50   REM LOAD THE ARRAY
60   PRINT "ITEM FOR LIST (USE 9999 TO FINISH)";
70   I = I + 1
80   INPUT LI(I)
90   IF LI(I) <> 9999 AND I <> 100 GOTO 60
110  E = I - 1
120  REM SEARCH
130  PRINT "ITEM FOR SEARCH";
140  INPUT IT
150  LI(E + 1) = IT
160  I = 0
170  I = I + 1
180  IF LI(I) = IT THEN F = 1
190  IF F = 0 GOTO 170
200  IF I <= E THEN PRINT "ITEM ";LI(I);" WAS FOUND IN THE "; I;" POSITION OF THE
        LIST"
210  IF I > E THEN PRINT "ITEM ";LI(E + 1);" WAS NOT FOUND"
```

The next program is the Pascal version of the WHILE loop pseudocode.

```
PROGRAM SEARCH(INPUT,OUTPUT);

{PROGRAM TO ILLUSTRATE SEQUENTIAL SEARCH USING WHILE}

VAR
   LIST : ARRAY[1..100] OF INTEGER;
   ELEMENTS : INTEGER;
   INDEX : INTEGER;
   FOUND : BOOLEAN;
   ITEM : INTEGER;

PROCEDURE LISTIN;
BEGIN {LISTIN PROCEDURE}
   INDEX := 1;
```

```
      WRITE('ITEM FOR LIST? ');
      READLN(LIST[INDEX]);
      WHILE (LIST[INDEX] <> 9999) AND (INDEX < 100) DO
         BEGIN
            INDEX := INDEX + 1;
            WRITE('ITEM FOR LIST (9999 TO FINISH)? ');
            READLN(LIST[INDEX]);
         END;
      ELEMENTS := INDEX - 1;
END; {LISTIN PROCEDURE}

BEGIN {MAIN PROGRAM}
   LISTIN;
   FOUND := FALSE;
   WRITE('ITEM TO FIND? ');
   READLN(ITEM);
   LIST[ELEMENTS + 1] := ITEM;
   INDEX := 1;
   WHILE (INDEX <= ELEMENTS) AND NOT FOUND DO
      IF ITEM = LIST[INDEX] THEN
         FOUND := TRUE
      ELSE
         INDEX := INDEX + 1;
   IF FOUND AND (INDEX <= ELEMENTS) THEN
      WRITELN('ITEM ',LIST[INDEX],' WAS FOUND IN
               THE ',INDEX:4,' POSITION')
      ELSE
         WRITELN('ITEM ',ITEM,' WAS NOT FOUND');
END. {MAIN PROGRAM}
```

ELEMENTS was set to INDEX minus 1 in LISTIN to get rid of the 9999 value used to end the list.

Pascal includes UNTIL, so coding the search with an UNTIL loop is an alternative. Remember, UNTIL assumes that the program passes through the loop at least once during each run, so an UNTIL loop is suitable for a search routine. The sequential search using UNTIL in Pascal looks like this:

```
PROGRAM SEARCH(INPUT,OUTPUT);

{PROGRAM TO ILLUSTRATE SEQUENTIAL SEARCH USING UNTIL}

VAR
   LIST : ARRAY[1..100] OF INTEGER;
   ELEMENTS : INTEGER;
   INDEX : INTEGER;
   FOUND : BOOLEAN;
   ITEM : INTEGER;

PROCEDURE LISTIN;
BEGIN {LISTIN PROCEDURE}
   INDEX := 1;
   WRITE('ITEM? ');
   READLN(LIST[INDEX]);
```

```
    WHILE (LIST[INDEX] <> 9999) AND (INDEX < 100) DO
        BEGIN
            INDEX := INDEX + 1;
            WRITE('ITEM (9999 to FINISH) ');
            READLN(LIST[INDEX]);
        END;
    ELEMENTS := INDEX - 1;
END; {LISTIN PROCEDURE}
BEGIN {MAIN PROGRAM}
  LISTIN;
  FOUND := FALSE;
  WRITE('Item to find? ');
  READLN(ITEM);
  LIST[ELEMENTS + 1] := ITEM;
  INDEX := 1;
  REPEAT
      IF ITEM = LIST[INDEX] THEN
          FOUND := TRUE
      ELSE
          INDEX := INDEX + 1;
  UNTIL (ITEM > ELEMENTS) OR FOUND;
  IF FOUND AND (INDEX <= ELEMENTS) THEN
      WRITELN('ITEM ',LIST[INDEX],' WAS FOUND IN THE ',INDEX:4,'POSITION')
  ELSE
      WRITELN('ITEM ',ITEM,' WAS NOT FOUND');
END. {MAIN PROGRAM}
```

BINARY SEARCHES

In a *binary search,* data must be ordered according to a key field. The order can be alphanumeric or numeric. A binary search uses the key field to find the desired item.

To understand binary searches, return to the telephone book analogy. A telephone book is in alphabetic order by last name. Last name is the key field. To do a binary search, begin by opening the book to its midpoint. If the names you find there precede the name you want, ignore the second half of the book. Divide the first part in half, and see whether the names on that page precede or follow the desired name. Choose the part of the book that is useful to you, divide it, and continue until you find the name or run out of pages.

The example that follows explains binary searching by using a list of 18 names.

1. ALEX
2. ARLENE
3. BETTY
4. CHARLIE
5. DONNA
6. FAY
7. GLENDA
8. HAL
9. HAROLD

10. KEN
11. LARRY
12. LINDA
13. MARGE
14. NANCY
15. PERRY
16. ROGER
17. STAN
18. YVONNE

Say you are searching for GLENDA. The steps that a program takes to implement the binary search follow.

1. Determine the length of the list—18 names.

2. Set the variable FIRST to 1 and LAST to 18 (the total). Set the variable FOUND to FALSE.

3. Divide (FIRST + LAST) by 2 and round the result down to the nearest integer. The result of rounding is 9.

4. Retrieve the name at that position. The name retrieved is HAROLD.

5. Is this the name you are searching for? If TRUE, set FOUND to TRUE and leave the search routine. If FALSE, continue searching. The value returned is FALSE.

6. Does HAROLD precede or succeed GLENDA? HAROLD succeeds GLENDA.

7. If the name retrieved precedes the desired name, then set FIRST to (current position + 1) or 10. If the name retrieved succeeds the desired name, then set LAST to (current position - 1) or 8.

8. Is LAST greater than FIRST? FALSE. If TRUE, then leave the search routine, returning FOUND as FALSE.

9. The new list is reduced to the names between position 1 (FIRST) and position 8 (LAST).

10. Now divide (FIRST + LAST) by 2 and round the result down to the nearest integer. The result of rounding is 4.

11. Retrieve the name at position 4. The name retrieved is CHARLIE.

12. Is this the name you are searching for? FALSE. If TRUE, set FOUND to TRUE and leave the search routine.

13. Does CHARLIE precede or succeed GLENDA? CHARLIE precedes GLENDA.

14. If the name retrieved precedes the desired name, then set FIRST to (current position + 1) or 5. If the name retrieved succeeds the desired name, then set LAST to (current position - 1) or 3.

15. Is LAST greater than FIRST? FALSE. If TRUE, then leave the search routine, returning FOUND as FALSE.

16. The list is reduced to names between position 5 (FIRST) and position 8 (LAST).

17. Now divide (FIRST + LAST) by 2 and round the result down to the nearest integer. The result of rounding is 6.

18. Retrieve the name at position 6. The name retrieved is FAY.

19. Is this the name you are searching for? FALSE. If TRUE, set FOUND to TRUE and leave the search routine.

20. Does FAY precede or succeed GLENDA? FAY precedes GLENDA.

21. If the name retrieved precedes the name desired, then set FIRST to (current position +1) or 7. If the name retrieved succeeds the name desired, then set LAST to (current position - 1) or 5.

22. Is LAST greater than FIRST? FALSE. If TRUE, then leave the search routine, returning FOUND as FALSE.

23. The new list is reduced to the names between position 7 (FIRST) and position 8 (LAST).

24. Now divide (FIRST + LAST) by 2 and round the result down to the nearest integer. The result of rounding is 7.

25. Retrieve the name at position 7. The name retrieved is GLENDA.

26. Is this the name you are searching for? TRUE. If TRUE, set FOUND to TRUE and leave the search routine.

    Now try searching for a name that isn't in the list. HARRY.

1. Determine the length of the list: 18 names

2. Set the variable FIRST to 1 and LAST to 18 (the total). Set the variable FOUND to FALSE.

3. Divide (FIRST + LAST) by 2 and round the result down to the nearest integer. The result of rounding is 9.

4. Retrieve the name at that position. The name retrieved is HAROLD.

5. Is this the name you are searching for? If TRUE, set FOUND to TRUE and leave the search routine. If FALSE, continue searching. The value returned is FALSE.

6. Does HAROLD precede or succeed HARRY? HAROLD precedes HARRY.

7. If the name retrieved precedes the name desired, then set FIRST to (current position + 1) or 10. If the name retrieved succeeds the name desired, then set LAST to (current position - 1) or 8.

8. Is LAST greater than FIRST? FALSE. If TRUE, then leave the search routine, returning FOUND as FALSE.

9. The new list is reduced to the names between position 10 (FIRST) and position 18 (LAST).

10. Now divide (FIRST + LAST) by 2 and round the result down to the nearest integer. The result of rounding is 14.

11. Retrieve the name at position 14. The name retrieved is NANCY.

12. Is this the name you are searching for? FALSE. If TRUE, set FOUND to TRUE and leave the search routine.

13. Does NANCY precede or succeed HARRY? NANCY succeeds HARRY.

14. If the name retrieved precedes the name desired, then set FIRST to (current position + 1) or 15. If the name retrieved succeeds the name desired, then set LAST to (current position - 1) or 13.

15. Is LAST greater than FIRST? FALSE. If TRUE, then leave the search routine, returning FOUND as FALSE.

16. The new list is reduced to the names between position 10 (FIRST) and position 13 (LAST).

17. Now divide (FIRST + LAST) by 2 and round the result down to the nearest integer. The result of rounding is 11.

18. Retrieve the name at position 11. The name retrieved is LARRY.

19. Is this the name you are searching for? FALSE. If TRUE, set FOUND to TRUE and leave the search routine.

20. Does LARRY precede or succeed HARRY? LARRY succeeds HARRY.

21. If the name retrieved precedes the name desired, then set FIRST to (current position + 1) or 12. If the name retrieved succeeds the name desired, then set LAST to (current position - 1) or 10.

22. Is LAST greater than FIRST? FALSE. If TRUE, then leave the search routine, returning FOUND as FALSE.

23. The new list is reduced to the names between position 10 (FIRST) and position 10 (LAST).

24. Now divide (FIRST + LAST) by 2 and round the result down to the nearest integer. The result of rounding is 10.

25. Retrieve the name at position 10. The name retrieved is KEN.

26. Is this the name you are searching for? FALSE. If TRUE, set FOUND to TRUE and leave the search routine.

27. Does KEN precede or succeed HARRY? KEN succeeds HARRY.

28. If the name retrieved precedes the name desired, then set FIRST to (current position + 1) or 11. If the name retrieved succeeds the name desired, then set LAST to (current position - 1) or 9.

29. Is LAST greater than or equal to FIRST? TRUE. If TRUE, then leave the search routine, returning FOUND as FALSE.

Note that seven of the instructions keep repeating. These are the elements of a program loop.

When using a binary search, be absolutely sure that the list being searched is really in alphanumeric or numeric order. If even one item is out of place, the search can fail.

The pseudocode for a binary search follows.

```
Begin binary search procedure
    Set LAST to number of items in list
    Set FIRST to 1
    Set FOUND to FALSE
    Read searched-for ITEM
    WHILE not found and FIRST <= LAST DO
        MIDDLE = (FIRST + LAST) / 2
        If ITEM > MIDDLE then
            FIRST = MIDDLE + 1
        Else
```

```
                        If ITEM < MIDDLE then
                            LAST = MIDDLE - 1
                Else
                        FOUND = TRUE
        End WHILE
End binary search procedure
```

The UNTIL loop is more suited to a search than WHILE, as the pseudocode that follows shows.

```
Begin binary search procedure
    Set LAST to number of items in list
    Set FIRST to 1
    Set FOUND to FALSE
    Read searched-for ITEM
    Repeat
        MIDDLE = (FIRST + LAST) / 2
        If ITEM > MIDDLE then
            FIRST = MIDDLE + 1
        Else
            If ITEM < MIDDLE then
                LAST = MIDDLE - 1
        Else
                FOUND = TRUE
        UNTIL FOUND or FIRST > LAST
End binary search procedure
```

BASIC implementations of the binary search use WHILE.

```
10   DIM LI(100)
20   L = 0
30   F1 = 1
40   F2 = 0
50   REM LOAD THE ARRAY
60   PRINT "ITEM FOR LIST (USE 9999 TO FINISH)";
70   L = L + 1
80   INPUT LI(L)
90   IF LI(L) <> 9999 AND L <> 100 GOTO 60
110  L = L - 1
120 REM SEARCH
130 PRINT "ITEM FOR SEARCH";
140 INPUT IT
150 WHILE F2 = 0 AND F1 <= L
160     M = INT((F1 + L) / 2)
170     IF IT > LI(M) THEN F1 = M + 1
180     IF IT < LI(M) THEN L = M - 1
190     IF IT = LI(M) THEN F2 = 1
200 WEND
210 IF F2 = 1 THEN PRINT "ITEM ";LI(M);" WAS FOUND IN THE ";M;" POSITION OF THE
    LIST"
220 IF F2 = 0 THEN PRINT "ITEM ";IT;" WAS NOT FOUND"
```

Binary searches in Pascal can use WHILE or UNTIL. The Pascal segment that follows uses WHILE.

```
PROGRAM BINSEARCH(INPUT,OUTPUT);

{PROGRAM TO ILLUSTRATE BINARY SEARCH USING WHILE}

VAR
   LIST : ARRAY[1..100] OF INTEGER;
   MIDDLE : INTEGER;
   FIRST : INTEGER;
   FOUND : BOOLEAN;
   LAST : INTEGER;
   INDEX : INTEGER;
   ITEM : INTEGER;

PROCEDURE LISTIN;
BEGIN {LISTIN PROCEDURE}
   INDEX := 1;
   WRITE('ITEM? ');
   READLN(LIST[INDEX]);
   WHILE (LIST[INDEX] <> 9999) AND (INDEX < 100) DO
       BEGIN
            INDEX := INDEX + 1;
            WRITE('ITEM (USE 9999 TO END) ');
            READLN(LIST[INDEX]);
       END;
   LAST := INDEX - 1;
END; {LISTIN PROCEDURE}

BEGIN {MAIN PROGRAM}
   LISTIN;
   FIRST := 1;
   FOUND := FALSE;
   WRITE('Item to find? ');
   READLN(ITEM);
   WHILE (LAST >= FIRST) AND NOT FOUND DO
   BEGIN
       MIDDLE := TRUNC((LAST + FIRST) / 2);
       IF ITEM > LIST[MIDDLE] THEN
           FIRST := MIDDLE + 1
       ELSE
           IF ITEM < LIST[MIDDLE] THEN
              LAST := MIDDLE - 1
           ELSE
              FOUND := TRUE;
   END;
   IF FOUND THEN
       WRITELN('ITEM ',LIST[MIDDLE],' WAS FOUND IN
              THE ',MIDDLE:4,' POSITION')
   ELSE
       WRITELN('ITEM ',ITEM,' WAS NOT FOUND');
END. {MAIN PROGRAM}
```

Substituting a REPEAT...UNTIL loop for the WHILE loop yields this Pascal segment:

```
PROGRAM BINSEARCH(INPUT,OUTPUT);

{PROGRAM TO ILLUSTRATE BINARY SEARCH USING UNTIL}

VAR
  LIST : ARRAY[1..100] OF INTEGER;
  MIDDLE : INTEGER;
  FIRST : INTEGER;
  FOUND : BOOLEAN;
  LAST : INTEGER;
  INDEX : INTEGER;
  ITEM : INTEGER;

PROCEDURE LISTIN;
BEGIN {LISTIN PROCEDURE}
  INDEX := 1;
  WRITE('ITEM? ');
  READLN(LIST[INDEX]);
  WHILE (LIST[INDEX] <> 9999) AND (INDEX < 100) DO
      BEGIN
          INDEX := INDEX + 1;
          WRITE('ITEM (USE 9999 TO END) ');
          READLN(LIST[INDEX]);
      END;
  LAST := INDEX - 1;
END; {LISTIN PROCEDURE}

BEGIN {MAIN PROGRAM}
  LISTIN;
  FIRST := 1;
  FOUND := FALSE;
  WRITE('Item to find? ');
  READLN(ITEM);
  REPEAT
      MIDDLE := TRUNC((LAST + FIRST) / 2);
      IF ITEM > LIST[MIDDLE] THEN
          FIRST := MIDDLE + 1
      ELSE
          IF ITEM < LIST[MIDDLE] THEN
              LAST := MIDDLE - 1
          ELSE
              FOUND := TRUE;
  UNTIL (FIRST > LAST) OR FOUND;
  IF FOUND THEN
      WRITELN('ITEM ',LIST[MIDDLE],' WAS FOUND IN
              THE ',MIDDLE:4,' POSITION')
  ELSE
      WRITELN('ITEM ',ITEM,' WAS NOT FOUND');
END. {MAIN PROGRAM}
```

As mentioned, a sequential search usually has to access half the items in the list when looking for an item. The binary search requires comparatively fewer accesses. The table that follows shows the maximum number of accesses for lists of different sizes.

List Size	Maximum Accesses
4	2
8	3
16	4
32	5
64	6
128	7
256	8
512	9
1024	10
2048	11

See the pattern? If you are familiar with the binary numbering system, you'll immediately see the connection and understand why this kind of search is called a binary search.

CASE STUDY: PAYROLL PROGRAM, SEARCHES

Managers often need to access the payroll records of individual employees. Therefore, this section shows how to add a search routine to the payroll example developed in prior chapters. The pseudocode that follows describes a binary search for an employee's name and a sequential search for the highest and lowest year-to-date earnings.

```
Add to processing procedure the following menu options:
     1. Process payroll
     2. Search for a name
     3. Search for highest and lowest year-to-date earnings
     4. Terminate program

If 1 is entered then
     do processing procedure
If 2 is entered then
     do binary search procedure
If 3 is entered then
     do sequential search procedure
If 4 is entered then
     do termination procedure


Begin binary search procedure
     Enter NAME to be located
     FOUND = FALSE
     LAST = NUMBER OF EMPLOYEES
     FIRST = 1
     While not FOUND and LAST > FIRST
          MIDDLE = (FIRST + LAST) / 2
```

```
                     If NAME to locate < NAME[MIDDLE] then
                          LAST = MIDDLE - 1
                     Else
                          If NAME to locate > NAME[MIDDLE] then
                               FIRST = MIDDLE + 1
                          Else
                               FOUND = TRUE
               End while
               If FOUND = TRUE then
                    Print data on employee
               Else
                    Report employee not FOUND
          End binary search procedure

     Begin sequential search procedure
               HIGH = 0
               LOW = 100000
               For INDEX = 1 to number of employees do
                    If YTD > HIGH then
                         HIGH = YTD. HIGH Position = INDEX
                    If YTD < LOW then
                         LOW = YTD. LOW Position = INDEX
               Next INDEX
               Print out data on employee with highest YTD
               Print out data on employee with lowest YTD
          End sequential search procedure
```

Most of the code for the BASIC and Pascal versions was supplied previously.

Modifying the program to handle ties in the YTD earnings search is left as an exercise. Another modification might be to find the second highest and lowest YTD earnings in the sequential search procedure.

CASE STUDY: INVENTORY PROGRAM, SEARCHES

This case study presents a simple inventory program that uses binary and sequential searches. It illustrates an inventory system that can be searched by item number or item name.

```
     Begin inventory program
          Do initialize procedure
          Do database procedure
          Do datain procedure
          Begin loop
               If PART ID # SEARCH then
                    Do binary search procedure
               If NAME SEARCH then
                    Do sequential search procedure
               If QUIT PROGRAM then
                    Terminate program
          End loop
     End inventory program
```

```
Begin initialize procedure
      Name variables and declare their type
      Assign initial values
End initialize procedure


Begin database procedure
      Read in ID #, name, quantity, and cost of items in inventory
End database procedure


Begin datain procedure
      Set up menu for 1 - PART ID # SEARCH
                       2 - NAME SEARCH
                       3 - QUIT PROGRAM
      Enter choice
End datain procedure


Begin binary search procedure
      Enter PART ID # to search for
      Set FIRST to 1
      Set LAST to number of ITEMS in inventory
      Set FOUND to FALSE
      While not FOUND and LAST > FIRST do
          MIDDLE = (FIRST + LAST) / 2
          If PART ID searched for > ITEMS[MIDDLE] then
              FIRST = MIDDLE + 1
          If PART ID searched for < ITEMS[MIDDLE] then
              LAST = MIDDLE - 1
          If PART ID searched for = ITEMS[MIDDLE] then
              FOUND = TRUE
      End while
      If FOUND then
          Print data about item
      Else
          Print "ITEM NOT FOUND"
End binary search procedure


Begin sequential search procedure
      Read in item name to search for
      Place item name to search for at end of LIST
      Set FOUND to FALSE
      Set INDEX to 1
      While not FOUND and INDEX <= number of ITEMS in
                                      list + 1 do
          If item name to find = ITEMS[INDEX] then
              Set FOUND to TRUE
          Else
              Set INDEX to INDEX + 1
      End while
      If INDEX <= number of items in list then
          Print name, ID #, quantity, and cost of item
      Else
      Print "ITEM NOT FOUND"
End sequential search procedure
```

Normally, an inventory list is found in a file. Because of the many different implementations of file I/O found in BASIC and Pascal, an array is used in the programs that follow. Keep in mind that the part numbers must be in numeric order for the binary search to work properly.

The BASIC version of the inventory program looks like this:

```
10 DIM ID(500),N$(500),Q(500),C(500)
20 I = 1
30 PRINT "INPUT ID (9999 TO QUIT): ";
40 INPUT ID(I)
50 WHILE ID(I) <> 9999
60    PRINT "INPUT NAME: ";
70    INPUT N$(I)
80    PRINT "INPUT QUANTITY: ";
90    INPUT Q(I)
100    PRINT "INPUT COST: ";
110    INPUT C(I)
120    I = I + 1
130    PRINT "INPUT ID (9999 TO QUIT): ";
140    INPUT ID(I)
150 WEND
160 REM TO ELIMINATE 9999
170 I = I - 1
180 T = I
1000 PRINT " INVENTORY PROGRAM FOR FUN FANTASIES"
1010 PRINT
1020 PRINT
1030 PRINT "WHICH DO YOU CHOOSE?"
1040 PRINT
1050 PRINT " SEARCH BY PART NUMBER   = 1"
1060 PRINT " SEARCH BY NAME          = 2"
1070 PRINT " TO QUIT                 = 3"
1080 PRINT
1090 PRINT "CHOOSE NOW: "
1100 INPUT X
1110 ON X GOSUB 2000,3000,4000
1120 GOTO 1000
2000 REM BINARY SEARCH FOR ID NUMBER
2010 REM
2020 PRINT "ENTER ID TO SEARCH FOR: ";
2030 INPUT IC
2040 F1 = 1
2050 L1 = T
2060 F = 0
2070 WHILE L1 >= F1 AND F = 0
2080    M = INT((F1 + L1) / 2)
2090    IF IC > ID(M) THEN F1 = M + 1
2100    IF IC < ID(M) THEN L1 = M - 1
2110    IF IC = ID(M) THEN F = 1
2120 WEND
2130 IF F = 1 THEN PRINT ID(M),N$(M),Q(M),C(M)
2140 IF F = 0 THEN PRINT "ITEM NOT FOUND - PLEASE TRY AGAIN"
2150 RETURN
3000 REM SEQUENTIAL SEARCH FOR NAME
```

```
3010 REM
3020 PRINT "ENTER NAME TO LOOK FOR: ";
3030 INPUT N1$
3040 N$(T + 1) = N1$
3050 F = 0
3060 I = 1
3070 WHILE F = 0 AND I <= T
3080    IF N1$ = N$(I) THEN F = 1 ELSE I = I + 1
3090 WEND
3100 IF F = 1 THEN PRINT ID(I),N$(I),Q(I),C(I)
3110 IF F = 0 THEN PRINT "ITEM NOT FOUND - PLEASE TRY AGAIN"
3120 RETURN
4000 REM TERMINATION PROCEDURE
4010 REM
4020 END
```

The Pascal version follows:

```
PROGRAM INVENTORY(INPUT,OUTPUT);
VAR
  NAME : STRING[20];
  ITEMS : ARRAY[1..500] OF STRING[20];
  ID : ARRAY[1..500] OF INTEGER;
  QUANTITY : ARRAY[1..500] OF INTEGER;
  COST : ARRAY[1..500] OF REAL;
  DONE : BOOLEAN;
  RESPONSE : INTEGER;
  ANS : CHAR;
  INDEX : INTEGER;
  SPACE : INTEGER;
  WANTID : INTEGER;
  WANT : STRING[20];
  MID : INTEGER;
  LAST : INTEGER;
  FIRST : INTEGER;
  FOUND : BOOLEAN;

PROCEDURE DATABASE;
BEGIN
  INDEX := 1;
  WRITE('ENTER ID # FOR INVENTORY ITEM: ');
  READLN(ID[INDEX]);
  WHILE (INDEX <= 500) AND (ID[INDEX] <> 9999) DO
    BEGIN
      FOR SPACE := 1 TO 20 DO
        NAME[SPACE] := ' ';
      WRITE('ENTER ITEM NAME: ');
      READLN(NAME);
      ITEMS[INDEX] := NAME;
      WRITELN;
      WRITE('ENTER ITEM QUANTITY: ');
      READLN(QUANTITY[INDEX]);
      WRITE('ENTER ITEM COST: ');
      READLN(COST[INDEX]);
      INDEX := INDEX + 1;
```

```
                    WRITELN('ENTER ID # FOR INVENTORY ITEM');
                    WRITELN('ENTER 9999 TO STOP');
                    READLN(ID[INDEX]);
            END; {WHILE}
        INDEX := INDEX - 1; {TO GET RID OF 9999}
END; {INVENTORY DATABASE READING PROCEDURE}


PROCEDURE NAMEIN;

BEGIN {INVENTORY ITEM TO SEARCH FOR PROCEDURE}
    FOR SPACE := 1 TO 20 DO
        WANT[SPACE] := ' ';
        WRITE('ENTER ITEM NAME: ');
        READLN(WANT);
END; {INVENTORY ITEM TO SEARCH FOR PROCEDURE}


PROCEDURE SEQUENCE;

BEGIN {SEQUENTIAL SEARCH PROCEDURE}
    NAMEIN;
    ITEMS[INDEX + 1] := WANT;
    FOUND := FALSE;
    SPACE := 1;
    WHILE (SPACE <= (INDEX + 1)) AND NOT FOUND DO
        IF WANT = ITEMS[SPACE] THEN
            FOUND := TRUE
        ELSE
            SPACE := SPACE + 1;
        IF SPACE < (INDEX + 1) THEN
            WRITELN(ID[SPACE]:6,ITEMS[SPACE]:20,COST[SPACE]:8:2,
                    QUANTITY[SPACE]:6)
        ELSE
            WRITELN('ITEM NOT IN LIST');
END; {SEQUENTIAL SEARCH PROCEDURE}


PROCEDURE PARTIN;

BEGIN
    WRITE('ENTER PART NUMBER: ');
    READLN(WANTID);
END;


PROCEDURE BINARY;

BEGIN
    PARTIN;
    FIRST:= 1;
    LAST := INDEX;
    FOUND:= FALSE;
    WHILE (LAST >= FIRST) AND NOT FOUND DO
        BEGIN
            MID := TRUNC((FIRST + LAST) / 2);
            IF WANTID > ID[MID] THEN
                FIRST := MID + 1
            ELSE
```

```
            IF  WANTID  <  ID[MID]  THEN
                LAST  :=  MID  -  1
        ELSE
                FOUND  :=  TRUE;
      END;
  IF  FOUND  THEN
      WRITELN(ITEMS[MID]:20,ID[MID]:6,COST[MID]:8:2,
              QUANTITY[MID]:6)
  ELSE
      WRITELN('ITEM  NOT  FOUND');
END;  {BINARY  PROCEDURE}

PROCEDURE  DATAIN;

BEGIN  {MENU  PROGRAM}
  WRITELN('INVENTORY  PROGRAM  FOR  FUN  FANTASIES');
  WRITELN;
  WRITELN;
  WRITELN('WHICH  DO  YOU  CHOOSE:');
  WRITELN;
  WRITELN('        SEARCH  BY  PART  ID  #  =  1');
  WRITELN('        SEARCH  BY  PART  NAME  =  2');
  WRITE('CHOOSE  NOW:    ');
  READLN(RESPONSE);
END;  {MENU  PROGRAM}

BEGIN  {MAIN  PROGRAM}
  DATABASE;
  DONE  :=  FALSE;
  DATAIN;
  WHILE  NOT  DONE  DO
      BEGIN
          IF  RESPONSE  =  1  THEN
              BINARY;
          IF  RESPONSE  =  2  THEN
              SEQUENCE;
          WRITE('SEARCH  FOR  ANOTHER?  ');
          READLN(ANS);
          IF  ANS  =  'Y'  THEN
              DATAIN
          ELSE
              DONE  :=  TRUE;
      END;
  END.  {MAIN  PROGRAM}
```

INDEXES

An index is used with very large data files to speed the search for the appropriate records. A search that uses an index is called an *indexed search*. An index works like its counterpart in a book. Rather than having to leaf through the whole book to find an item, you can look it up in the index, which points you to the correct page. A file or array index works in the same way. For example, suppose you have an inventory file consisting of records or array elements. Each file contains a part number, description, quantity on hand, price, cost, and much more data. These records are stored in the inventory file or array in no particular order. Each record or array position is designated by a number—record 1, record 2, and so forth. The index file consists of a list of part numbers, and the number of the record containing the data about that part. A file or array of records can use more than one index.

The index can be in a file, but it is usually stored in an array for fast access. Storing the index in an array is especially common when the index relates to a database. With the index in an array, the program can access records according to different fields, without sorting the whole file by that field.

Of course, you could store the inventory records in part number order—then you wouldn't need the index because you could use a binary search on the file itself. However, arranging the records by part number means you can index only one part of the record. You cannot have one index on part numbers and another on descriptions. A second disadvantage is that when you add a new record, you have to move some of the existing records to make room for it. If you use an index, you can just append the record to the end of the file and rearrange the index entries, which are shorter than the record. If you store records by part number, you must move records again when you delete a record. All records after the deleted record must move up one "slot" to fill the space.

If you use an index, you can delete the *index entry* from the list. Of course, you must move all the index entries after the deleted entry to fill the space, but the short index entries can be moved faster than the long file records, especially if they are stored in an array. Can you see the advantage of using an index when a part number is changed?

Frequently, indexes are stored in ordered arrays or files and accessed using a binary search. Another popular index system is called the binary tree, or B-tree. You can investigate this interesting system when you are ready for advanced programming techniques.

Change to an Ordered Array

As mentioned earlier, you must change the index as records are inserted, changed, and deleted. First, look at inserting.

Inserting. First, you must find the correct insertion point. This is the same as the value LAST, which is available from the binary search routine. Then you must use this value to rearrange the array contents to make room for the new item. This consists simply of moving all the items after LAST down one position to provide the room. The pseudocode that follows shows how insertion works.

```
Procedure MAKE_ROOM
Begin procedure
    Set X to number of items in LIST
    While X > LAST + 1 do
        LIST[X + 1] = LIST[X]
        X = X - 1
```

```
     End while
     LIST[LAST]  =  ITEM  TO  ADD
End procedure
```

Deleting. To delete an item from an array, use the binary search to find the item. If found, use the following procedure:

```
Procedure DELETE_ITEM
Begin procedure
     Set X to LAST
     Do while X < number of items in LIST - 1
          LIST[X]  =  LIST[X + 1]
          X = X + 1
     End while
End procedure
```

Long Indexes

Sometimes, if the index is too long for the array, only the appropriate portion of the index is loaded into the array. This entails dividing the index into several small segments and then placing them in a separate index array. A search of this kind is called a *long-indexed search.*

The search continues through the index file until it finds the segment that contains the item. The initial values for FIRST and LAST are:

FIRST = One more than last value in preceding segment

LAST = The last element in the segment to be searched further

To understand how to apply this algorithm, suppose you have a file of 500 items ordered on I.D. number from 0001 to 9999. The program picks out the values located at every 50th element of the file. These values are placed in a index array. The table that follows shows the position of the values in the array.

Position	Value
50	864
100	1279
150	2401
200	3987
250	5678
300	6245
350	7003
400	8214
450	8876
500	9985

After a binary or sequential search of this array, the first and last numbers are determined. If you are searching for item 7421, you find it in the eighth segment of the list. LAST equals 8214; FIRST equals 7004. Then the binary search takes over.

SUMMARY

This chapter introduces common searching algorithms that locate data according to different fields. Sequential searches are used for unordered data. Binary searches are used for ordered data. Indexed searches allow searching on any field that has been indexed. The long-indexed search is used for long lists and divides the list into segments.

Key Terms

Binary search	Long-indexed search
Indexed search	Sequential search

Review Questions

1. What are the basic searching methods?

2. a. Which searching method(s) work(s) on ordered data?
   b. Which searching method works best on ordered data?
   c. Which searching method(s) work(s) on unordered data?
   d. Which searching method works best on unordered data?

3. Write pseudocode for a basic sequential search.

4. Return to the text of this chapter to review the table that contains the maximum number of searches needed to find an item in arrays of different sizes. What is the maximum number of searches needed for a list of 4096 items?

Problem-Solving Assignments

1. Modify the payroll search modules presented in the case study in this chapter to incorporate the logic to handle ties in the year-to-date earnings search.

2. Code the pseudocode you created in assignment 1.

3. Modify the pseudocode of assignment 1 to obtain the second highest YTD and the lowest YTD earnings. Use a sequential search routine.

4. Code the pseudocode you created in assignment 3.

5. Modify the inventory control pseudocode presented in the case study in this chapter to incorporate files. Code the changes.

6. Take the pseudocode for indexing and apply it to the following problem:

   You have a list of 20 records. Each record contains a name, I.D. number, and a person's yearly salary. The 20 records are not ordered by any of the three fields.

   a. Create indexes for each field.
   b. Add a record and reindex each index.
   c. Delete a record and reindex each file.

7. Take the pseudocode in problem 6, code it, and test it to ensure it works.

8. Write the pseudocode for the following long-index problem.

Long Index	Data
97	1, 3, 11, 27, 39, 97
120	101, 102, 103, 104, 120
289	210, 270, 289
378	317, 377, 378
378	317, 377, 378

   a. Create the long-index file indicated.
   b. Add the number 140 to the data.
   c. Search for the numbers 270 and 187.

9. Take the pseudocode in problem 8, code it, and test it to ensure it works.

10. Recode the search program on page 162 to get rid of the GOTO statement on line 90 (if your BASIC allows).

11. Recode the search program on page 163 to get rid of the GOTO statements on lines 90 and 190 (if your BASIC allows).

8

Sorts and Merges

Sorting puts items in an array or a file in numeric or alphabetic order. Many different end-users employ sorts to arrange data in many different ways. There are many sort routines. Some, such as the bubble sort, are very simple but slow; others, such as the shell sort, are a bit more complex but very much faster. There are so many different sort routines that it would be impossible to describe them all here; there are entire books on the subject. The sorts described in this chapter are some of those most commonly used.

Here's an example of sorting in use. When considering the contents of a database, different users might be interested in seeing the data in different patterns. For example, if a database listed part sales over a period of time, some viewers might be interested in the identification numbers of the parts sold, some might be interested in the people who sold the parts, and another group might prefer to view the sales by date. Assuming all these fields were available in the database records, you could sort the database on the field of interest, thus grouping the information as the viewer prefers.

In a parts sales database, each sale is stored in a record. The different sections of the record—such as the part number, the quantity sold, the date sold, the salesperson, and so forth—are called *fields*. (Some database programs use other terms for databases, records, and fields.)

Obviously, it takes time to re-sort the database for each viewer. Sorting a large database in a disk file can take quite a while, depending on the speed of the computer, disk drive, and the number of records. In this case the usual method is to create a sorted index for each field of interest, as described in Chapter 7. Of course the database program must maintain the indexes correctly as new records are added, fields of interest changed, and records deleted.

If the indexes are stored in an array in memory, the sorts can be accomplished quickly, since sorting in memory and making changes to the index is much faster than manipulating the data directly on the disk. The sorted indexes can then be stored on disks and erased from memory when not in use. This practice cuts down on the computer memory required.

Sorts can arrange data in increasing (ascending) order or decreasing (descending) order. For example, when sorting records by date, does the viewer wish to see the most recent dates first or the oldest? Sorts can easily be designed to work in either order.

When setting up database fields, remember the characteristics of each field. If you set the field up incorrectly, it may be unsuitable for sorting. When it comes to sorting, setting up a date field can be tricky. Consider the list that follows. The dates are in MM/DD/YY (month/date/year) format.

```
12/28/88
12/17/84
11/12/87
09/23/85
```

If you sort the dates in alphanumeric order, you end up with

```
09/23/85
11/12/87
12/17/84
12/28/88
```

The years are out of sequence. However, suppose you change the date format to YY/MM/DD.

```
88/12/28
84/12/17
87/11/12
85/09/23
```

Now the dates sort correctly. The sort yields the correct order:

```
84/12/17
85/09/23
87/11/12
88/12/28
```

Another way to represent times is through the use of *Julian dates*. Sometimes a Julian date is the number of days elapsed since some starting date. Sometimes a Julian date is a five-digit number—the first two digits represent the current year and the last three digits represent the number of days elapsed that year. Thus, February 1, 1990 is 90032. Dates stored in this format can be sorted easily.

How do we sort? Let's look at a bubble sort first.

THE BUBBLE SORT

The simplest version of the *bubble sort* works by going through an entire list, comparing each pair of values in turn. Consider an ascending bubble sort. The bubble sort routine compares the first and second values, placing the lower of the pair first. Then the sort compares the second and third values and puts that pair in ascending order. The sort continues through the list, comparing pairs. Each time the sort works through the whole list, the sort has made a *pass* through the list. Say the list contains a total of *n* elements. The total number of passes in any bubble sort is *n* minus 1. After making *n* minus 1 passes, the list is sorted.

Figure 8.1 shows the five passes of an ascending sort through a list of six elements. The square brackets in the figure show which values are being tested in each comparison. The sort begins by comparing the values in positions A and B. The values are 7 and 4. The value 4 is less than the value 7, so 7 and 4 swap places. The next comparison is between the values in positions B and C. The value in B is now 7, so 7 is compared with 8. These two values are already in ascending order, so the routine does not swap them. The sort continues, making comparisons and swaps as shown in passes 2 through 5.

By studying passes 2 through 5, you can see that the last value is never swapped after pass 1. The second-to-last value is never swapped after the second pass, and so forth. An efficiently programmed sort does not make unnecessary comparisons.

So, after the first pass, the sort no longer performs the last comparison. After the second pass, the sort no longer performs the second-to-last comparison, and so forth.

To understand another feature of an efficient sort, consider a list in which all the values are in order before the last pass. Rather than making *n* minus 1 passes, the efficient sort routine stops after a pass without swaps. The means for stopping is a Boolean value.

The pseudocode that follows describes an ascending bubble sort that does not make unnecessary comparison. The Boolean value NOEXCHANGE prevents unnecessary passes.

```
Repeat
   NOEXCHANGE = TRUE
   For INDEX A = 1 to number of elements - 1
      INDEX B = INDEX A + 1
      If ARRAY [INDEX B] < ARRAY [INDEX A]
         TEMP = ARRAY [INDEX A]
         ARRAY [INDEX A] = ARRAY [INDEX B]
         ARRAY [INDEX B] = TEMP
         NOEXCHANGE = FALSE
   Next INDEX A
Until NOEXCHANGE = TRUE
```

The BASIC code of an ascending bubble sort looks like this:

```
10 DIM A(100)
20 REM ENTER LIST OF NUMBERS TO SORT
30 E = 0
40 PRINT "NUMBER TO SORT (9999 TO QUIT): "
50 E = E + 1
60 INPUT A(E)
70 IF A(E) <> 9999 AND E < 100 GOTO 40
80 E = E - 1
90 REM SORT
100 NO = 1
110 WHILE NO = 1
```

Figure 8.1

Passes 1 through 5 of an ascending bubble sort

Posi-tion	List Ele-ment	1st Com-parison	2nd Com-parison	3rd Com-parison	4th Com-parison	5th Com-parison	
A	7	4	4	4	4	4	
B	4	7	7	7	7	7	
C	8	8	8	6	6	6	Pass 1
D	6	6	6	8	3	3	
E	3	3	3	3	8	1	
F	1	1	1	1	1	8	

List Ele-ment	1st Com-parison	2nd Com-parison	3rd Com-parison	4th Com-parison	5th Com-parison	
4	4	4	4	4	4	
7	7	6	6	6	6	
6	6	7	3	3	3	Pass 2
3	3	3	7	1	1	
1	1	1	1	7	7	
8	8	8	8	8	8	

List Ele-ment	1st Com-parison	2nd Com-parison	3rd Com-parison	4th Com-parison	5th Com-parison	
4	4	4	4	4	4	
6	6	3	3	3	3	
3	3	6	1	1	1	Pass 3
1	1	1	6	6	6	
7	7	7	7	7	7	
8	8	8	8	8	8	

List Ele-ment	1st Com-parison	2nd Com-parison	3rd Com-parison	4th Com-parison	5th Com-parison	
4	3	3	3	3	3	
3	4	1	1	1	1	
1	1	4	4	4	4	Pass 4
6	6	6	6	6	6	
7	7	7	7	7	7	
8	8	8	8	8	8	

List Ele-ment	1st Com-parison	2nd Com-parison	3rd Com-parison	4th Com-parison	5th Com-parison	
3	1	1	1	1	1	
1	3	3	3	3	3	
4	4	4	4	4	4	Pass 5
6	6	6	6	6	6	
7	7	7	7	7	7	
8	8	8	8	8	8	

```
120     NO = 0
130     FOR I1 = 1 TO E - 1
140        I2 = I1 + 1
150        IF A(I2) > A(I1) THEN 200
160        T = A(I1)
170        A(I1) = A(I2)
180        A(I2) = T
190        NO = 1
200     NEXT I1
210 WEND
220 REM PRINT SORTED LIST
230 FOR X = 1 TO E
240     PRINT A(X);
250 NEXT X
260 PRINT
```

The BASIC code that follows performs a bubble sort to yield descending order. Line 150 defines the routine as a descending sort.

```
10 DIM A(100)
20 REM ENTER LIST OF NUMBERS TO SORT
30 E = 0
40 PRINT "NUMBER TO SORT (9999 TO QUIT): "
50 E = E + 1
60 INPUT A(E)
70 IF A(E) <> 9999 AND E < 100 GOTO 40
80 E = E - 1
90 REM SORT
100 NO = 1
110 WHILE NO = 1
120     NO = 0
130     FOR I1 = 1 TO E - 1
140        I2 = I1 + 1
150        IF A(I2) < A(I1) THEN 200
160        T = A(I1)
170        A(I1) = A(I2)
180        A(I2) = T
190        NO = 1
200     NEXT I1
210 WEND
220 REM PRINT SORTED LIST
230 FOR X = 1 TO E
240     PRINT A(X);
250 NEXT X
260 PRINT
```

If you are using a two-dimensional array, the second dimension must be swapped along with the first dimension. The BASIC program that follows illustrates an ascending sort on the first element of a two-dimensional array. The new line numbers end in 5.

```
10 DIM A(100,2)
20 REM ENTER LIST OF NUMBERS TO SORT
```

```
30 E = 0
40 PRINT "NUMBER TO SORT (9999 TO QUIT): "
50 E = E + 1
60 INPUT A(E,1)
65 A(E,2) = A(E,1) + 1
70 IF A(E,1) <> 9999 AND E < 100 GOTO 40
80 E = E - 1
90 REM SORT
100 NO = 1
110 WHILE NO = 1
120    NO = 0
130    FOR I1 = 1 TO E - 1
140       I2 = I1 + 1
150       IF A(I2,1) > A(I1,1) THEN 200
160       T = A(I1,1)
165       T1 = A(I1,2)
170       A(I1,1) = A(I2,1)
175       A(I1,2) = A(I2,2)
180       A(I2,1) = T
185       A(I2,2) = T1
190       NO = 1
200    NEXT I1
210 WEND
220 REM PRINT SORTED LIST
230 FOR X = 1 TO E
240    PRINT A(X,1);A(X,2)
250 NEXT X
```

Line 65 provides a value for the second element. The value is one greater than the first. The program shows how the second element follows the first as required.

An ascending bubble sort of two parallel arrays are handled in much the same way, as this BASIC program segment shows.

```
10 DIM A(100),B(100)
20 REM ENTER LIST OF NUMBERS TO SORT
30 E = 0
40 PRINT "NUMBER TO SORT (9999 TO QUIT): "
50 E = E + 1
60 INPUT A(E)
65 B(E) = A(E) + 1
70 IF A(E) <> 9999 AND E < 100 GOTO 40
80 E = E - 1
90 REM SORT
100 NO = 1
105 PRINT E
110 WHILE NO = 1
120    NO = 0
130    FOR I1 = 1 TO E - 1
140       I2 = I1 + 1
150       IF A(I2) > A(I1) THEN 200
160       T = A(I1)
165       T1 = B(I1)
170       A(I1) = A(I2)
175       B(I1) = B(I2)
```

```
180      A(I2) = T
185      B(I2) = T1
190      NO = 1
200    NEXT I1
210 WEND
220 REM PRINT SORTED LIST
230 FOR X = 1 TO E
240    PRINT A(X);B(X)
250 NEXT X
```

Here is the Pascal version of the ascending bubble sort pseudocode:

```
PROGRAM BUBBLE(INPUT,OUTPUT);
VAR
  NUMELEMENTS : INTEGER;
  INDEXA : INTEGER;
  INDEXB : INTEGER;
  LIST : ARRAY [1..100] OF INTEGER;
  NOEXCHANGES : BOOLEAN;
  TEMP : INTEGER;

PROCEDURE LOADNUM;

BEGIN
  NUMELEMENTS := 1;
  WRITE('NUMBER TO SORT: ');
  READLN(LIST [NUMELEMENTS]);
  REPEAT
     NUMELEMENTS := NUMELEMENTS + 1;
     WRITE('NUMBER TO SORT (9999 TO QUIT): ');
     READLN(LIST [NUMELEMENTS]);
  UNTIL (NUMELEMENTS = 100) OR (LIST [NUMELEMENTS] = 9999);
  NUMELEMENTS := NUMELEMENTS - 1;
END;

PROCEDURE BSORT;

BEGIN
  REPEAT
     NOEXCHANGES := TRUE;
     FOR INDEXA := 1 TO NUMELEMENTS - 1 DO
        BEGIN
           INDEXB := INDEXA + 1;
           IF LIST [INDEXA] > LIST [INDEXB] THEN
              BEGIN
                 TEMP := LIST [INDEXA];
                 LIST [INDEXA] := LIST [INDEXB];
                 LIST [INDEXB] := TEMP;
                 NOEXCHANGES := FALSE;
              END;
        END;
     UNTIL NOEXCHANGES;
END;
BEGIN {MAIN PROGRAM}
  LOADNUM;
```

```
   BSORT;
   FOR INDEXA := 1 TO NUMELEMENTS DO
       WRITELN(LIST [INDEXA]);
 END.
```

So far, you have focused on using the bubble sort on numeric arrays. An alphanumeric sort uses the same principles as the numeric sort. By testing pairs of values, the alphanumeric sort compares characters in the array to determine correct order. The primary difference is in how you declare the array. In BASIC, declare a string array; in Pascal, declare a character array or a string array. The kind of array you choose in Pascal depends on whether you can use strings in your implementation. Try it!

THE EXCHANGE SORT

The *exchange sort* works by selecting the first value in the array and then checking it against each of the other values until the routine finds the lowest value that is less than the first. If the routine finds such a value, it swaps the positions of the first value and the value it found. The routine then moves to the second value. The sort looks for the lowest value that is less than the second value. If it finds such a value, the second value and the found value swap positions. This procedure continues until the next-to-last element has been compared. The array is now sorted.

Figure 8.2 shows an ascending exchange sort. The boxed value in each column is the first value of the tested pair. The pseudocode for an ascending exchange sort looks like this:

```
For INDEXPOSITION = 1 to number of array elements
   CHANGE POSITION = INDEX POSITION
   For INDEX = INDEX POSITION + 1 to number of array elements
       If ARRAY [INDEX] < ARRAY [CHANGE POSITION] then
          CHANGE POSITION = INDEX
       End of index loop
   If CHANGE POSITION <> INDEX POSITION then
       TEMP = ARRAY [INDEX POSITION]
       ARRAY [INDEX POSITION] = ARRAY [CHANGE POSITION]
       ARRAY [CHANGE POSITION] = TEMP
End of index position loop
```

Here is the BASIC version of the ascending exchange sort.

```
10 DIM A(100)
20 REM ENTER LIST OF NUMBERS TO SORT
30 E = 0
40 PRINT "NUMBER TO SORT (9999 TO QUIT): "
50 E = E + 1
60 INPUT A(E)
70 IF A(E) <> 9999 AND E < 100 GOTO 40
80 E = E - 1
90 REM SORT
```

```
100 FOR IP = 1 TO E
110    CP = IP
120    FOR I = IP + 1 TO E
130        IF A(I) < A(CP) THEN CP = I
140    NEXT I
150    IF CP <> IP THEN GOSUB 300
160 NEXT IP
170 REM PRINT SORTED ARRAY
180 FOR X = 1 TO E
190    PRINT A(X);
200 NEXT X
210 PRINT
220 END
299 REM SWAP VALUES SUBROUTINE
300 T = A(IP)
310 A(IP) = A(CP)
320 A(CP) = T
330 RETURN
```

The Pascal version of the ascending exchange sort follows.

```
PROGRAM EXCHANGE(INPUT,OUTPUT);
VAR
    NUMELEMENTS : INTEGER;
    INDEXPOSITION : INTEGER;
    CHANGEPOSITION : INTEGER;
    INDEX : INTEGER;
    LIST : ARRAY [1..100] OF INTEGER;
    TEMP : INTEGER;

PROCEDURE LOADNUM;

BEGIN
    NUMELEMENTS := 1;
```

Figure 8.2

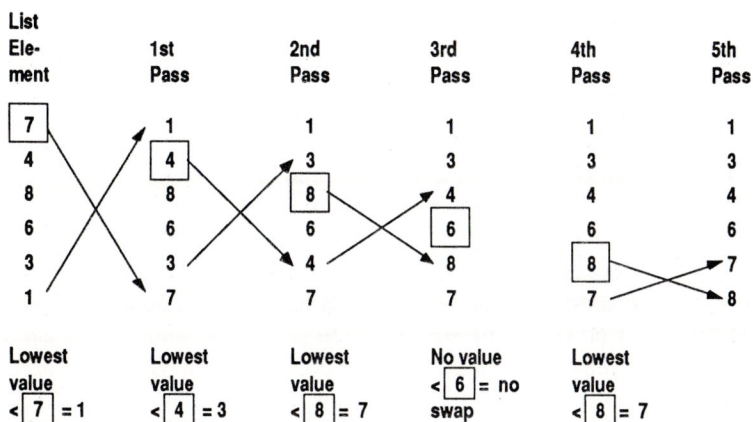

An ascending exchange sort

List Element	1st Pass	2nd Pass	3rd Pass	4th Pass	5th Pass
7	1	1	1	1	1
4	4	3	3	3	3
8	8	8	4	4	4
6	6	6	6	6	6
3	3	4	8	8	7
1	7	7	7	7	8

Lowest value $< \boxed{7} = 1$ Lowest value $< \boxed{4} = 3$ Lowest value $< \boxed{8} = 7$ No value $< \boxed{6} =$ no swap   Lowest value $< \boxed{8} = 7$

```
        WRITE('NUMBER TO SORT: ');
        READLN(LIST [NUMELEMENTS]);
        REPEAT
           NUMELEMENTS := NUMELEMENTS + 1;
           WRITE('NUMBER TO SORT (9999 TO QUIT): ');
           READLN(LIST [NUMELEMENTS]);
        UNTIL (NUMELEMENTS = 100) OR (LIST [NUMELEMENTS] = 9999);
        NUMELEMENTS := NUMELEMENTS - 1;
    END;


PROCEDURE ESORT;

BEGIN
    FOR INDEXPOSITION := 1 TO NUMELEMENTS DO
        BEGIN
            CHANGEPOSITION := INDEXPOSITION;
            FOR INDEX := INDEXPOSITION + 1 TO NUMELEMENTS DO
                IF LIST [INDEX] < LIST [CHANGEPOSITION] THEN
                    CHANGEPOSITION := INDEX;
            IF CHANGEPOSITION <> INDEXPOSITION THEN
                BEGIN
                    TEMP := LIST [INDEXPOSITION];
                    LIST [INDEXPOSITION] :=
                                        LIST [CHANGEPOSITION];
                    LIST [CHANGEPOSITION] := TEMP;
                END;
        END;
END;

BEGIN {MAIN PROGRAM}
    LOADNUM;
    ESORT;
    FOR INDEX := 1 TO NUMELEMENTS DO
        WRITELN(LIST [INDEX]);
END.
```

Note that, in BASIC and Pascal, much of the exchange sort code is the same as the bubble sort code.

THE SHELL SORT

The *shell sort* is the fastest sort you have studied so far. An out-of-place value finds its ultimate home quickly because the shell sort can move the value farther than other sorts. The means to these long moves is the *gap*.

The gap is the distance between compared values. The shell sort begins with a big gap, comparing values that are far apart. The gap gets smaller as the sort continues. Eventually, the sort compares contiguous values just like the bubble sort.

Figure 8.3 shows an ascending shell sort. In pass 1 the value of the gap is 3. In passes 2 and 3, the value of the gap is 1. The boxed value in each comparison is the first value in the tested pair. As you can see, the values in the tested pair swap positions if the second value is lower than the first. The pseudocode for the ascending shell sort shown in Figure 8.3 looks like this:

```
GAP = ELEMENTS / 2
STEP = 1
NUMBER = ELEMENTS MINUS GAP
Repeat
   COUNTER = STEP
   Repeat
      NOEXCHANGE = TRUE
      OFFSET = COUNTER + GAP
      If ARRAY [OFFSET] < ARRAY [COUNTER] then
         TEMP = ARRAY [COUNTER]
         ARRAY [COUNTER] = ARRAY [OFFSET]
         ARRAY [OFFSET] = TEMP
         COUNTER = COUNTER MINUS GAP
         NOEXCHANGE = FALSE
```

Figure 8.3

An ascending shell sort

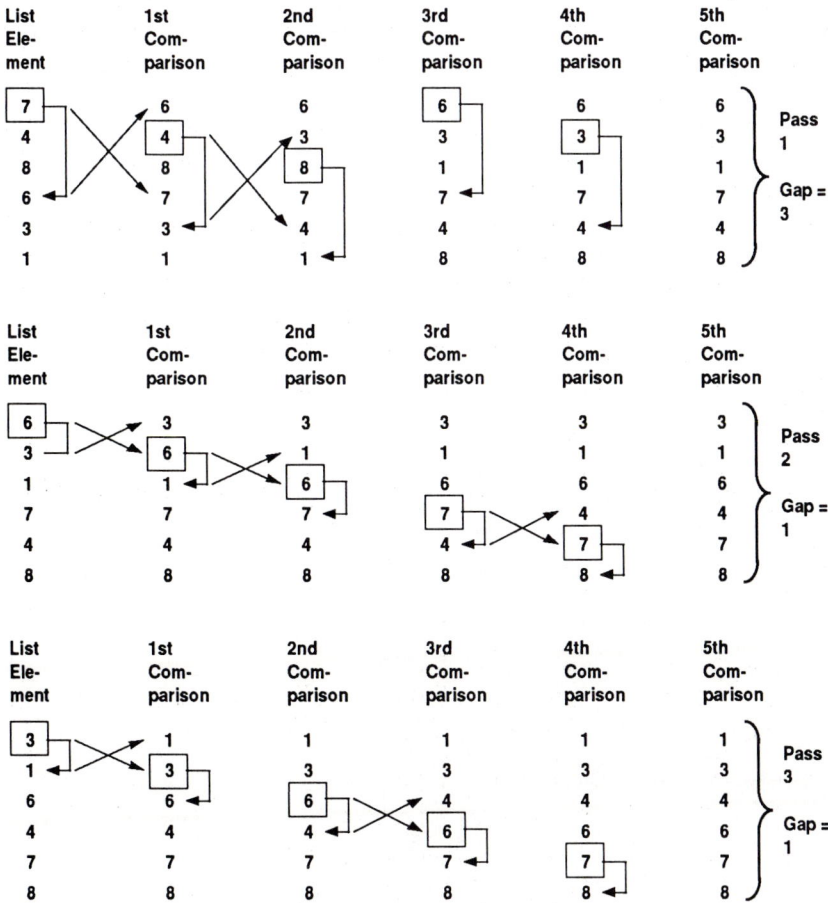

```
   End if
  Until COUNTER < 0 or NOEXCHANGE = TRUE
  STEP = STEP + 1
  If STEP > NUMBER then
    GAP = GAP / 2
    STEP = 1
    NUMBER = ELEMENTS MINUS GAP
  End if
Until GAP < 1
```

The BASIC code for the ascending shell sort shown in Figure 8.3 follows.

```
10 DIM L(100)
20 REM ENTER LIST OF NUMBERS TO SORT
30 E = 0
40 PRINT "NUMBER TO SORT (9999 TO QUIT): "
50 E = E + 1
60 INPUT L(E)
70 IF L(E) <> 9999 AND E < 100 GOTO 40
80 E = E - 1
90 REM SORT
100 G = INT(E / 2)
105 S = 1
110 N = E - G
120 WHILE G > 0
125    C = S
130    O = C + G
140    IF L(C) < L(O) THEN 170
150    GOSUB 300
160    C = C - G
165    IF C > 0 THEN 130
170    S = S + 1
175    IF S <= N   THEN 195
180    G = INT(G / 2)
185    S = 1
190    N = E - G
195 WEND
200 REM PRINT SORTED ARRAY
210 FOR X = 1 TO E
220    PRINT L(X);
230 NEXT X
240 PRINT
250 END
299 REM SWAP SUBROUTINE
300 T = L(O)
310 L(O) = L(C)
320 L(C) = T
340 RETURN
```

The Pascal code for the ascending shell sort shown in Figure 8.3 looks like this:

```
PROGRAM SHELLSORT(INPUT,OUTPUT);

VAR
    ELEMENTS : INTEGER;
```

```
      NUMBER : INTEGER;
      STEP : INTEGER;
      COUNTER : INTEGER;
      LIST : ARRAY [1..100] OF INTEGER;
      GAP : INTEGER;
      OFFSET : INTEGER;
      TEMP : INTEGER;
      NOEXCHANGE : BOOLEAN;

PROCEDURE LOADNUM;

BEGIN
   ELEMENTS := 1;
   WRITE('NUMBER TO SORT: ');
   READLN(LIST [ELEMENTS]);
   REPEAT
      ELEMENTS := ELEMENTS + 1;
      WRITE('NUMBER TO SORT (9999 TO QUIT): ');
      READLN(LIST [ELEMENTS]);
   UNTIL (ELEMENTS = 100) OR (LIST [ELEMENTS] = 9999);
   ELEMENTS := ELEMENTS - 1;
END;

PROCEDURE SSORT;

BEGIN
   GAP := TRUNC(ELEMENTS / 2);
   STEP := 1;
   NUMBER := ELEMENTS - GAP;
   REPEAT
      COUNTER := STEP;
      REPEAT
         NOEXCHANGE := TRUE;
         OFFSET := COUNTER + GAP;
         IF LIST [COUNTER] > LIST [OFFSET] THEN
            BEGIN
               TEMP := LIST [COUNTER];
               LIST [COUNTER] := LIST [OFFSET];
               LIST [OFFSET] := TEMP;
               COUNTER := COUNTER - GAP;
               NOEXCHANGE := FALSE;
            END;
      UNTIL (COUNTER < 1) OR NOEXCHANGE;
      STEP := STEP + 1;
      IF STEP > NUMBER THEN
         BEGIN
            GAP := TRUNC(GAP / 2);
            STEP := 1;
            NUMBER := ELEMENTS - GAP;
         END;
   UNTIL GAP < 1;
END;

BEGIN {MAIN PROGRAM}
   LOADNUM;
   SSORT;
```

```
        FOR COUNTER := 1 TO ELEMENTS DO
            WRITELN(LIST [COUNTER]);
    END.
```

THE QUICKSORT

The *quicksort* continually divides the list in half so that the routine sorts small groups instead of large groups. The quicksort routine described in this section makes three passes. Each pass divides each group in half until all groups are single numbers. As Figure 8.4 shows, each pass is the result of a division operation.

The pseudocode for Figure 8.4 follows. By studying the pseudocode, you can learn the calculations involved in each division.

```
STEPS:
1. Scan list of numbers
2. Determine lowest value
3. Determine highest value
4. MID = HIGH + LOW / 2
5. Place all lower to MID in one group
6. Place all higher than MID in second group

Take first group
Repeat steps 2 - 6 ABOVE

Repeat until all groups = 1

Take second group and repeat steps 2 - 6 until all groups = 1
```

See if you can develop a more sophisticated pseudocode for Figure 8.4 as well as a working BASIC or Pascal program. When implemented properly, the quicksort is the fastest of the sorts described in this chapter.

Figure 8.4

Results of each pass of an ascending quicksort

List Element	1st Pass	2nd Pass	3rd Pass
7	4	3	1
4	3	1	3
8	1	4	4
6	7	6	6
3	8	7	7
1	6	8	8

CASE STUDY: PAYROLL PROGRAM, SORTS

With a few modifications you can add sorting to the payroll program you have developed in preceding chapters.

Begin by adding this new option to the main menu:

```
SORT DATA = 7
```

When the user chooses the new option, the program branches to the sort module. The first part of the sort module branches control to the lower levels as needed. The pseudocode that follows describes the new sort module. Notice the use of the top-down programming technique.

```
Begin sort menu procedure
      1 - Sort by alpha A - Z
      2 - Sort by alpha Z - A
      3 - Sort by ytd high to low
      4 - Sort by payrate high - low
      5 - Sort by number of hours work high - low
      6 - Quit sort procedure
   Select now
Repeat
   If SELECTION = 1 then do ALPHAAZ sort procedure
      Else if SELECTION = 2 do ALPHAZA sort procedure
         Else if SELECTION = 3 do YTD HILO sort procedure
            Else if SELECTION = 4 do PAYRATE HILO sort procedure
               Else if SELECTION = 5 do #HRS HILO sort procedure
   Until SELECTION = 6
End sort menu procedure

Begin ALPHAAZ sort procedure
   For INDEX 1 = 1 to #ELEMENTS MINUS 1
      INDEX 2 = INDEX 1 + 1
      If NAME [INDEX 2] < NAME [INDEX 1] of EXCHANGE
                              procedure (INDEX 1,INDEX 2)
   Next INDEX 1
End ALPHAAZ sort procedure

Begin ALPHAZA sort procedure
   For INDEX 1 = 1 to #ELEMENTS MINUS 1
      INDEX 2 = INDEX 1 + 1
      IF NAME [INDEX 2] > NAME [INDEX 1] do EXCHANGE
                              procedure (INDEX 1,INDEX 2)
   Next INDEX 1
End ALPHAZA sort procedure

Begin YTD HILO sort procedure
   For INDEX 1 = 1 to #ELEMENTS MINUS 1
      INDEX 2 = INDEX 1 + 1
      If YTD [INDEX 1] > YTD [INDEX 2] do EXCHANGE procedure
                                    (INDEX 1,INDEX 2)
```

```
      Next INDEX 1
End YTD HILO sort procedure

Begin PAYRATE HILO sort procedure
   For INDEX 1 = 1 to #ELEMENTS MINUS 1
      INDEX 2 = INDEX 1 + 1
      If PAYRATE [INDEX 1] > PAYRATE [INDEX 2] do EXCHANGE
                                 procedure (INDEX 1,INDEX 2)
   Next INDEX 1
End PAYRATE HILO sort procedure

Begin #HRS HILO sort procedure
   For INDEX 1 = 1 to #ELEMENTS MINUS 1
      INDEX 2 = INDEX 1 + 1
      If hours work [INDEX 1] > hours work [INDEX 2] do
                        EXCHANGE procedure (INDEX 1,INDEX 2)
   Next INDEX 1
End #HRS HILO sort procedure
```

CASE STUDY: MAILING LIST

A regional newspaper, *The Insurance Paper,* has a huge database of the names and addresses of 21,000 subscribers and prospective subscribers. The database program must sort on name and ZIP code for different operations and reports. A complete sort would be inefficient for this file because each record contains twenty fields. Thus, you must implement an index sort.

To make the problem simpler, suppose that each record consists of the six fields: NAME, ID, STREET ADDRESS, CITY, STATE, ZIP.

Pseudocode for the sort menu follows.

```
1. Sort by name A-Z
2. Sort by ZIP LOHI
3. End sort procedure

Begin NAME AZ sort procedure
    NOEXCHANGE = TRUE
    Repeat
        For INDEX 1 = 1 to NUMBER OF RECORDS - 1
            INDEX 2 = INDEX 1 + 1
            If NAME [INDEX 1] > NAME [INDEX 2] then
                Exchange pointer positions
                NOEXCHANGE = FALSE
    Until NOEXCHANGE = TRUE
End NAME AZ sort procedure

Begin ZIP LOHI sort procedure
    NOEXCHANGE = TRUE
    Repeat
        For INDEX 1 = 1 to NUMBER OF RECORDS MINUS 1
            INDEX 2 = INDEX 1 + 1
```

```
         If ZIP [INDEX 1] > ZIP [INDEX 2] then
            Exchange pointer positions
               NOEXCHANGE = FALSE
      Until NOEXCHANGE = TRUE
End ZIP LOHI sort procedure
```

The point is that once you understand sorting it makes little difference where it is used. All you need to know is where the data come from, what type of data are to be sorted, how the data are to be sorted, and where they go once the sort is over.

MERGES

Up until this point you have been dealing with arrays that need to be reordered according to one criteria or another. This reordering is often a preliminary step toward a processing module that performs *merging*. Merging combines two lists into a single list.

Appends

The easiest merge technique is to simply add new items to the end of an old list. This is called *appending*. When this technique is used, the two lists are appended and then sorted or reindexed into the correct order. Figure 8.5 shows an append and sort.

True Merges

Many applications use the merge to update files. In this situation a *true merge* is needed. A true merge takes two sorted lists and combines them on a case-by-case basis. The result is a new list in sorted order.

The true merge begins with two lists that are sorted according to the same key field. Suppose both lists contain names sorted in alphabetic order.

The program must take the first record from each file and determine which goes first. Figure 8.6 shows this first comparison.

Figure 8.5

An append and sort

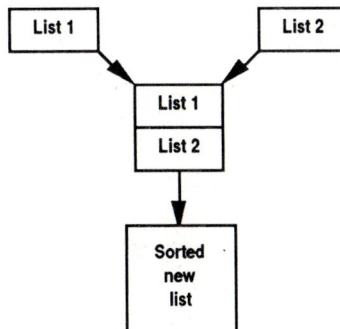

There are three options in a true merge:

- List 1 > List 2. If ADAIR precedes AARON, ADAIR is placed on the new list and the next name on List 1, BAIN, is accessed.
- List 2 < List 1. If AARON precedes ADAIR, AARON is placed on the new list and the next name on List 2, ADAIR, is accessed.
- List 1 = List 2. If ADAIR is the same as AARON, then ADAIR is added to the new list and the next names on List 1 and List 2, BAIN and ADAIR, are accessed.

In this case List 2 < List 1; AARON precedes ADAIR. Therefore, AARON is placed on the new list, and the next name on List 2 is accessed.

In the second comparison in this true merge, the names are ADAIR and ADAIR. This time List 1 = List 2. Thus, ADAIR is added to the list, and the next names on both lists are accessed. The next comparison is between BAIN and BAKER.

This process continues until you run out of names on List 1, List 2, or both at the same time. If List 1 finishes first, then the rest of List 2 is added to the end of the new list. If List 2 finishes first, then the rest of List 1 is added to the end of the new list. If both lists end at the same time, then the new list is complete.

Thus, at the end of the run, the new list consists of AARON, ADAIR, BAIN, BAKER, CARTER, DAVIS, and LEWIS. The pseudocode that follows outlines this true merge in detail.

```
TOTAL1 = Number of items in first array
TOTAL2 = Number of items in second array
Create DESTINATION_ARRAY with a size of TOTAL1 + TOTAL2
COUNTER1 = 0
COUNTER2 = 0
COUNTER3 = 0

While COUNTER1 < TOTAL1 and COUNTER2 < TOTAL2 do
    If ARRAY1 [COUNTER1 + 1] < ARRAY2 [COUNTER2 + 1] then
```

Figure 8.6

First comparison of a true merge

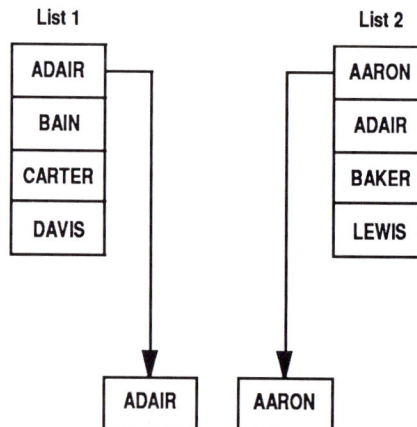

```
            COUNTER1 = COUNTER1 + 1
            COUNTER3 = COUNTER3 + 1
            DESTINATION_ARRAY [COUNTER3] = ARRAY1 [COUNTER1]
        Else
            COUNTER2 = COUNTER2 + 1
            COUNTER3 = COUNTER3 + 1
            DESTINATION_ARRAY [COUNTER3] = ARRAY2 [COUNTER2]
        End if
End while

If COUNTER1 < TOTAL1 then
    For INDEX = COUNTER1 + 1 to TOTAL1
        COUNTER3 = COUNTER3 + 1
        DESTINATION_ARRAY [COUNTER3] = ARRAY1 [INDEX]
    Next INDEX
Else
    For INDEX = COUNTER2 + 1 to TOTAL2
        COUNTER3 = COUNTER3 + 1
        DESTINATION_ARRAY [COUNTER3] = ARRAY2 [INDEX]
    Next INDEX
End if
```

The pseudocode calls for the program to begin by setting to 0 the element counters of each array to be merged. The program then compares the items pointed to by the element counter + 1. The program selects the lower value. The element counter in the selected array is incremented, and the array element pointed to by the element counter is copied to the destination array. If the value of the element counter matches the total number of items in that array, the first phase of the merge has been completed. The next step is to copy all the items in the array that has not already been completely transferred to the destination array. The merge is now completed.

The BASIC and Pascal implementations of the preceding pseudocode include routines to load the arrays to be merged. (Real-life programs usually merge files, not arrays, and you will find that merging files is easier.) In BASIC or Pascal, be sure the numeric values are in ascending order; otherwise, the merge will not work correctly.

The BASIC code that follows merges two arrays into a third array in ascending order.

```
10  REM ARRAY 1 AND 2
20  DIM A1(100)
30  DIM A2(100)
40  T1 = 0
50  INPUT "ITEM FOR ARRAY 1:";I
60  WHILE I <> 9999 AND T1 <= 100
70      T1 = T1 + 1
80      A1(T1) = I
90      INPUT "ITEM FOR ARRAY 1 (9999 TO QUIT):";I
100 WEND
110 T2 = 0
120 INPUT "ITEM FOR ARRAY 2:";I
130 WHILE I <> 9999 AND T2 <= 100
140     T2 = T2 + 1
150     A2(T2) = I
```

```
160    INPUT "ITEM FOR ARRAY 2 (9999 TO QUIT):";I
170 WEND
180 REM MERGE
190 DIM A3(T1 + T2)
200 C1 = 0
210 C2 = 0
220 C3 = 0
230 WHILE C1 < T1 AND C2 < T2
240    IF A2(C2 + 1) < A1(C1 + 1) THEN 290
250    C1 = C1 + 1
260    C3 = C3 + 1
270    A3(C3) = A1(C1)
280    GOTO 320
290    C2 = C2 + 1
300    C3 = C3 + 1
310    A3(C3) = A2(C2)
320 WEND
330 IF C2 < T2 THEN 390
340 FOR I = C1 + 1 TO T1
350    C3 = C3 + 1
360    A3(C3) = A1(I)
370 NEXT I
380 GOTO 440
390 FOR I = C2 + 1 TO T2
400    C3 = C3 + 1
410    A3(C3) = A2(I)
420 NEXT I
430 REM PRINT RESULTING MERGED ARRAY
440 FOR I = 1 TO C3
450    PRINT A3(I);
460 NEXT I
470 PRINT
480 END
```

The Pascal code that follows implements the ascending merge of two arrays.

```
PROGRAM MERGE(INPUT,OUTPUT);
VAR
   ARRAY1,
   ARRAY2 : ARRAY [1..100] OF INTEGER;
   ARRAY3 : ARRAY [1..200] OF INTEGER;
   COUNTER1,
   COUNTER2,
   COUNTER3,
   INDEX,
   TOTAL1,
   TOTAL2,
   ITEM : INTEGER;

PROCEDURE LOAD1;
BEGIN
   TOTAL1 := 0;
   WRITE('ITEM FOR ARRAY 1: ');
   READLN(ITEM);
   WHILE (ITEM <> 9999) AND (TOTAL1 < 100) DO
      BEGIN
```

```
                 TOTAL1 := TOTAL1 + 1;
                 ARRAY1 [TOTAL1] := ITEM;
                 WRITE('ITEM FOR ARRAY 1 (9999 TO QUIT): ');
                 READLN(ITEM);
            END;
   END;


PROCEDURE LOAD2;
BEGIN
      TOTAL2 := 0;
      WRITE('ITEM FOR ARRAY 2: ');
      READLN(ITEM);
      WHILE (ITEM <> 9999) AND (TOTAL2 < 100) DO
         BEGIN
             TOTAL2 := TOTAL2 + 1;
             ARRAY2 [TOTAL2] := ITEM;
             WRITE('ITEM FOR ARRAY 2 (9999 TO QUIT): ');
             READLN(ITEM);
         END;
   END;


PROCEDURE MERGE_ARRAY;
BEGIN
      COUNTER1 := 0;
      COUNTER2 := 0;
      COUNTER3 := 0;
      WHILE (COUNTER1 < TOTAL1) AND (COUNTER2 < TOTAL2) DO
         BEGIN
            IF ARRAY1 [COUNTER1 + 1] < ARRAY2 [COUNTER2 + 1] THEN
                  BEGIN
                      COUNTER1 := COUNTER1 + 1;
                      COUNTER3 := COUNTER3 + 1;
                      ARRAY3 [COUNTER3] := ARRAY1 [COUNTER1];
                  END
            ELSE
                  BEGIN
                      COUNTER2 := COUNTER2 + 1;
                      COUNTER3 := COUNTER3 + 1;
                      ARRAY3 [COUNTER3] := ARRAY2 [COUNTER2];
                  END;
         END;
         IF COUNTER1 < TOTAL1 THEN
            BEGIN
                  FOR INDEX := COUNTER1 + 1 TO TOTAL1 DO
                      BEGIN
                          COUNTER3 := COUNTER3 + 1;
                          ARRAY3 [COUNTER3] := ARRAY1 [INDEX];
                      END;
            END
         ELSE
            BEGIN
                  FOR INDEX := COUNTER2 + 1 TO TOTAL2 DO
```

```
                              BEGIN
                                  COUNTER3 := COUNTER3 + 1;
                                  ARRAY3 [COUNTER3] := ARRAY2 [INDEX];
                              END;
                   END;
        END;

        BEGIN {MAIN PROGRAM}
           LOAD1;
           LOAD2;
           MERGE_ARRAY;
           { DISPLAY RESULTS OF MERGE }
           FOR INDEX := 1 TO COUNTER3 DO
              WRITE(ARRAY3 [INDEX]:8);
           WRITELN;
        END.
```

The next chapter discusses file processing. In that chapter you must use the sort and merge techniques explained in this chapter. Make sure you thoroughly understand sorting and merging before moving on.

SUMMARY

This chapter introduces the bubble sort, exchange sort, shell sort, and quicksort. The first three are similar, with minor differences in the control code lines. The last requires a more complex pseudocode solution. Sorting is an essential routine. It allows the rearrangement of data so that various end-users can view it in their own ways.

This chapter also introduces merging. There are two types of merges, the append and the true merge. The append combines two lists into a new one and then sorts if necessary. The true merge begins with two sorted lists and combines them in a new sorted list.

Key Terms

Appending	Merging
Bubble sort	Pass
Exchange sort	Quicksort
Gap	Shell sort
Julian date	True merge

Review Questions

1. How are the bubble and shell sort similar? How are they different?

2. How are the bubble and the exchange sort similar? How are they different?

3. How do you change a sort from ascending to descending?

4. How do numeric and alphanumeric sort routines differ?

5. Why are indexes used instead of sorts?

6. What are the types of merging and how do they differ?

1. Expand the pseudocode for the quicksort to show all details.

2. Code the quicksort created in assignment 1.

3. Code the sort module discussed in the payroll case study.

4. Code the mailing list discussed in the mailing list case study.

5. Expand the *Insurance Paper* sort menu and code the pseudocode. Send trial data through the program to test it.

6. Given the two lists that follow, create an append sort routine that provides a new list sorted by last name. Use top-down modular design techniques to create pseudocode for the problem. Once you are satisfied that your pseudocode is correct, code the solution.

List 1

Name	City/Town	State
ADAIR	MANLIUS	NY
BAKER	WYOMING	OH
CARTER	EL CAJON	CA
DAVIS	GRANVILLE	OH
ELBA	LANCASTER	CA
ZINZER	NEWTON	MA

List 2

Name	City/Town	State
AARON	NICHOLS HILLS	OK
BAIN	CAMBRIDGE	MA
DAVIS	GRANVILLE	OH
MANTEE	ALBUQUERQUE	NM
WINGER	TOPEKA	KA

7. Merge two unordered lists. Mix up the items on the lists given in assignment 6. Then add a sort routine prior to the merge in your pseudocode.

8. Append list 1 to list 2, then sort. In this assignment, you must account for duplicates. How do you do this?

9

Files

Files are collections of related material. Some files contain executable code; others contain data used by programs. This discussion of file processing considers data file processing.

One of the hardest things about file processing is that different language implementations frequently use different disk I/O commands. This is especially true of BASIC and Pascal. Obviously, this book can't show all the implementations. However, this chapter does present examples of the most popular versions of BASIC and Pascal for the microcomputer. The BASIC versions discussed are Microsoft interpreted BASIC, as provided for microcomputers and supplied with MS-DOS, and GWBASIC for IBM compatibles. The Pascal version discussed is Borland's Turbo Pascal release 4.0 for IBM microcomputers and compatibles. If you are using a different version of either language, the pseudocode shown here applies, but you will have to modify the program code.

In this book so far, all data have been stored as variables and arrays in memory. This was fine for discussions but not very practical for real programs. In the examples that follow, files are more appropriate than variables and arrays.

- A payroll program requiring a list of employees and their deductions and keeping a history of payments made to date during the current year.

- An inventory program requiring a list of all the items in stock, their quantities, price, and so forth.

- A word processing program having a dictionary for checking spelling as well as a thesaurus.

- A point-of-sale program requiring an inventory list and sometimes a customer list. The program usually retains a record of all the sales transactions for some period of time.

- An accounting program keeping a record of the income and expenses for the current year.

- A computer-assisted drawing (CAD) program generating a file containing a drawing.

These are just a few examples of the types of programs that use data files. There are many, many more.

TYPES OF FILES

There are two main types of files: sequential and random access. Each has advantages and disadvantages.

Sequential Files

In a *sequential file* the data are stored in serial order. As each item is put in the file, the item is positioned immediately following the previous item. No space separates them. The items can be surrounded by delimiters, usually commas or quotation marks, so that the program reading the file can distinguish them. Sometimes, all the items are of the same type and the same length, permitting the program reading the file to separate them by their size. In some cases, paragraphs of text can be separated by carriage returns (ASCII 13); pages can be separated with the form-feed character (ASCII 12). As long as the program reading the file can interpret the data correctly, any separation scheme can be used.

One advantage of sequential files is that they do not waste file space, since all the data are stored without gaps between the items. Any type of data—numeric, Boolean, or character—can be stored in a sequential file. You can mix types together if you desire.

Sequential files are ideal for blocks of text, such as documents, and for lists of data that will be read into an array when the program needs them.

The main disadvantage of sequential files is that you cannot access a specific item in the file by moving directly to it. Since the items in the file are theoretically of different sizes and types, the computer has no way of knowing where an item will be found. For example, the fifth value in a file can only be found by starting at the beginning of the file and reading the file until the item is found or the end of the file is reached. This is how the sequential search described in Chapter 7 works.

As you can see, you cannot conveniently delete an item from the middle of a sequential file or make any changes to the item. Theoretically, if the requested change does not change the item's length, the change should be allowed. In reality, in most cases the language designer has already decided that no changes are permitted. However, the designers of some languages or versions trust the programmer's good sense and permit changes. An example of a language that gives the programmer great freedom (to get into trouble) is C.

Whatever the language, when you write to a sequential file, the writing process usually starts at the beginning of the file. The file's prior contents are replaced by the new data. Thus, you wipe out the previous contents. The danger of losing needed data when writing to a sequential file is one reason for having a backup of the file. Most languages now also permit you to append data to an existing file.

Random-Access Files

When a random-access file is created, record sizes and, usually, field sizes are specified. The data items are then stored in records and subdivided into fields if required. Sometimes, the record consists of a single field. Records are designated by consecutive numbers, starting with 0 or 1, depending on the language implementation. Since the record size is known, the computer can access any record by multiplying the record number by the record size, advancing that number of bytes into the file, and retrieving the entire record from the file. This is done either by system software or by the language itself. The user normally needs only to request a specific record; they need not be concerned with how retrieval takes place.

Storing data in a random-access file is slightly more complicated. The record number where the data is to be written must be specified. If the record is divided into fields, the programmer must indicate which portion of the record belongs in which field. Sometimes, the programmer must decide if the data is to be right- or left-justified within the field's allocated space. Any data previously in that record location will be overwritten when the storing operation takes place. In spite of this, deleting or changing the contents of any record is a relatively simple matter.

Of course, all this flexibility has disadvantages as well. The major disadvantage is that the record size specified must be large enough to hold the longest item(s) expected; for all shorter items record (disk) space will be wasted. Also, some language versions permit only character data in random-access files; one of these versions is Microsoft BASIC. Functions are provided to convert numeric values to characters for file storage and back to numeric values when used by the program; however, the extra steps can be a nuisance.

SEQUENTIAL FILE EXAMPLE

This example is a simple one. The goal is to copy a numeric array to a sequential file, erase the array, and copy the file back into the array. The pseudocode that follows shows the necessary routines.

```
Create ARRAY for 10 numeric values
Create SEQUENTIAL FILE to hold ARRAY
SIZE = Number of elements in ARRAY

REM Save ARRAY
Open SEQUENTIAL FILE for writing
For INDEX = 1 to SIZE
    Write ARRAY [INDEX] to FILE
```

```
Next INDEX
Close SEQUENTIAL FILE

REM Erase ARRAY
For INDEX = 1 to SIZE
    ARRAY [INDEX] = 0
Next INDEX

REM Load ARRAY
Open SEQUENTIAL FILE for reading
For INDEX = 1 to SIZE
    Read ARRAY [INDEX] from SEQUENTIAL FILE
Next INDEX
Close SEQUENTIAL FILE
```

The same routines work for a character array; just change the array and variable types to character.

The BASIC and Pascal segments that follow include the code to load the array and print it and/or the file after each step, so you can see that the program does indeed work. The BASIC implementation of the pseudocode looks like this:

```
10 DIM A(10)
20 S = 10
30 REM LOAD ARRAY
40 FOR I = 1 TO S
50    INPUT "NUMBER FOR ARRAY: ",A(I)
60 NEXT I
70 PRINT "TRANSFERRING ARRAY TO FILE"
80 OPEN "O",1,"TESTFILE"
90 FOR I = 1 TO S
100    WRITE #1, A(I)
110 NEXT I
120 CLOSE 1
130 PRINT "HERE'S THE CONTENTS OF THE ARRAY"
140 FOR I = 1 TO S
150    PRINT A(I);
160 NEXT I
170 PRINT
180 PRINT "HERE'S THE CONTENTS OF THE FILE"
190 OPEN "I",1,"TESTFILE"
200 FOR I = 1 TO S
210    INPUT #1,X
220    PRINT X;
230 NEXT I
240 PRINT
250 CLOSE 1
260 PRINT "THE ARRAY HAS BEEN ERASED"
270 FOR I = 1 TO S
280    A(I) = 0
290    PRINT A(I);
300 NEXT I
310 PRINT
320 PRINT "TRANSFERRING THE FILE BACK TO THE ARRAY"
```

```
330 OPEN "I",1,"TESTFILE"
340 FOR I = 1 TO S
350     INPUT #1,A(I)
360 NEXT I
370 PRINT
380 CLOSE 1
390 PRINT "THE ARRAY NOW CONTAINS: "
400 FOR I = 1 TO S
410     PRINT A(I);
420 NEXT I
430 PRINT
```

In the OPEN commands in lines 80, 190, and 330, the first argument determines whether the file is to be written to or read from. The "O" stands for output, which writes from the CPU to the disk drive. "I" stands for input, which reads from the disk drive to the CPU. The second argument, 1, is the file number. Each open file must be assigned a different number; that is, two files cannot be opened with the same number at the same time. A file can have a different number each time it is opened. The number can be contained in a numeric variable. (The number of open files permitted depends on a number of conditions that are too MS-DOS specific to delve into here.) The last argument is the name of the file. The file name can be stored in a variable if desired.

Note how the file is always closed when the program has finished working with it. It is necessary to close a file when switching from reading to writing or vice versa. It is also necessary to close the file if you wish to start reading or writing again from the beginning. The WRITE # and INPUT # commands, which write to and read from the sequential file, must include the file number. If the CLOSE command does not include a file number, all open files will be closed.

Here's the same program in Pascal.

```
PROGRAM SFILE(INPUT,OUTPUT);

VAR
    SIZE,
    X,
    INDEX : INTEGER;
    LIST : ARRAY [1..10] OF INTEGER;
    ARRAY_FILE : FILE OF INTEGER;

PROCEDURE CREATEFILE;
BEGIN
    ASSIGN(ARRAY_FILE,'TESTFILE');
    REWRITE(ARRAY_FILE);
    CLOSE(ARRAY_FILE);
END;

PROCEDURE LOADVALUES;
BEGIN
    FOR INDEX := 1 TO SIZE DO
```

```
                    BEGIN
                        WRITE('NUMBER FOR ARRAY: ');
                        READ(LIST [INDEX]);
                    END;
        END;

        PROCEDURE SAVEARRAY;
        BEGIN
            RESET(ARRAY_FILE);
            FOR INDEX := 1 TO SIZE DO
                WRITE(ARRAY_FILE,LIST [INDEX]);
            CLOSE(ARRAY_FILE);
        END;

        PROCEDURE SHOWARRAY;
        BEGIN
            FOR INDEX := 1 TO SIZE DO
                WRITE(LIST [INDEX]:8);
            WRITELN;
        END;

        PROCEDURE SHOWFILE;
        BEGIN
            RESET(ARRAY_FILE);
            FOR INDEX := 1 TO SIZE DO
                BEGIN
                    READ(ARRAY_FILE,X);
                    WRITE(X:8);
                END;
            WRITELN;
            CLOSE(ARRAY_FILE);
        END;

        PROCEDURE ERASEARRAY;
        BEGIN
            FOR INDEX := 1 TO SIZE DO
                LIST [INDEX] := 0;
        END;

        PROCEDURE GETARRAY;
        BEGIN
            RESET(ARRAY_FILE);
            FOR INDEX := 1 TO SIZE DO
                READ(ARRAY_FILE,LIST [INDEX]);
            CLOSE(ARRAY_FILE);
        END;

        BEGIN {MAIN PROGRAM}
            SIZE := 10;
            CREATEFILE;
            LOADVALUES;
            WRITELN('TRANSFERRING ARRAY TO FILE');
            SAVEARRAY;
            WRITELN('HERE''S THE CONTENTS OF THE ARRAY');
            SHOWARRAY;
            WRITELN('HERE''S THE CONTENTS OF THE FILE');
```

```
    SHOWFILE;
    ERASEARRAY;
    WRITELN('THE ARRAY HAS BEEN ERASED');
    SHOWARRAY;
    WRITELN('TRANSFERRING THE FILE BACK TO THE ARRAY');
    GETARRAY;
    WRITELN('THE ARRAY NOW CONTAINS:');
    SHOWARRAY;
END.
```

The ASSIGN command is used to equate a disk file name, in this case TESTFILE, to a variable of type FILE or ARRAY_FILE. The REWRITE command is used to create and open a new file; the RESET command opens an existing file.

RANDOM-ACCESS EXAMPLE

The random-access file is slightly more difficult to work with. This example expands on the inventory program introduced in Chapter 7. As much as possible, the structures shown in Chapter 7 are left intact so you can easily compare the differences.

```
Begin inventory program
     Do INITIALIZE procedure
     Do DATAIN procedure
     Begin loop
          If PART ID # SEARCH then
               Do binary search procedure
          If NAME SEARCH then
               Do sequential search procedure
          If INPUT DATA then
               Do database procedure
          If CREATE FILE
               Do create file procedure
          If QUIT PROGRAM then
               Terminate program
     End loop
End inventory program

Begin initialize procedure
     Name variables and declare their type
     Assign initial values
End initialize procedure

Begin create file procedure
     Create file
End create file procedure

Begin database procedure
     Read in ID #, name, quantity, and cost of items in inventory
End database procedure
```

```
Begin DATAIN procedure
      Set up menu for 1 - PART ID # SEARCH
                       2 - NAME SEARCH
                       3 - INPUT DATA
                       4 - CREATE FILE
                       5 - QUIT PROGRAM
      Enter choice
End DATAIN procedure

Begin binary search procedure
      Enter ID # to search for
      Set FIRST to number of first record
      Set LAST to number of ITEMS in inventory (subtract 1 if FIRST is 0)
      Set FOUND to FALSE
      While NOT FOUND and LAST > FIRST do
            MIDDLE = (FIRST + LAST) / 2
            Move to RECORD AT MIDDLE position in file
            If ID # searched for > RECORD AT MIDDLE then
                  FIRST = MIDDLE + 1
            If ID # searched for < RECORD AT MIDDLE then
                 LAST = MIDDLE MINUS 1
            If ID # searched for = RECORD AT MIDDLE then
                 FOUND = TRUE
      End while
      If FOUND then
            Print data about item
      Else
            Print "ITEM NOT FOUND"
End binary search procedure

Begin sequential search procedure
      Read in item name to search for
      Set FOUND to FALSE
      Set INDEX to first record number
      Move to first record in file
      While not FOUND and end of file not reached do
            If item name to find = RECORD # INDEX then
                  Set FOUND to TRUE
            Else
                  Set INDEX to INDEX + 1
            Move to next record
      End while
      If FOUND then
            Print name, ID #, quantity, and cost of item
      Else
            Print "ITEM NOT FOUND"
End sequential search procedure
```

Remember, enter the items in the order of their I.D. numbers. The program does not sort the records, and they must be in order for the binary search to work. You might wish to rewrite the program to include an I.D. number index so the program can search the index instead of the file. You can create the index in an array as described in Chapter 7 and save the array to the disk as a sequential file, as illustrated earlier in this chapter.

Inventory is spelled "INVENTRY" as a file name because the disk operating system used does not accept file names over eight characters long.

Here is the BASIC version of the random-access inventory pseudocode.

```
10 OPEN "R",1,"INVENTRY.DAT",32
20 FIELD 1, 4 AS ID$,20 AS DESCRIPTION$,4 AS QUANTITY$, 4 AS COST$
30 I = 0
40 PRINT "INPUT ID (9999 TO QUIT): ";
50 INPUT ID
60 WHILE ID <> 9999
70   PRINT "INPUT NAME: ";
80   INPUT D$
90   PRINT "INPUT QUANTITY: ";
100   INPUT Q
110   PRINT "INPUT COST: ";
120   INPUT C
130   I = I + 1
140   GOSUB 5000
150   PRINT "INPUT ID (9999 TO QUIT): ";
160   INPUT ID
170 WEND
180 T = LOF(1)/32
1000 CLS:PRINT " INVENTORY PROGRAM FOR FUN FANTASIES"
1010 PRINT
1020 PRINT
1030 PRINT "WHICH DO YOU CHOOSE?"
1040 PRINT
1050 PRINT "     SEARCH BY PART NUMBER= 1"
1060 PRINT "     SEARCH BY NAME       = 2"
1070 PRINT "     TO QUIT              = 3"
1080 PRINT
1090 PRINT "CHOOSE NOW: "
1100 INPUT X
1110 ON X GOSUB 2000,3000,4000
1120 GOTO 1000
2000 REM BINARY SEARCH FOR ID NUMBER
2010 REM
2020 CLS:PRINT "ENTER ID TO SEARCH FOR: ";
2030 INPUT IC
2040 F1 = 1
2050 L1 = T
2060 F = 0
2070 WHILE L1 >= F1 AND F = 0
2080   M = INT((F1 + L1) / 2)
2090   GET 1,M
2100   IF IC > CVS(ID$) THEN F1 = M + 1
2110   IF IC < CVS(ID$) THEN L1 = M - 1
2120   IF IC = CVS(ID$) THEN F = 1
2130 WEND
2140 IF F = 1 THEN PRINT CVS(ID$),DESCRIPTION$,CVS (QUANTITY$),CVS (COST$)
2150 IF F = 0 THEN PRINT "ITEM NOT FOUND - PLEASE TRY AGAIN"
2160 RETURN
3000 REM SEQUENTIAL SEARCH FOR NAME
3010 REM
```

```
3020 CLS:PRINT "ENTER NAME TO LOOK FOR: ";
3030 INPUT D1$
3040 F = 0
3050 I = 1
3060 WHILE F = 0 AND I <= T
3070 GET 1,I
3080 IF D1$ + SPACE$(LEN(DESCRIPTION$) - LEN(D1$)) = DESCRIPTION$ THEN F = 1
     ELSE I = I + 1
3090 WEND
3100 IF F = 1 THEN PRINT CVS(ID$),DESCRIPTION$,CVS (QUANTITY$),CVS (COST$)
3110 IF F = 0 THEN PRINT "ITEM NOT FOUND - PLEASE TRY AGAIN"
3120 RETURN
4000 REM TERMINATION PROCEDURE
4010 REM
4020 CLOSE 1
4030 END
5000 REM SAVE INVENTORY RECORD TO FILE
5010 LSET ID$ = MKS$(ID)
5020 LSET DESCRIPTION$ = D$
5030 LSET QUANTITY$ = MKS$(Q)
5040 LSET COST$ = MKS$(C)
5050 PUT 1,I
5060 RETURN
```

The N\$ and N1\$ variables were changed to D\$, DESCRIPTION\$, and D1\$ because NAME is a reserved word and cannot be used for a variable name. The MKS\$ functions in lines 5010, 5030, and 5040 convert the numeric values to four-byte strings for the file. The CVS functions found here and there convert those strings back to numerics. Remember, Microsoft BASIC will not accept numeric variables in a random-access file.

The LSET commands in lines 5010 through 5040 place the variables in the fielded positions (line 20) in the record. The L in LSET means left justify.

The R in the OPEN statement (line 10) stands for random access; the 32 at the end of the line is the record size. The 32 was calculated as the total of field sizes in the FIELD statement in line 20.

A statement like GET 1,M means get the field values assigned to record number M from the file opened with the file number 1. PUT works the same way, but it puts the LSET and/or RSET fields into the record position.

The contortions in line 3080 are necessary to add spaces to the name being searched for so it matches the name in the field. The name is right-padded with spaces as necessary to fill a 20-byte field (line 20). The string comparison operator includes trailing spaces in the strings being compared. Another alternative is to delete the trailing spaces from DESCRIPTION\$.

```
WHILE RIGHT$(DESCRIPTION$,1) = " "
   DESCRIPTIONS$ = LEFT$(DESCRIPTION$,LEN(DESCRIPTION$) - 1)
WEND
```

CLS means clear the screen.

Finally, in line 180 the function LOF(1) (last of file 1) returns the number of bytes stored in the file assigned the number 1. The 32 is the number of bytes in the record. By dividing LOF(1) by 32, the number of records in the file is assigned to T. This is done so that the program can be run again once items are placed in the file. Just enter 9999 for the first ID number on subsequent program runs. Unfortunately, you can't add new records on a subsequent run with this program. However, one small change (two lines) would enable you to do so. Can you figure out what the change would be?

The Pascal version of the random-access inventory program looks like this:

```
PROGRAM RAINVENTORY(INPUT,OUTPUT);
USES CRT;
TYPE
   INVENTORY = RECORD
      NAME : STRING[20];
      ID : INTEGER;
      QUANTITY : INTEGER;
      COST : REAL;
   END;

VAR
   NAME : STRING[20];
   INV : INVENTORY;
   ID : INTEGER;
   DONE : BOOLEAN;
   RESPONSE : INTEGER;
   ANS : CHAR;
   INDEX : LONGINT;
   SPACE : LONGINT;
   WANTID : INTEGER;
   WANT : STRING[20];
   MID : LONGINT;
   LAST : LONGINT;
   FIRST : LONGINT;
   FOUND : BOOLEAN;
   LIST : FILE OF INVENTORY;

PROCEDURE CREATEFILE;
BEGIN
   ASSIGN(LIST,'INVENTRY.DAT');
   REWRITE(LIST);
   CLOSE(LIST);
END;

PROCEDURE DATABASE;
BEGIN
   ASSIGN(LIST,'INVENTRY.DAT');
   RESET(LIST);
   INDEX := FILESIZE(LIST) - 1;
   WRITE('ENTER ID # FOR INVENTORY ITEM: ');
   READLN(ID);
   WHILE ID <> 9999 DO
      BEGIN
         INV.ID := ID;
         FOR SPACE := 1 TO 20 DO
```

```
              INV.NAME[SPACE] := ' ';
          WRITE('ENTER ITEM NAME: ');
          READLN(INV.NAME);
          WRITELN;
          WRITE('ENTER ITEM QUANTITY: ');
          READLN(INV.QUANTITY);
          WRITE('ENTER ITEM COST: ');
          READLN(INV.COST);
          INDEX := INDEX + 1;
          SEEK(LIST,INDEX);
          WRITE(LIST,INV);
          WRITELN('ENTER ID # FOR INVENTORY ITEM');
          WRITE('ENTER 9999 TO STOP ');
          READLN(ID);
        END; {WHILE}
        CLOSE(LIST);
END; {INVENTORY DATABASE READING PROCEDURE}


PROCEDURE NAMEIN;
BEGIN {INVENTORY ITEM TO SEARCH FOR PROCEDURE}
   FOR SPACE := 1 TO 20 DO
      WANT[SPACE] := ' ';
   WRITE('ENTER ITEM NAME: ');
   READLN(WANT);
END; {INVENTORY ITEM TO SEARCH FOR PROCEDURE}


PROCEDURE SEQUENCE;
BEGIN {SEQUENTIAL SEARCH PROCEDURE}
   ASSIGN(LIST,'INVENTRY.DAT');
   RESET(LIST);
   NAMEIN;
   FOUND := FALSE;
   SPACE := 0;
   SEEK(LIST,SPACE);
   WHILE NOT EOF(LIST) AND NOT FOUND DO
      BEGIN
         READ(LIST,INV);
         IF WANT = INV.NAME THEN
            FOUND := TRUE
         ELSE
            SPACE := SPACE + 1;
         SEEK(LIST,SPACE);
      END;
   IF FOUND THEN
      WRITELN(INV.ID:6,INV.NAME:20,INV.COST:8:2,INV.QUANTITY:6)
   ELSE
      WRITELN('ITEM NOT IN LIST');
   CLOSE(LIST);
END; {SEQUENTIAL SEARCH PROCEDURE}


PROCEDURE PARTIN;
BEGIN
   WRITE('ENTER PART NUMBER: ');
   READLN(WANTID);
END;
```

```
PROCEDURE BINARY;
BEGIN
   ASSIGN(LIST,'INVENTRY.DAT');
   RESET(LIST);
   PARTIN;
   FIRST := 0;
   LAST := FILESIZE(LIST) - 1;
   FOUND := FALSE;
   WHILE (LAST >= FIRST) AND NOT FOUND DO
      BEGIN
         MID := (FIRST + LAST) DIV 2;
         SEEK(LIST,MID);
         READ(LIST,INV);
         IF WANTID > INV.ID THEN
            FIRST := MID + 1
         ELSE
            IF WANTID < INV.ID THEN
               LAST := MID - 1
            ELSE
               FOUND := TRUE;
      END;
        IF FOUND THEN
            WRITELN(INV.NAME:20,INV.ID:6,INV.COST:8:2, INV. QUANTITY:6)
      ELSE
            WRITELN('ITEM NOT FOUND');
      CLOSE(LIST);
END; {BINARY PROCEDURE}

PROCEDURE DATAIN;
BEGIN {MENU PROGRAM}
   CLRSCR;
   WRITELN('INVENTORY PROGRAM FOR FUN FANTASIES');
   WRITELN;
   WRITELN;
   WRITELN('WHICH DO YOU CHOOSE:');
   WRITELN;
   WRITELN('        SEARCH BY PART ID # = 1');
   WRITELN('        SEARCH BY PART NAME = 2');
   WRITELN('        INPUT DATA         = 3');
   WRITELN('        CREATE FILE        = 4');
   WRITE('CHOOSE NOW:   ');
   READLN(RESPONSE);
END; {MENU PROGRAM}

BEGIN {MAIN PROGRAM}
   DONE := FALSE;
   DATAIN;
   WHILE NOT DONE DO
      BEGIN
         IF RESPONSE = 1 THEN
            BINARY;
         IF RESPONSE = 2 THEN
            SEQUENCE;
         IF RESPONSE = 3 THEN
            DATABASE;
         IF RESPONSE = 4 THEN
```

```
            CREATEFILE;
            WRITE('RETURN TO MENU? ');
            READLN(ANS);
            IF ANS = 'Y' THEN
                DATAIN
            ELSE
                DONE := TRUE;
        END;
    END. {MAIN PROGRAM}
```

The USES CRT at the beginning of the program makes the CLRSCR (clear screen) function available. CLRSCR is used after the menu is displayed.

The SEEK function moves the file pointer to a specific record. EOF(LIST) (end of file LIST) returns true when a SEEK moves to a record beyond the end of the file.

The record type INVENTORY is used to combine all the inventory record data into a single structure. Since INV is assigned to INVENTORY in the VAR list, you can use INV followed by a period and the name of the variable in the INVENTORY structure to refer to that specific record field.

Note that records in Pascal are numbered starting at 0. Therefore, the binary search variable FIRST is set to 0 and LAST is set to the number of records minus 1. The sequential search is also set to start at 0.

Some of the INTEGER variable types were changed to LONGINT because the SEEK function requires a LONGINT record number.

SUMMARY

This chapter discusses two types of file processing: sequential and random. Sequential files are the easiest to understand and use; however, they can take longer to process. Random files are more complicated to code and can take up more storage, but they are much faster at processing large amounts of data. Sequential files store and access data in sequence. When you write to a sequential file, you lose everything that was there before. A random file can store and access data directly because it does not have to read through each preceding file. When you write to a random file, you write over only that record, not the whole file.

Key Terms

ASSIGN	OPEN "I"
CLOSE	OPEN "R"
CLRSCR	Random-access file
EOF(LIST)	RESET
FIELD	REWRITE
GET	SEEK
LONGINT	Sequential file
LSET	USES CRT
MKS$	

1. What is a data file?

2. What is a sequential file?

3. Describe how the 10th record is accessed in a sequential file.

4. Describe how the 10th record is written to a sequential file.

5. Describe how to change one field in a sequential file record.

6. What are the strengths and weaknesses of sequential files?

7. What is a random file?

8. Describe how the 10th record is accessed in a random file.

9. Describe how the 10th record is written to a random file.

10. Describe how to change one field in a random-file record.

11. What are the strengths and weaknesses of random files?

12. Compare random and sequential files.

Problem-Solving Assignments

1. Change the payroll program to incorporate sequential and direct-access files.

2. Build pseudocode to update the payroll program so that it uses the sort and merge modules to combine and update a transaction (change) file and a master file (payroll).

3. The PB Electric Company has hired you to write a program to computerize their billing system. Your program must do the following:

   a. Read the kilowatt per hour (KWH) rate schedule into an array or arrays so that, later, the program can look up the appropriate rate.

   b. Read in individual customer meter readings along with customer names. These records are stored to a transaction file that is later sorted in alphabetic order.

c. Calculate the amount due by accessing the master file, which contains first and last name, old meter reading, customer rate code, and past due amount. The master file is sorted in last-name order. Take the new reading and subtract the old reading. Then multiply the result by the proper rate.

d. Charge 5 percent interest for overdue payments.

e. Calculate total amount due, which is equal to the overdue amount plus the amount due.

f. Replace the old meter reading with the new meter reading.

g. Print a report that includes name, number of kilowatt hours used, amount due, amount past due, interest charged, and total amount due.

h. Calculate summary totals and print them out for the number of kilowatts used, amount due, amount past due, interest charged, and total amount due.

The KWH rate schedule is:

Code	$ per KWH	Type
1	.0525	Residential, partial electric
2	.0485	Residential, all electric
3	.0850	Commercial, usage under 50,000 KWH
4	.0750	Commercial, usage between 50,001 and 100,000 KWH
5	.0659	Commercial, over 100,001 KWH

The Master file looks like this:

Last	First	Old Readings	Rate Code	Amt. Past Due
DOVER	EILEEN	27648	1	0.00
DOVER	BEN	42615	2	45.20
DOVER	SEN	314625	3	0.00
TURKEY	IMA	615700	3	0.00
DUNNE	UR	800500	3	300.00

The transaction file looks like this:

DUNNE UR	1025500
DOVER EILEEN	28648
TURKEY IMA	695700
DOVER SEN	354625
DOVER BEN	45115

You are free to design your own output format.

10

Testing, Debugging, and Maintenance Programming

It is a rare program that does not require debugging, testing, and maintenance. Debugging is finding syntax errors and the source of logic mistakes. Testing ensures that there are no logic errors in the program. By testing, a programmer can be certain that the program works as intended. Maintenance is required when the program's requirements change. For example, maintenance can be as simple as changing a tax or interest rate or as complex as adding a new feature or changing one already present.

TESTING

First of all, document your test data before you start testing. Use the same set of test data each time you test. If you use the same data each time, you won't forget anything, you will be able to verify that you checked, and you will know exactly what should be in each variable at any time during the test. This is useful when debugging. Sometimes you can arrange to feed the test data into the program from a disk file instead of the keyboard; this speeds up the testing significantly. When you're done, be sure to save the test data—you'll need it when you modify the program someday.

Be sure to test every menu choice.

Don't assume one segment works just because another segment works and they both supposedly use the same code.

Don't assume anything!

Be sure the test data you use cover the range of input allowed for each input item. For example, if your program requires a number from 1 to 1000, try 1 and 1000 as well as some values in between. Also try 0, negative numbers, 1001, and greater values; make sure they are rejected. (A good program should always check every item of data supplied to it, whether the data comes from the keyboard or a data file.) Try a value like 123.4567 if the program expects two decimal places. Try a number with a few decimal places if the program expects an integer.

If your program expects a character value, try pressing the Return key without typing in any characters. Does the program respond properly? It probably should show the user an error message unless a null string is a usable input value. If the program expects a numeric value, try pressing Return. Try entering letters instead of digits.

If your program uses date input, be sure that the dates are valid; that is, not 11/31/88 or 02/29/87. Try an invalid number of characters, like 2/3/88. Watch out for leap years. Try each program feature several times in a row; sometimes failure occurs after one or more repetitions. Also try to test all the features in different orders; sometimes an attempt to run one feature immediately before or after another turns up a problem. These tests should reveal uninitialized variables, among other things.

A really thorough test helps you sleep better once the program is released for use out in the real world. Use your imagination when testing—users can think of the darndest things to try! If you can manage it, get someone without computer experience to attempt to run your pride and joy once you think it is bug-free.

In a formal programming environment, a program design may be subjected to periodic formal or informal reviews. These may be conducted by your supervisors, fellow programmers, or both. Here the algorithms chosen, design strategies, user interface, test data, and other aspects of the program design will be critiqued.

PROGRAMMING TIPS

Testing always brings the focus to prudent programming practice. Whether you are writing code or correcting it, the principles that follow apply.

Don't jump out of a FOR...NEXT loop; always let the loop terminate normally. If you need to jump out, use a WHILE or UNTIL loop instead.

Always initialize the variables. Be especially careful to set accumulators and flag variables correctly.

Some languages (C, for example) don't initialize variables, especially local arrays and structures, to 0 or null when they are created. If your program expects this condition, you'll have to do the initializing yourself.

Watch out for duplicated variable names. Remember, in some language implementations, only a certain number of variable characters are significant. Sometimes as few as the first two are significant, even though you are permitted to use longer variable names.

Always use RETURN when you code each GOSUB in BASIC. Use the equivalent statement in other languages. Don't jump from subroutine to subroutine via GOTOs, intending to use the last subroutine's RETURN. Leaving a subroutine via a GOTO is very tempting when an error condition occurs and breaks the normal program sequence. Don't do it. Set a flag and return normally, using the flag to indicate the error to the calling portion of the program.

Don't use GOTO at all in well-structured languages like Pascal and C and in some of the modern BASIC compilers.

Put values that are the same throughout the program in a variable or constant at the beginning of the program; don't keep entering the literal value. If the value of a defined variable or constant changes or has to be changed, then you need only to modify it in one easy-to-find location. This is especially useful for values that represent tax rates, interest rates, and other such volatile items. It's no fun going through a 20-page program, trying to find all the .05s pertaining to a tax rate to change them to .055.

Use intervals of at least 10 between consecutive BASIC line numbers, if your version of BASIC uses them. This interval gives you room to expand the code later if necessary.

Anticipate errors whenever possible. Have an ON ERROR...GOTO or the equivalent set correctly whenever you open or access a file. Use IORESULT in Pascal. Or have a generalized error routine that tests the error code number and branches accordingly to catch mistakes such as an instruction to divide by zero. You don't want your program to ever terminate unexpectedly (crash), no matter what the user enters.

If you're using floppy disks, have the program check to be sure the user didn't swap disks before the program writes to a floppy. Most modern disk operating systems have a way of labeling a disk—the volume names in MS-DOS are a way of labeling, for example. Writing to a changed disk can cause enormous damage to the disk contents.

Comments and Headers

Be sure to use plenty of comments in your code. If you are using a compiler, you can be especially thorough because the comments are not included in the executable program. Put a header at the beginning of each program. In the header include program creation and modification dates, the version number, and the programmer's name. Also include an explanation of what each global variable does. Use a similar heading at the beginning of each subroutine, function, procedure, etc. to explain argument requirements, the uses of all the variables, and the purpose of the segment. Use a log to keep track of the date of each modification to the code and what was changed. (Software programs called version control systems can do this for you automatically.) Try to keep copies of at least two previous versions; these copies can save you a lot of grief if you change a working program and suddenly find that things have quit working correctly. If you write programs regularly, you'll find that you won't recognize code you wrote a month ago—much less understand how it works.

Program Stubs

When you write the program, you should, of course, follow structured programming principles. It is easier to write the basic portions of the program first, without worrying about details. You can later implement the detailed modules. To do this, you'll need to incorporate stubs in your program. A stub is simply a module that returns valid data without doing any processing.

Here's an example. Say a portion of your program checks to see if a payment was made within 30 days of the billing date. If it was, the program goes on; otherwise, it adds an interest charge to the transaction file and to the customer's balance due. A module is used to retrieve the billing date from a transaction file. Another module recovers the payment date from the transaction file. A third module uses the two dates to calculate the number of days between them. Finally, if the number of days exceeds 30, a fourth module calculates the interest charge and adds it to the transaction file and the customer's balance.

When you begin, write the first and second modules written to return only preset dates. Write the third module to return only a number less than 30. Write the fourth module to consist of only a return command with no changes made to the transaction file and customer balance.

After the program works correctly with no interest charges, rewrite the day counter stub to return a value higher than 30. Then write the fourth module as it will be in the final program. See if the interest charges are correctly calculated and added to the transaction file and customer balance.

Next write the third module. See if it returns the correct value to represent days between dates. Test various dates. Be sure to test for dates crossing February 29th in leap years and nonleap years. When you're sure the third module works, write the first two modules.

See how using program stubs simplifies program writing? They allow you to gradually incorporate more and more detail, testing each new module as you add it.

DEBUGGING

Most of these suggestions assume you are not using a source code debugger with breakpoints and the ability to watch variables. If your language has a debugger, learn to use it; the debugger can save you many hours of debugging.

Sometimes debugging can be the most frustrating part of a programmer's job. You can look and look and not see an error that—in hindsight—seems obvious.

Syntax errors are usually easy to find; just check your program language reference. Don't assume something is legal, however, just because it's not forbidden in the reference. Reference manuals can contain errors; be sure to read any errata sheets that you receive. If you still have a problem after you check your manual, sneak up on the error by starting with a version of the command you know is legal. Then change the syntax a little at a time until the error occurs.

If you're unsure about some code in a large program, write a very small program that incorporates the code in question. It's much easier to verify the operation of a few lines of code than 20 pages. If you're using an interpreter, try the code in direct mode.

If you are using an interpreter, put some STOP statements or equivalent structures in your program and display the appropriate variables when each one triggers. In general, you can continue the program after stopping. Be careful not to change any program code, or you won't be permitted to go on; you are usually permitted to change variables' values.

Sprinkle PRINT statements through the part of the code that is causing the error, displaying the value of the variables that could possibly be causing the bug. Be sure to preface each displayed variable with its name and where you are in the program. Use line numbers as locators in BASIC.

```
299 PRINT "AT LINE 299 T = ";T
```

The debugging statements might serve better if they are directed to the printer instead of the screen.

If your program is hanging or crashing and you're not sure exactly where, put a PRINT statement at the beginning of each function, subroutine, subprogram, procedure, or whatever is called by the portion of the program that is failing. Note the last portion that is printed. Your problem is between the PRINT statement that produced the display and the next PRINT statement. Subdivide that area with more display lines until you pin down the bug.

Try letting someone else look at the problem portion of your code. Sometimes you see what you expect to see, not what's actually there.

Try explaining your code to someone else; this is a very effective way to find a bug. If there are no human volunteers or draftees available, explain it to your cat, dog, or goldfish. Remember, though: most goldfish have rather short attention spans.

Another method is called desk checking. Go through the problem area of the program writing down the contents of each variable as you go. This may help you discover where things are going wrong. This is a slow process and should be used as a last resort.

PROGRAM MAINTENANCE

When you attempt to modify an existing running program, you'll see why a multitude of comments helps. You'll be thankful for all the hints you can get when you try to change a program, no matter whether it is an old one of yours or someone else's.

First, be sure to make a copy of the program you are modifying so you'll have a point of return if things go wrong.

As you complete each change, test it thoroughly before you start changing the next. If available, use the test data originally created for the program. You may have to modify the test data slightly so they will work with your changes. Once you are sure the test data work, modify the data to test your changes. When you are sure all is well, save the modified version of the revised program (don't erase the original copy) and start on the next change. Be sure to save the new version of the test data too, but retain the original data. Continue this process until your modifications are complete. Above all, don't make all the modifications before you test. If you do, you'll have a much harder time locating errors. Be sure to use plenty of comments.

There are several types of maintenance programmng:

- In *corrective maintenance,* you find all the bugs and eliminate them. Methods were discussed earlier in the chapter.

- In *adaptive maintenance,* you adapt the program to changes in the environment. Such changes could includes new taxes, pay scales, etc. This was also discussed earlier.

- *Preventive maintenance* makes the program run faster and take up less space in memory. This type of maintenance frequently is needed when a new release of the application is planned.

- A *conversion* requires you to translate the program to another language, a new version of the old language, or perhaps to another computer.

- If you program an *upgrade,* you add new features to match or exceed those of a similar competing program.

DESIGN DOCUMENTATION

In addition to the comments placed in the program, formal programming often requires additional documentation. Professional programmers are required to keep a program log. It should contain detailed information about all changes made in a program and the reasons why the changes were made. If the program modifications need approval, professional programmers include copies of the approval forms with the documentation. As mentioned, retain the data used to test the program. Describe this data with the documentation.

Of course, include a copy of the current program listing when you submit the revised program. In addition, provide a copy of the pseudocode and any flowcharts that would be helpful.

SUMMARY

Chapter 10 discussed the skills of testing, debugging, and maintaining programs. It also provided helpful hints for creating error-free programs. Testing is the practice of trying to make your program not work so that you can improve it. Debugging is the art of finding out what went wrong before the program is put into production. Maintaining is the continual updating and modification of a program to keep up with current needs. Together, these skills will ensure that a program is working correctly.

Key Terms

Adaptive maintenance
Conversion
Corrective maintenance
Desk checking

Preventive maintenance
Stubs
Upgrade
Version control system

1. What are the differences between debugging and maintaining a program?

2. In testing a program, what kind of data do you use? Give examples.

3. You have a program that does not work. You do not know where the program is going wrong. You do not have a debugger at your disposal. How would you go about finding the program error(s)?

4. List the different kinds of maintenance.

5. A program has been used by your company for a number of years. It has worked correctly during that time. Suddenly it gives strange results. You are called in to correct it. First, what are you doing? Second, what steps would you take to solve the problem?

6. What are stubs? How and why are they used?

7. What is an upgrade?

8. What is desk checking?

Problem-Solving Assignments

1. The program that follows allows you to estimate total costs for a small business. It estimates total costs in several categories; rental costs are fixed.

```
5    DIM M$(12)
10   L9 = 0
20   R9 = 0
30   U9 = 0
40   S9 = 0
50   O9 = 0
60   T9 = 0
70   R = 1500
80   FOR I = 1 TO 12
90         READ M$(I)
100 NEXT I
110 DATA "JAN","FEB","MAR","APR","MAY","JUN"
120 DATA "JUL","AUG","SEP","OCT","NOV","DEC"
130 PRINT "MONTH";TAB(10);"LABOR";TAB(20);"RENT";TAB(30);
140 PRINT "UTILITIES";TAB(40);"SUPPLIES";TAB(50);"OTHER";
150 PRINT TAB(60);"TOTAL"
160 PRINT
170 FOR I = 1 TO 12
180        L = INT(RND(0) * 1001 + 2000)
190        U = INT(RND(0) * 301 + 200)
```

```
200          S = INT(RND(0) * 201 + 500)
210          O = INT(RND(0) * 501 + 1500)
215          T = L + R + U + S + O
220          T9 = T9 + T
230          L9 = L9 + L
240          R9 = R9 + R
250          U9 = U9 + U
260          S9 = S9 + S
270          O9 = O9 + O
280          PRINT M$(I);TAB(10);L;TAB(20);R;TAB(30);U;TAB(40);
290          PRINT S;TAB(50);O;TAB(60);T
300 NEXT I
305 MA = T9 / 12
310 PRINT
320 PRINT "TOTALS";TAB(10);L9;TAB(20);R9;TAB(30);U9;TAB(40);
330 PRINT S9;TAB(50);O9;TAB(60);T9
340 PRINT
350 PRINT "MONTHLY AVERAGE ";MA
360 END
```

a. Create the pseudocode for this program.

b. Change the program to reflect increased rental costs of 12 percent, increased utility costs of 15 percent, and increased supply costs of 8 percent.

c. Now keep the 12-month total and calculate new totals with 5 percent, 10 percent, and -5 percent increases in labor costs. To do this you must do more than multiply the totals by the appropriate percentages; instead you must make 12 new monthly cost estimates and a new total to compare with the old total.

2. Change the payroll program developed in previous chapters to reflect changes in taxes and health costs. Also add a new procedure to take out savings to be put in a retirement fund.

3. Change the search routine in the payroll program or rearrange the ordering to allow speedier searching.

4. Convert a program from BASIC into Pascal or vice versa.

Programmer's Tools

There are a number of useful tools available to help programmers design, code, and document their programs. This appendix is designed to give you an overview of commonly used forms and techniques.

TOOLS FOR DESCRIBING OUTPUT

Output to be printed can be described using a *print chart*. This is simply a page with 52 rows and 80 to 142 columns. Each row-by-column cell represents a position at which a character can be placed on a page.

If output is to be directed to a terminal, also referred to as a CRT (cathode ray tube) or VDT (visual display terminal), it can be plotted using a *display system layout sheet*. This sheet is just like a print chart, except that it has 24 rows and 80 columns corresponding to the 24 rows and 80 columns on the screen.

USING PSEUDOCODE TO PREPARE AN ALGORITHM

Pseudocode is used to show the details of the processing done by the program. There are no generally accepted standards for pseudocode.

Pseudocode is short English phrases or sentences detailing the necessary steps for execution of the program. Pseudocode has been used throughout the text to illustrate programming logic.

This appendix was written by Janet E. Spears.

Pseudocode has a number of advantages as a tool in the development of programming logic. It is easier for the programmer to write source code from pseudocode than from a flowchart. Pseudocode is language-independent, so it can be used no matter what language the programmer will use to code the program.

Some programmers show key words in capital letters and indent lines to make the pseudocode easier to read. This procedure has been used throughout this text.

Here is an example of simple pseudocode to add numbers that will be input from the keyboard would be:

1. Start.
2. Identify variables to be used.
3. Start loop to read five numbers.
4. Read the numbers
5. Accumulate the total of the numbers input.
6. End the loop.
7. Print the total.
8. End.

In the text, the outline form of pseudocode has been used, but the steps can also be numbered.

FLOWCHARTS

When the algorithm is correct, a program *flowchart* is prepared. A flowchart is a pictorial representation of the algorithm created.

Flowcharting symbols have been standardized by the American National Standards Institute (ANSI). There are plastic templates available that contain the flowchart symbols.

The processing to be done at each step is written inside the appropriate outline. A flowchart should be read from top to bottom and from left to right. Every program flowchart starts and ends with the single terminal symbol.

Names used to identify data items in the symbols should be consistent and meaningful to the programmer.

A decision symbol should contain the two items being compared. Also, each exit from the decision symbol should be labeled with the appropriate condition: <, >, <=, =, or < >.

Flowlines show the direction of the flowchart, and there should be only one flowline into a symbol. Flowlines entering and exiting from the symbol should be positioned in the center of the symbol. There should be only one flowline out of a symbol except on two occasions: One occasion is the decision diamond. The other is when the End of File (EOF) condition may be represented by a labeled flowline that exits from the symbol.

The process symbol is used for operations performed on data, and the preparation symbol is used for operations performed on the program itself.

The annotation symbol is used for programmer documentation.

Drawing a flowchart helps the programmer visualize each step necessary for the program to work correctly.

Flowcharts are a form of programmer documentation and are used as a reference by other programmers and users to determine the flow of the program. Flowcharts also allow a programmer to try out alternative solutions to a problem before coding the program.

Flowcharts are frequently used by programmers, but they are time-consuming to construct. Also, there is no universal way to flowchart a program; two programmers solving the same problem may have two completely different flowcharts that achieve the same output.

Flowchart Symbols

The standard symbols used in flowcharting are shown in Figure A.1. Following is a more detailed explanation.

Process. Used to denote an operation involved in the actual processing of data. The process symbol is used for all arithmetic and data transfer operations.

Input/Output. Used for an instruction to either input or output data to a device.

Preparation. Used to define data names and formats used in input, output, and work areas, and to assign initial values to work areas.

Decision. Used to designate that different logic paths will be followed based on a condition in the program.

Terminal. Used to designate the beginning or the end of the program or routine.

Connector. Used to connect parts of the flowchart when the use of flowlines could be confusing. In structured programming it is used only to designate a continuation of the flowchart to another page.

Offpage Connector. Used to connect parts of a flowchart from one page to another.

Annotation. Used to further describe or comment on the flowchart.

Flowlines. Used to link symbols and to indicate the sequence of operations. The flowline symbol consists of a line with an arrowhead at the end.

External Subroutine. Used to access a subroutine that exists outside the program.

Internal Subroutine. Used to access a subroutine that exists within the program.

Figure A.1

ANSI flowchart symbols

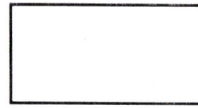

Process
represents any manipulation of data,
such as arithmetic operations

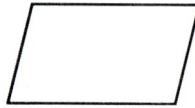

Input/output
represents any data input or output operation

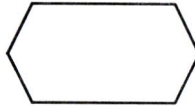

Preparation
represents any manipulation performed on the program,
such as initializing counters

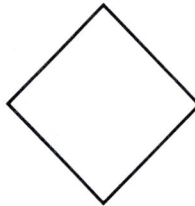

Decision
represents the comparison of two values

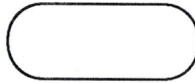

Terminal
represents the start and end of the program

Connector
represents the exit to or entry from another part of the program

Off page connector
used to show that the flowchart extended to another page

Annotation
defines an area for comments to explain processing steps

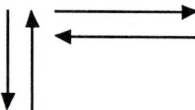

Flowline
Indicates the flow of the program

External subroutine
used to call a subroutine that exists outside the program

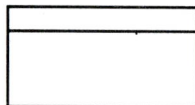

Internal subroutine
used to call a subroutine thet exists within the program

STRUCTURED PROGRAMMING FLOWCHARTS

The flowcharts illustrated up to this point are straight-line or sequential flowcharts (Figure A.2). In other words, the logic flows from START to STOP with very few subroutines and with as many GO TO instructions as the programmer wishes. Straight-line flowcharts work fine for short programs, but not for long, complex programs. For structured programs with a number of modules, programmers need more complex documentation techniques. The most commonly used of these is the structure, or hierarchy, chart. But HIPO charts, Nassi-Schneiderman charts, decision tables, and truth tables are also useful tools.

Structure (Hierarchy) Charts

A structure chart organizes a program into a series of levels (Figure A.3). Modules are identified as rectangles and are executed from the top down and from left to right at every level. The structure chart shows the routines used and their relationships.

Many programmers number their modules by level or location in the hierarchy chart.

Once the hierarchy chart is complete, the programmer can then flowchart or write the pseudocode for the routines shown in the chart.

Hierarchy Plus Input-Processing-Output (HIPO) Charts

Hierarchy charts are often expanded to form a HIPO chart (Figure A.4). This design tool includes three types of diagrams that expand the modules defined in a hierarchy chart.

1. The table of contents is an annotated version of the hierarchy chart; it contains reference numbers and a brief description of each module.
2. The overview diagram details the specific steps involved in input, processing, and output for the entire program. These steps are cross-referenced to the module numbers used in the table of contents.
3. The detail diagram lists in detail what is done in each module.

The HIPO chart is an excellent form of documentation because it contains detailed, step-by-step information about what each module is expected to do. HIPO charts combine structure-chart and pseudocode techniques.

A page, or IPO chart, is prepared for each module (Figure A.5). It shows what data is used by the module, the processing steps performed by the module, and the output written by the module.

Between the input and process sections, the numbers of any module that can call the module being documentated can be entered; and between the process and output sections, the numbers of any modules called by this module may be entered.

HIPO charts provide the input and output for each module. They also determine what modules call the module being read.

However, HIPO charts are time-consuming to prepare, and the documentation for the program gets lengthy because there is a page for each module, regardless of the size of the module.

238

Figure A.2

A straight-line flowchart

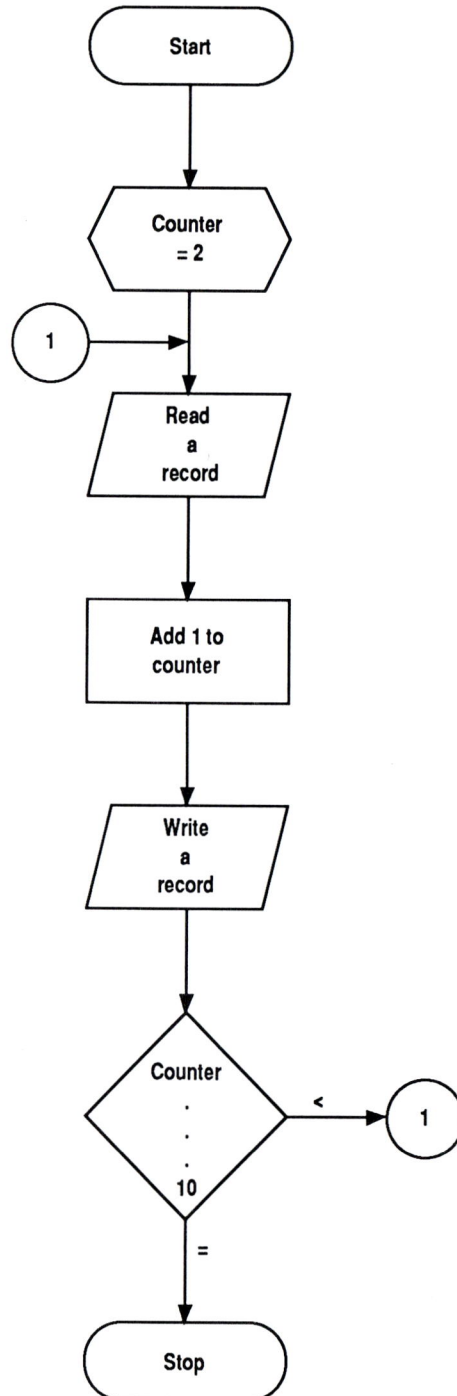

A structure chart

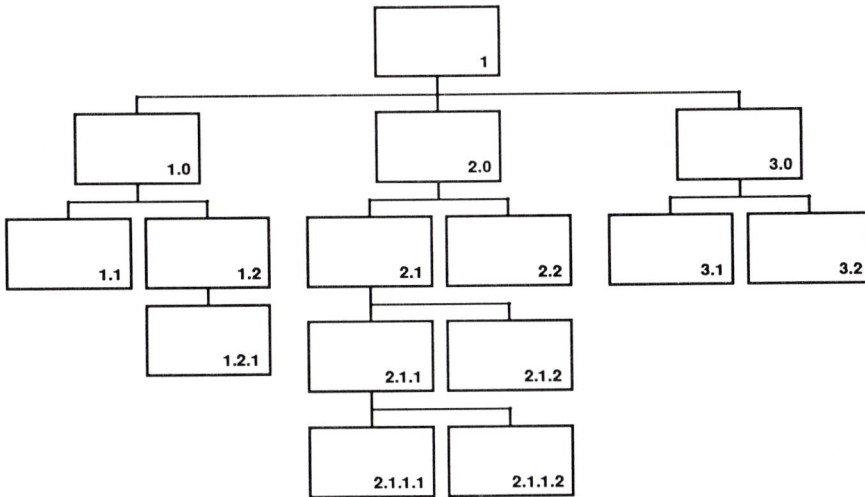

A HIPO chart

Nassi-Schneiderman Charts

The Nassi-Schneiderman chart (Figure A.6) was developed by I. Nassi and Ben Schneiderman. Each routine in a Nassi-Schneiderman chart is shown using a rectangle. This chart is used to show sequence, decision, and iteration structures. Only the DO-WHILE looping structure is used. There is no way to show a GO TO or unconditional branch. A separate chart is developed for each routine in the program.

TOOLS FOR ANALYZING PROGRAM LOGIC

Decision Tables

Programmers find decision tables (Figure A.7) useful when analyzing complicated decision logic, but a flowchart cannot be replaced by decision tables. A decision table is divided into four quadrants, each of which is separated by double lines. These quadrants are called the *condition stub, condition entry, action stub,* and *action entry.*

The conditions to be tested for decisions are shown in the top half of the table along with their possible values (true or false). If the outcome of a decision does not affect the action, a hyphen (-) can be used instead of true or false.

The actions to be taken based on the decision are indicated in the bottom half of the table by an X in the appropriate action entry.

Truth Tables

The truth table (Figure A.8) is used to represent the possible values of combinations of conditions. The letters T and F stand for true and false, the two possible values of a condition.

Figure A.5

An IPO chart

IPO Chart		
Program:	Programmer:	Date:
Module Name:	Module Function:	
Input	Processing	Output
1.	1.	1.
2.	2.	2.
3.	3.	3.
	4.	4.
	5.	5.
	6.	

Figure A.6

A Nassi-Schneiderman
chart

Main routine

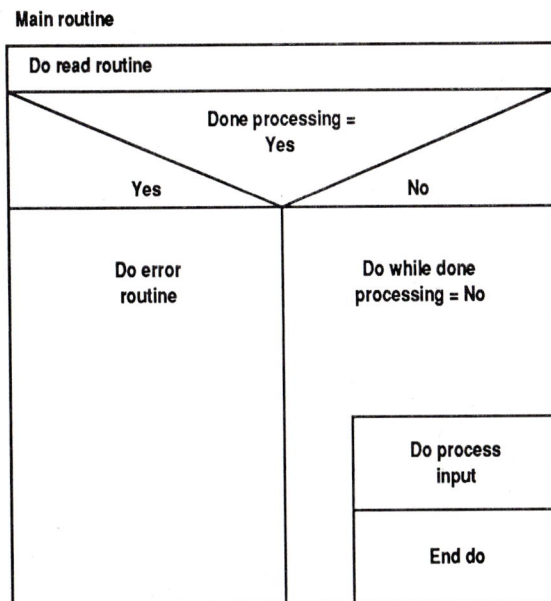

Figure A.7

A decision table

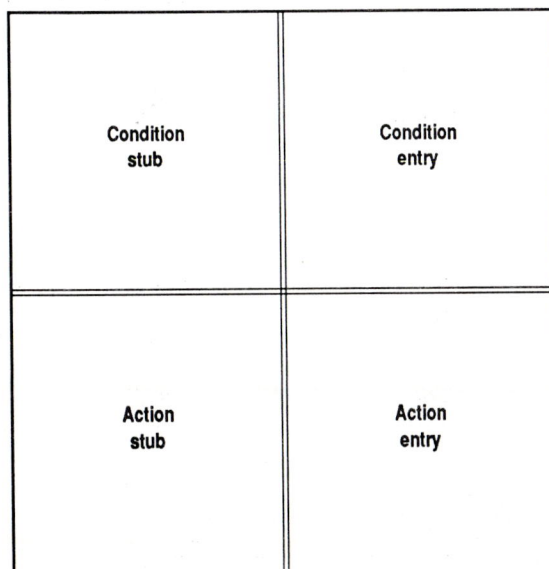

Figure A.8

A truth table

A	B	A and B	A or B	Not A	Not B
T	T	T	T	F	F
T	F	F	T	F	T
F	T	F	T	T	F
F	F	F	F	T	T

The method for developing a truth table is as follows:

1. Set up a column for each condition.
2. List all possible combinations of conditions, one combination to a row.
3. Write each expression to be evaluated as a column heading.
4. Under each of the column headings, write the value of the expression in the heading for the combination of conditions given for that particular row.

If there are n conditions, the number of possible combinations of the values of the conditions will be equal to 2 to the power of n. If there are two conditions (A and B), there will be four ways in which their values can be combined, and four rows in the truth table.

SUMMARY

The importance of documentation cannot be overemphasized. Any program that is used will undoubtedly have to be modified sometime in the future. When the time comes to change the program, even the original programmer will have difficulty remembering the details of the program unless it has been well documented.

This appendix reviewed the basic tools of program design and documentation: pseudocode, straight-line flowcharting, structured flowcharting (hierarchy charts, HIPO charts, and Nassi-Schneiderman charts), and programming logic tools (decision tables and truth tables).

Index

Syntax, 16
    errors, 19
System programs, 11

Tables, 129-152
Tape, magnetic, 116-117
Termination modules, 88, 148-149
Termination value, 40-41
Testing programs, 19, 225-226
Tips for programming, 226-228
Top-down programming, 47-49
Tracks, 96
Trailing read, 40
Troubleshooting, 225-230
True merges, 201-206
Truth tables, 242, 244

Unconditional branching, 33
UNTIL command, 170
Updating files, with merging, 201-206
Upgrades, program, 230
Users
    defining, 8
    designing output for, 94, 98

Users (continued)
    interacting with screen, 111-115
    support group for, 20
USES CRT command, 222

Value check, 121
Values, setting, 227
VAR statements, 71, 86
Variable loops, 42-43
Variables, 59
    initializing correctly, 226
Verification of data, 120-122
Version control systems, 227

Wedge, to connect peripherals to PCs, 115
WHILE command, 170
WHILE(...WEND) statements, 85-86, 87
Widows, 96
Window packages, for screen design, 118
WRITE command, 84, 86, 103
WRITE #, 84, 100, 213
WRITELN command, 78, 86, 103

Notes

Notes

Notes

Notes